D0207802

# MOTHER 3 HANDBOOK
## 2nd Edition

*The English gamers' guide to the world of MOTHER 3*

The MOTHER 3 Handbook is written, designed, published, and distributed by Fangamer LLC. This first edition copy was printed and bound in November, 2011 by the good folks at Bang Printing in Brainerd, MN.

ISBN-10: 0-9845032-9-3
ISBN-13: 978-0-9845032-9-2

Errors? Follow the 'Forum' link at http://handbook.fangamer.com and make a report there, please.

## CREDITS

**Jon Kay**: *Art Direction, Design, Layout*
**Reid Young**: *Editor-in-Chief*
**Andrew Rogers**: *General Editor*
**Clyde Mandelin**: *General Editor*
**Camille Young**: *Clay Models, Misc Artwork*
**Emilio Orsi**: *Character Illustrations*
**Sebastian Hardy**: *Editor CH 2, Item Illustrations*
**Marty Elmer**: *Character Illustrations (Back View)*
**Steven Campos**: *Graphics, General Editor*
**Christopher Warriner**: *Editor CH 3, Data*
**Brian Jaworski**: *Editor CH 4+5*
**Charlie Verdin**: *Editor CH 7*
**Kevin Williams**: *Editor CH 8*
**Jeff Erbrecht**: *Data*
**Ryan Alyea**: *Technical Support*

## SPECIAL THANKS

Starmen.Net staff and community; Christopher Thomas; The Big N; Ben Carignan; Heidi Yolmeh; Toby Fox; patient wives and significant others; House Industries; Emigre; sxc.hu; various old school Rareware game soundtracks.

## EXTRA SPECIAL THANKS

Shigesato Itoi; The entire M3FT team; The Dave; preorder customers who helped scan for errors; fans who supported us with, encouraging words comments, preorders, and links

**Dedicated to the EarthBound fans who waited for 16 years to play this game.**

# MOTHER 3

## HANDBOOK

# FOREWORD

This handbook was independently designed, written, and produced from scratch by MOTHER (EarthBound) fans with the same kind of care that creator Shigesato Itoi put into the series. MOTHER 3 has not been made officially available outside of Japan, but with this book we hope to give it the recognition we feel it deserves.

This would not be possible without the creative energy of the fans who are constantly producing art in every medium imaginable. If you're feeling inspired, the community at Starmen.Net is filled with fans (both artistic and otherwise) who would love to hear/see your thoughts about the game.

This handbook is not designed to help you beat the game; it's designed to help you enjoy it. Take time to appreciate this book and hopefully you'll find yourself appreciating the game that much more.

...............................................................................

*"MOTHER 3 is a playground with plenty of room for your imagination to run free. The more you think about it, the greater MOTHER 3 will become. The more you feel it, the deeper it will become. The more fun you have, the more you'll grow."*

*Shigesato Itoi*

WELCOME TO THE WORLD OF

# MOTHER3

PROLOGUE

# WELCOME!

## PROLOGUE

# MEET THE FAMILY

As with any introduction, you begin by meeting everyone and learning their names—except that you're providing the material. You get to name the family, as well as your favorite food and favorite "thing." Pick anything you want, or use the "Don't Care" options for an easy out.

## WELCOME TO THE WORLD OF MOTHER 3

*Welcome to the Nowhere Islands!*

Our story takes place in Tazmily Village, a tiny town nestled among the Nowhere Islands. North of town, beyond the Sunshine Forest, a cozy log cabin sits high atop rocky Mt. Oriander.

### Tired Attire

Your brother, Claus, wakes you up from a peaceful slumber. Amble downstairs to see what's up, greeting your mother along the way. She stops you before you even go outside and scoots you upstairs to change out of your PJs.

### HINAWA    A gentle, protective mother.

The beautiful Hinawa nourishes her family with a lot of love and a little bit of home cooking. The twins keep her busy while her husband Flint tends the livestock back home.

## LOOKIN' HANDSOME

A boy has to look his best for a play date with the Drago family. Change your clothes and check yourself out in the mirror before you leave.

## STOP LOAFING AROUND

It's hard to get moving when you roll out of bed, but changing out of your pajamas has a way of waking you up—and enabling the B Button dash! Get a loaf of Nut Bread by dashing into Hinawa's chair in the kitchen.

## LUCAS A young mama's boy.

Lucas has earned a reputation for being a bit of a weakling, but his mother is confident he'll grow to be a strong young man. He should change out of his jammies first, though.

ORIANDER PLATEAU

ALEC'S HOUSE

STOMPING GROUNDS

SUNSHINE VALLEY

# A REGULAR DR. DOLITTLE

Throughout the game, you'll meet many animal friends. Don't be afraid to talk to them, too! Most animals will communicate in their own language, but translations are helpfully provided in parentheses.

# ALEC   An ornery old jokester.

Hinawa's father is well-acquainted with the outskirts of the Nowhere Islands. His great sense of humor helps him to make the best out of any situation, a lesson he hopes to pass on to his grandsons.

# FROGS

These affectionate amphibians have excellent memories and great networking skills. They're always happy to listen to your tales and pass the stories on to other frogs, functioning as 'Save Points'.

## STOMPING GROUNDS

◀ ORIANDER PLATEAU

# DRAGOS

Huge beasts with big hearts, these dinos are friendly and gentle, despite their appearances.

# A Dashing Tutorial

Claus has been up all morning playing with a family of Dragos, gentle beasts who roam the mountainsides. Claus and Alec are happy to provide a quick lesson in dashing, so shed your fears and try it out for yourself!

# CLAUS    Lucas's rambunctious twin.

Unlike his brother, Claus is an ambitious go-getter, always ready for action. Even though he sometimes pokes fun at his brother's innocence, he'll always stand up for his family.

# DASH-TARDLY DEEDS

After you learn your new colliding skill, why not test it on other things? Those other Dragos look like good targets. Now's your chance to get back at Claus for his jokes earlier.

# A SPARRING MATCH

Talk with Claus after you've had a chance to perfect your skills—you'll be interrupted by a pompous mole cricket who claims to be a passionate and determined fighter. If you lose, fear not. The mole cricket may not be a gracious winner, but at least he'll give you credit for your guts.

# MINI-BOSS

## MOLE CRICKET

He may talk tough, but even against a couple of kids this insect does not stand much of a chance. It's your first battle, so take it slow and keep it simple!

| HP: 45 | PP: 0 | OFF: 10 | DEF: 3 | EXP: 2 |

# Crunch for Lunch

Hinawa rounds up the boys for a family lunch, inadvertently heaping injury upon the mole cricket's insult – he won't soon forget this defeat! As Hinawa and Alec discuss the return trip, Alec gives Lucas a little good-natured teasing.

## Dear Flint,

Just like you said they would, the children have been running around the mountains and fields tirelessly since the moment we arrived.

Claus is as daring and full of energy as ever, while Lucas is still abit coddled. But neither one seems tired of playing at all.

My father seems sad to say goodbye to his grandchildren after seeing them for the first time in so long, but we should be home ___ this evening.

I ha___ ___ ni___nd refreshing the mountain air is. ___ ___ smell of sheep back in Tazmily ___ have been here to take in this air.

___ one of our neighbors to tend ___ here as a family.

___ thinking about you. When we ___ start cooking some of your favorite ___.

With love, your dearest
### Hinawa

# CHAPTER

## № 1

*The Night of the Funeral*

# CHAPTER № 1

## PART №1

# FOREST ON FIRE

Mysterious soldiers scramble throughout Tazmily's Sunshine Forest, terrorizing the wildlife and leaving fiery explosions in their wake.

## Rounding up the Troops

With the unfolding destruction in the forest, Tazmily's one-man panic brigade dons his firefighter hat and springs into action. Thomas battles valiantly with an insidious doorknob and eventually succeeds in convincing Flint to join him on his quest. Lighter has a shack deep in the woods where the black smoke is already billowing. There's no time to waste!

## THOMAS  *Tazmily's excitable but goodhearted watchman.*

"Bad times like this call for reckless nice guys like you!" Panicked and worrisome, Thomas is prepared to sound the alarm and rally the troops in response to any situation. Unfortunately, that's about the extent of his usefulness; he's too preoccupied with the latest emergency to offer any assistance during battles.

# LEGEND OF THE DOORKNOB

From time to time there comes a tale so compelling, so real, and so fraught with danger that it is transformed from a simple story into a legend.

*The time for that legend has come.*

# FLINT

### A strong, kind, and dependable father.

Father of young twins and husband to the lovely Hinawa, Flint is a quiet and reliable family man. His obligations as a shepherd keep him busy.

## SOUTH SHORE

TAZMILY SQUARE

B

FLINT'S HOUSE

S

A

| **A** | Stick |
|---|---|
| **B** | Nut Bread |
| **S** | Save Frog |

## GIVE HIM THE STICK!

Before you dash off to save Lighter, talk to your faithful companion Boney. He's hiding a simple Stick you'll be able to equip for a slightly more powerful attack.

### STICK
Offense +2

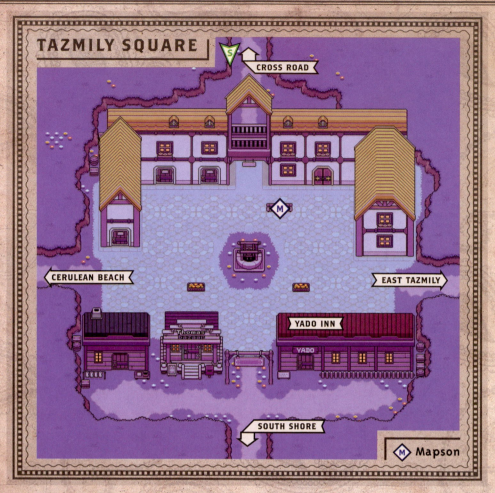

TAZMILY SQUARE

CROSS ROAD

CERULEAN BEACH

EAST TAZMILY

YADO INN

YADO

SOUTH SHORE

Ⓜ Mapson

## Mapfather

On your way to the Sunshine Forest, you'll want to stop to speak with Mapson, who circles the location of Lighter's shack. Press the 'R' button to pull up the map at any time.

## MAPSON

The aptly-named cartographer.

"If you need something from map-owning and map-loving Mapson, it must be a map, yes?" True to his name, Mapson is a valuable source of information. Whenever you're not sure where to go, ask for a map and he'll make a few quick notes to keep you on the right track.

## Follow the Leder

The constant, familiar clanging of Leder's bell fills the air with a strange mixture of calm and alarm. Stop to see if you can get any useful information out of ol' Beanstalk, the stoic.

### LEDER
The tallest man in town as well as the quietest.

### JACKIE
An innkeeper and self-conscious coward.

### JONEL
A superstitious and slightly selfish older fellow.

### ED
A smart and helpful townie with a sense of style.

### BUTCH
A chubby and somewhat oblivious young man.

### OLLIE
A helpful guy who is always in the wrong place.

## CROSS ROAD

SUNSET CEMETERY

A

FOREST GROTTO

X

BELL TOWER

B

TAZMILY SQUARE

| A | Nut Bread |
| B | Edible Mushroom |

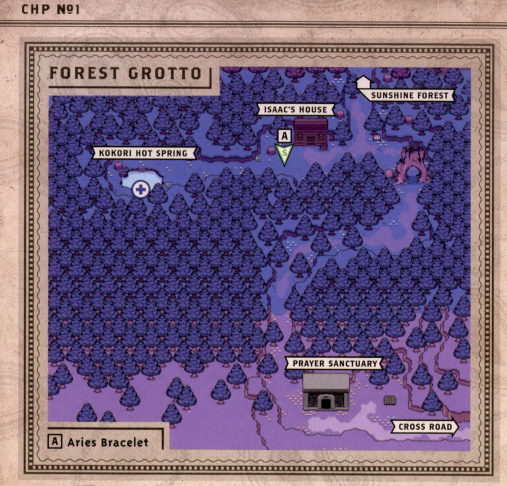

# FOREST GROTTO

SUNSHINE FOREST

ISAAC'S HOUSE

KOKORI HOT SPRING

A
S

PRAYER SANCTUARY

CROSS ROAD

A  Aries Bracelet

## Sweet Hour of Prayer

As you approach the forest, you'll want to stop momentarily to offer a quick prayer in the sanctuary next to Jonel. With that out of the way, Ed ushers you into the forest.

# A FOREST SANCTUARY

The Prayer Sanctuary is a mysterious place which demands quiet reverence. That is, until the sanctuary busts through the fourth wall and demands to know your name, at which point you better speak up. That's right, you! The one playing the game!

## MIKE'S HOME-MADE CREEPY COOKIES

On your way into the forest you'll come across Mike, who offers you some cookies. Beggars can't be choosers, so take him up on the offer and don't be shy about asking for seconds and thirds. When your life is on the line, even slightly unclean cookies are better than nothing!

*All-natural (plus some) is better for you... right?*

## Smoke Inhalation

On your way into the blaze you'll come across Bronson, who has inhaled too much smoke. He confirms that Lighter and Fuel are still unaccounted for, ordering you to go on ahead without him. Smoke thick enough to put an ironworker out of commission!

### BRONSON

An ironworker and take-charge kinda guy.

### MATT

An unassuming local guy with gigantic hair.

## ✚ HOT SPRINGS OF NOWHERE

The beautiful Kokori Hot Springs of Nowhere Island are renowned across all 3 square miles of this fine country! A short dip restores your health.

## RESTORING!

- ☛ HP & PP!
- ☛ ALL-HEALING!
- ☛ PLAY HOST TO STRANGERS!

No need to rush - 5 seconds rejuvenates!

## Chilling at the Hot Spring

Lighter's shack isn't too far away, but you might get worn down by the fire and enemies. Chow down on some of your food or, if you're running low, head back to the hot spring to get your health back up.

# BEWARE!
## OF THE FIRES

As you pick your way through the forest, proceed with caution. There are fires burning everywhere, and it's HOT —you'll take 1 HP damage each time you get too close!

## Through the Flames

The forest is ablaze, and on your way to Lighter's shack you catch a glimpse of a strange character loosing a trio of mean-looking bugs from an iron box. What's going on here? What kind of bug needs to be kept in an iron box...?

### A GUIDE TO BRAWN & TECHNIQUES

# FIGHTING STYLE

**FLINT** is a solid fighter whose greatest strength is his powerful melee attack. Regrettably he is a bit slow, so he'll sometimes be the last to attack. His wide variety of special battle moves makes up for this deficit, so use them wisely!

## Get the Facts

· Sticks and boards compose most of Flint's arsenal.
· Flint really likes cheese, so hang on to the snack for a quick recharge.
· Flint's battle instrument is the saxophone.

**SWING** Flint swings his weapon in every direction, hitting each enemy once. The only drawback is that he has no opportunity to perform timed attacks, making this ability useful only for battles with 2 or more enemies.

**STRENGTHEN UP**

Flint gathers his strength, increasing his offense by 5-12 points. This amazing skill, if used at the start of a battle, enables Flint to make quick work of enemies with lots of HP or high defense. Unfortunately, this increase cannot be stacked, and Flint's offense goes back to normal after the battle ends. If his offense falls during the battle for any reason, however, the skill can be re-used to bring it back up.

**POWER SMASH** Flint puts all of his strength behind his attack, but with increased attack power comes decreased accuracy: this attack misses most of the time. When it connects, though, it can deliver a blow roughly 4x stronger than normal attacks, making it useful for battles against enemies with lots of HP.

**TOUGHEN UP** Flint stiffens his body, increasing his defense by 4-7 points. With this skill, Flint can avoid defense/healing and concentrate on fighting—another great 'opening' attack for battles with powerful enemies. Like the 'Strengthen Up' skill, this lasts only for the duration of the battle and cannot be stacked, but it can be re-used if Flint's defense is lowered.

## SUNSHINE FOREST FIRE

LIGHTER'S CABIN

**A** Nut Bread
**B** Lighter's Lumber

X

FOREST GROTTO

### PIGMASKS

Who—or what—are these things?

# ENEMIES

## MR. BATTY

It's nothing more than an average bat, man. A few simple swats at this nocturnal nuisance will send it back to its cave.

Nut Cookie (2%) | Nut Bread (20%)

| HP: 56 | OFF: 41 | DEF: 14 | EXP: 20 |
|---|---|---|---|

## YAMMONSTER

This deranged tuber won't chase you, but it might get in the way. Take advantage of its poor depth perception by dashing up when it's not looking—you'll get plenty of Exp. and, often, a Nut Bread.

Nut Bread (60%)

| HP: 33 | OFF: 35 | DEF: 22 | EXP: 26 |
|---|---|---|---|

## FIREFLIES

It's up to you to handle these heated hellions alone, but it's not like you needed Thomas anyway. These bugs attack in packs of three with powerful charges in addition to their weaker fire attacks. Use Flint's special 'Swing' ability twice to extinguish them in two turns, and reward yourself by chowing down on the Nut Bread they leave behind.

Nut Bread (100%)

| HP: 53 EA. | OFF: 35 | DEF: 10 | EXP: 51 |
|---|---|---|---|

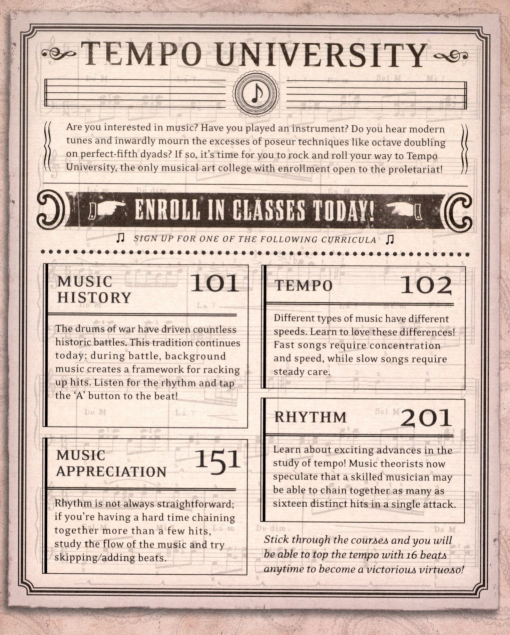

# TEMPO UNIVERSITY

Are you interested in music? Have you played an instrument? Do you hear modern tunes and inwardly mourn the excesses of poseur techniques like octave doubling on perfect-fifth dyads? If so, it's time for you to rock and roll your way to Tempo University, the only musical art college with enrollment open to the proletariat!

## ENROLL IN CLASSES TODAY!

♫ *SIGN UP FOR ONE OF THE FOLLOWING CURRICULA* ♫

### MUSIC HISTORY 101

The drums of war have driven countless historic battles. This tradition continues today; during battle, background music creates a framework for racking up hits. Listen for the rhythm and tap the 'A' button to the beat!

### MUSIC APPRECIATION 151

Rhythm is not always straightforward; if you're having a hard time chaining together more than a few hits, study the flow of the music and try skipping/adding beats.

### TEMPO 102

Different types of music have different speeds. Learn to love these differences! Fast songs require concentration and speed, while slow songs require steady care.

### RHYTHM 201

Learn about exciting advances in the study of tempo! Music theorists now speculate that a skilled musician may be able to chain together as many as sixteen distinct hits in a single attack.

*Stick through the courses and you will be able to top the tempo with 16 beats anytime to become a victorious virtuoso!*

## Lighter then Fuel

Lighter is down for the count, and worse yet, his son is still trapped in the house. Lighter mutters something about being attacked by the strange bugs, but there's no time to worry about that—Fuel needs help!

## LIGHTER's LUMBER

Be sure to grab Lighter's fallen weapon before you attempt to save Fuel – it will slow you down a little, but it's worth it for the extra heft!

**LIGHTER'S LUMBER**
Offense +6
Speed –3

# LIGHTER

Flint's childhood friend, this lumberjack is tough as nails.

# ENEMIES

## FLYING MOUSE

### MINI-BOSS

This flying menace thrives on destruction, so a burning house is an appropriate venue for your first encounter. You can fight him in a conventional style, but a single hit from Flint's 'Power Smash' will work just as well.

Peculiar Cheese (20%)

| HP: 110 | OFF: 46 | DEF: 20 | EXP: 45 |
|---------|---------|---------|---------|

SMAAAASH!!
138

## Fuel in a Fire

With the Fireflies put out you'll discover Fuel trapped in the burning house. To make matters worse, he's got company! The front door is jammed, so you'll have to dash straight through it to make your entrance.

## Saving Fuel

With the rodent out of the way, it's time to save Fuel. Go upstairs and dash through the debris near the southern window to reach him. On your way out of the house the infrastructure begins to collapse, so beat a hasty retreat!

# FUEL   Lighter's optimistic son, a friend of Claus and Lucas.

Fuel is a plucky young kid determined to be as great a man as his father. He's not afraid to get his hands dirty in battle, frequently throwing rocks (deals 2-3 HP damage to enemies) and lending support when you're down (restores 6-10 HP to Flint).

## Alive & Well

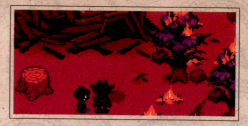

You've rescued Fuel and Thomas has taken Lighter to safety, so it's time to get back to the village. Be careful of the flames; they are still burning as hot as when you entered. Make your way back to the Forest Grotto and the Sanctuary.

# HOT·SPRINGS
# HEALTHY AND
# BEAUTY-FUL!

You may be aware of the Hot Spring's health-rejuvenating effects, but did you know that it also works wonders for your skin? Jump in to heal up after those boss battles and wash off the soot. Well, some of it anyway.

Disclaimer: Heads not included. No rain checks.

## ABBOT & ABBEY

A cute couple who live in the town square. They seem nice enough, but poor Abbey sure is accident-prone...

## Family Reunion

Exiting the forest, Fuel sprints over to his dad's side. Lighter has sustained some injuries, but nothing which will keep him down for long. After a brief reunion with his son, Lighter thanks you, an occasion so rare that only an unexpected rainstorm could really top it...

## BUD & LOU

This "comedy" duo is always on hand with comments to lighten up any situation. They work for Lighter, whom they refer to as "the boss".

# CHAPTER Nº 1

## PART Nº 2

# DESPERATE SEARCH

A calming rain patters against the secure Yado Inn as thoughts of Hinawa and the children race through everyone's minds.

## Everyone's Inn Recovery

When you come to, you'll find that Tessie has fixed up everyone's injuries at the Yado Inn. When you leave, Isaac will stop you to chat about a worrisome series of events. Now would be a good time to head back home to see if Hinawa has gotten back...

## A STATIC SECRET

On your way home, head east to Wess's house. If you sneak a peek behind the structure, you'll find a hidden Thunder Bomb. This prize refills

every time you visit Cross Roads or beyond, so use this boundary as an easy way to refill the box. These babies are especially useful in the first few chapters.

## Late for Supper

Hinawa's homing pigeon has appeared with a letter; but the news is grim. Hinawa's expected arrival time passed long ago. Take Boney along with you as a traveling companion and set out to search the woods for your family.

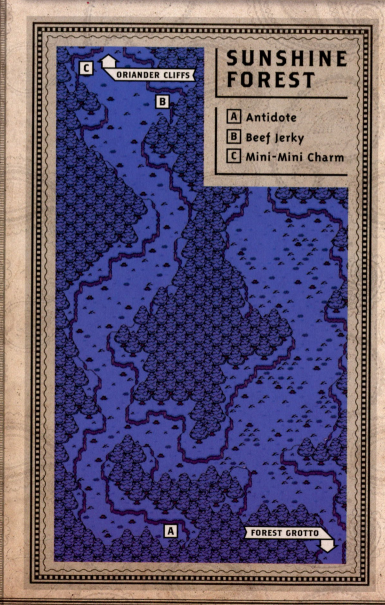

# BONEY

The family's lovable and dependable dog.

Boney may not have the best offense, but his speed is second to none. This canine has a special sniffing sense to boot, enabling you to learn the weaknesses of any foe in his range of scent. Good dog!

## SUNSHINE FOREST

**A** Antidote
**B** Beef Jerky
**C** Mini-Mini Charm

ORIANDER CLIFFS

FOREST GROTTO

## The Great Hinawa Hunt

The entire town is worried with the news of your family's disappearance. Most of the town is restless and decides to help out. Check on everyone's progress as you trudge deeper into the forest, but walk carefully! The forest seems much more alive with disturbed creatures now that the fire's been put out.

# DOTED ON WITH ANTIDOTES

Along the way, be sure to talk with Lisa. She'll give you an Antidote in case you get bit by a poisonous snake. If you need more, stop by Isaac's house: he has a box full of them, free for the taking!

## ISAAC

A rugged woodsman with a background as a lumberjack.

# ENEMIES

## BAKED YAMMONSTER

This bitter sweet potato-like foe may look sinister, but it's not much of a fighter. A few attacks ought to put it one step closer to dinner.

*Baked Yam (50%)*

| HP: 154 | OFF: 48 | DEF: 8 | EXP: 42 |
|---------|---------|--------|---------|

## MIGHTY BITEY SNAKE

This is one snake that will make you ache in its wake! Its fangs can secrete a deadly poison, so take it out quickly!

*Antidote (20%)*

| HP: 74 | OFF: 46 | DEF: 11 | EXP: 28 |
|--------|---------|---------|---------|

# BETTER BAKED BATTLES

While their form is somewhat different, Baked Yammonsters are still easy to sneak up on. When you see one on-screen, quickly walk or run up and around the planted yam to meet its back as it pulls itself out of the earthy soil.

# A Thunderous Finding

With sudden squalls of lightning, you'll soon come across a ghastly sight. Someone – or some*thing* – has completely destroyed some trees, barring your path forward. As Isaac and Lighter try their hardest to push the trees aside, head west. There, you find more chilling destruction. Townspeople will start theorizing about the perpetrator when suddenly Boney gets a whiff of something important.

## I Hate Cliffhangers!

High above the scene, a red scrap of cloth hangs perilously from a tree branch. This is a possible clue! Wess arrives on the scene at last, unable to stay at home while everyone else is helping. He offers the services of his son, Duster, in the scaling of the cliff.

## WESS

A kind-hearted old thief with a mean streak.

The only thing gruffer than Wess's appearance is his attitude! A retired thief, he spends his days training his son in the Thief Arts. However, there's nothing that'll keep this old man out of the action!

## Every Dog Has His Day

Using a sock as an odiferous identifier, Wess prepares Boney for a mission. The prerogative? To find and bring Duster to the scene from his deep sleep. Run Boney, run!

## DUSTER

A limping thief proficient in many skills, yet lacking in personal hygiene.

Duster may seem to be lazy at first, but he's truly quite a reliable friend. His tough father, Wess, constantly berates him with negative comments, but give him a chance and he'll pull through in the end. His mastery of the 'Wall Staple' technique is quite impressive to see.

## A Staple for Exploration

After his stapling show, meet Duster at the top of the cliff. The rain will finally stop and, now that it's in reach, you can check out the cloth. You'll find it to be both familiar and foreboding. There's only one way to go from here, though, and that's onward.

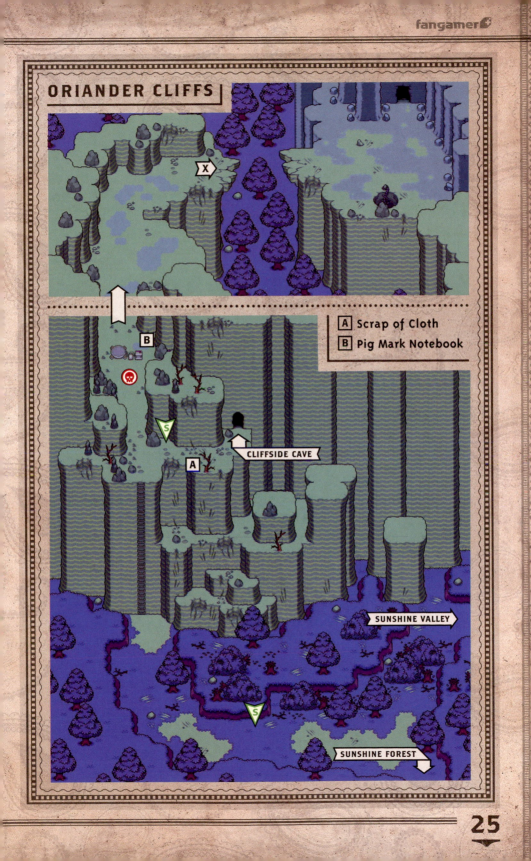

# ORIANDER CLIFFS

A Scrap of Cloth
B Pig Mark Notebook

X

B

A

CLIFFSIDE CAVE

SUNSHINE VALLEY

SUNSHINE FOREST

## BOSS WARNING!

### A GREEDY STASH

There's a small cave east of the tree that had the cloth on it. If you explore inside, you'll find some helpful food for the road ahead. Be sure to give some to Duster in case emergency healing is needed. Isn't the shape of this cave oddly familiar?

## RECONSTRUCTED
# AWESOME??

Nearby, some Pigmasks are huddled over something suspicious…. Your confrontation with the masked soldiers heads south after they flip the switch. Live from the slab rises a truly heinous creation – the Reconstructed Caribou!

## A Close Encounter of the Second Kind

In their hurried retreat, the Pigmasks drop some sort of notebook containing a set of heinous and disturbingly immature plans to mutilate the creatures living in the area. Your attempt to stop the escaping soldiers is seconds too late.

# THE SUSPICION BULLETIN!

*WATCH OUT*

## PIGMASKS?! - MEDDLESOME MYSTERIES

### ALERT!

*As recent tragedies strike our town of Tazmily, a group of masked soldiers seem to be behind the terrible events. Our townspeople have recorded the following evidence:*

- TROOPS WERE SEEN LAYING EXPLOSIVES IN THE SUNSHINE FOREST, RESULTING IN THE RECENT FIERY FIASCO.
- PIGMASKS WERE SEEN RELEASING STRANGE ANIMALS WHICH INJURED LIGHTER, DESTROYED HIS HOME, AND ENDANGERED HIS SON.
- RESIDENT ANIMALS WERE ABUSED AND MODIFIED INTO TERRIBLE FIGHTING MACHINES AGAINST THEIR WILL.
- 'THE FASCINATING CHIMERA PROJECT', A BOOKLET FULL OF THREATS AND INSTRUCTIONS FOR DEFORMING OUR WILDLIFE, WAS RECENTLY RECOVERED FROM A FLEEING PIGMASK.

It is believed that these invaders are behind the destruction of the northern cliffs and the disappearance of Flint s family. Keep a careful eye out, report mysterious activity, and stay vigilant until these perpetrators are caught!

## The Boys are Back in Town

At the base of the cliff, Jonel has has some good news! The tree blocking the way has been successfully moved and your sons Lucas and Claus have been found by the riverside! Head east to find them huddled around a warm fire under Tessie's care. After a touching reunion, you decide to stay with your boys while the other search parties comb the area for Hinawa.

## TESSIE

A kindhearted woman proficient as a medical nurse.

## Bitter Realization

As you attempt to extract information from the boys, a harried Bronson arrives with both good and bad news. Bronson tries to offset his revelation with something positive, but tactlessly blurts out his dark discovery. Hinawa has been found -- dead. Flint, overcome with rage, lashes out in every direction with a fiery plank until Lighter subdues him.

# ENEMIES

## MISCHIEVOUS MOLE

This rodent shouldn't give you too much trouble- it will probably give you bread instead! They never team up, so don't worry about getting into big fights.

Nut Bread (70%)

| HP: 103 | OFF: 50 | DEF: 17 | EXP: 31 |

# RECONSTRUCTED CARIBOU

### MINI BOSS

Duster's Wall Staples are the most useful skill to use here. If successful, the Caribou will be temporarily paralyzed. The effect wears off after a turn or two, so don't be shy to do it again. Also make sure Boney has the lion's share of food. His speed will ensure that your party has the first shot at healing.

| HP: 512 | OFF: 57 | DEF: 21 | EXP: 112 |

# CHAPTER №1

## PART №3

# TORN APART

The aftermath of a tragedy sets a family drifting apart, forever transforming cherished memories into bittersweet reminders.

## Flint Behind Bars

When you wake, Bronson will chat with you a bit about last night's events. As the first prisoner of Tazmily, he's not sure what to do with you, so he tells you to cool off a bit before retrieving the Drago Fang from him. To pass the time, check your surroundings and the door.

## An Apple a Day

After a short while, Claus will show up. With the funeral nearly over, he leaves you an apple and a hint before leaving. Bite into the apple to discover a tool to help you escape!

CERULEAN BEACH

SHERIFF'S OFFICE

→ TAZMILY SQUARE

A Edible Mushroom
B Nut Bread
C Manly Bandana

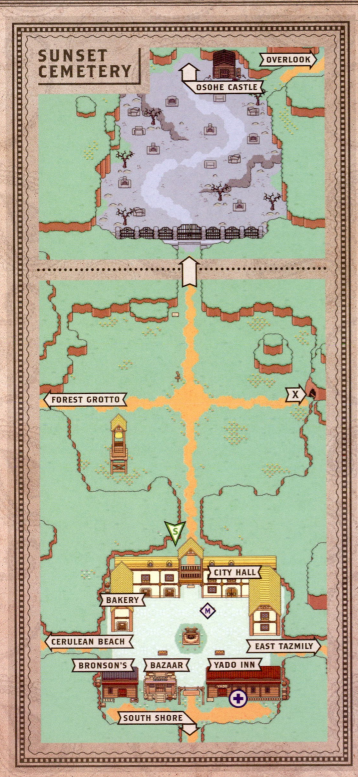

## SUNSET CEMETERY

OSOHE CASTLE
OVERLOOK
FOREST GROTTO
X
CITY HALL
BAKERY
M
CERULEAN BEACH
EAST TAZMILY
BRONSON'S
BAZAAR
YADO INN
SOUTH SHORE

# A Grave Situation

The air in town is heavy indeed. Heading over to the cemetery, you find Hinawa's father, Alec. A quick family discussion sets a plan in motion: Claus must be found! First, however, you ought to prepare for your journey.

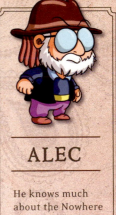

# ALEC

He knows much about the Nowhere Islands, including the mysterious Magypsies. His sense of humor is great and he cares deeply for his family. With a laid-back disposition, he often tries to lighten any tension he may sense. "Come on, now. That's no good. Smile! And relax!"

# HINAWA

Daughter of Alec
Wife to Flint
Mother to the twins
Lucas & Claus

# VILLAGE OF TAZMILY

The denizens of Tazmily are intertwined with relationships, friendships and other 'ships' yet to be discovered. Some in Tazmily have formed strong bonds while others remain to themselves.

BLOOD RELATED / FAMILY
MARRIED / OFFSPRING
FRIENDSHIP / RELATIONSHIP
EMPLOYED & WORKING FOR

WESS  PUSHER  ELMORE  SCAMP  ALEC  NIPPOLYTE  MAPSON  MIKE  BRONSON

DUSTER  OLLIE  NAN  ED  HINAWA  FLINT  LIGHTER  THOMAS  LISA

KUMATORA  SEBASTIAN  ALLE  BONEY  LUCAS  CLAUS  FUEL  RICHIE  NICHOL

BATEAU  CAROLINE  JONEL  BRENDA  MATT  JILL  TESSIE  REGGIE  ISAAC

NANA  ANGIE  BOB  DONA  BIFF  BUTCH  BUD  LOU

ABBOT  ABBEY  PAUL  LINDA  JACKIE  BETSY  LEDER  ???  ???

## Fang You Very Much

Bronson has been keeping his mind off of last night's events by forging a weapon from the Drago Fang. He entrusts you with it, knowing that it's the only weapon capable of piercing a Drago's hide.

# MASCULINE
## EQUIPMENT

After the funeral Lighter will leave the scene. Go to Cerulean Beach to find him and chat for a bit. He'll give you the Manly Bandana.

## BIRDS ON THE WING

Perched upon the beach is a group of pigeons. If you try to talk to or walk by these birds, they will flee into the sky. Nothing's more satisfying than dashing into them, however!

## SCATTERED SEEDS

You may have noticed small nuts scattered around Tazmily. While they only recover 5 HP a pop, they refill and move every time you enter Cross Road.

## NUTTY COMBINATIONS

Got a handful of nuts burning a hole in your pockets? Well, bring 'em in to Caroline's Bakery and cook them into something more useful!

*1 nut = Nut Cookie  |  3 nuts = Nut Bread*

**A** WESS'S HOUSE
**B**
← TAZMILY SQUARE

**A** Thunder Bomb
**B** Peculiar Cheese

CATTLE FARM

## EAST TAZMILY

TAZMILY VILLAGE — THOMAS'S BAZAAR — BARTERING SHOP

# THOMAS's BAZAAR

- Organic & Fresh!
- Only Top Quality!
- FREE!

In this town, everything's up for grabs—take what you need, no need for money! Items are set out right before you walk in the door, so once you see the wares, they don't change. However, if you happen to visit before viewing Hinawa's grave, the shop will restock, so be sure to come back later! The items potentially available include:

**Flea Charm**
Defense +5
*(always present on your first visit)*

**Running Bomb**
Battle Item
*(always present on your first visit)*

**Better Stick**
Offense +20
*(very rare!)*

**Fresh Milk**
Recovers 80 HP
*(spoils quickly)*

**Innit Tea**
Restores 15 HP

**Antidote**
Cures Poison Status

**Nut**
Restore 5 HP

**Ancient Banana**
Battle Item

**Edible Mushroom**
Restores 20 HP

**Anti-Paralysis**
Cures Paralysis status

## A NEW GUEST

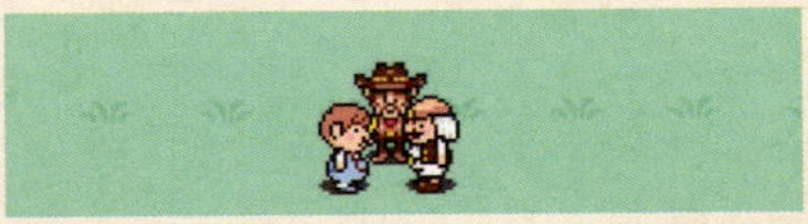

If you explore the southeast cattle farm, you'll find an unfamiliar face. Just who is this strange merchant?

## T-BOMB'S AWAY!

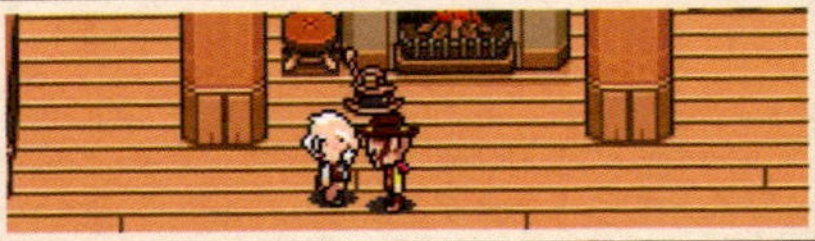

Before heading to Alec's house, talk to Wess (east of town). He'll give you another Thunder Bomb. Get the one out back too!

SUNSHINE FOREST

ORIANDER CLIFFS

FOREST GROTTO

## Just a Sunshine Day

Fully prepared for the journey ahead, Flint must now trek up to Alec's house to start his search. Have Mapson mark your map to make the trip through Sunshine Forest easier, but be wary about the new wildlife that emerged in the daylight!

Grab the items in the giftboxes if you haven't already!

## JUST PASSING THROUGH »

If you dash at enemies, you may find some pushovers - literally! This is based on your strength relative to theirs. You'll completely knock out weak enemies, while stronger enemies will only be temporarily stunned. Sadly you won't gain any experience from these maneuvers.

# BEANY BABIES

Beanlings are fast, tiny enemies which jump out of the ground. Run one down and beat it for a huge Exp. payoff!

# A DIRTY SECRET

Small spherical foes called Soot Dumplings roll around the wreckage of Lighter's scorched property. If you have skill in music combos, their Exp. yield will shoot your levels through the roof!

# ⊕ FRIENDLY
## FOLIAGE

The Walking Bushie appears near the cliff where you found the scrap of Hinawa's dress. This odd character heals your party and then politely runs away, so be kind and don't attack him!

# ENEMIES

## PRAYING MANTIS

It's a cool bug in concept but not much of a fighter in practice. Perhaps it should be praying for your mercy!

Nut (50%)

| HP: 34 | OFF: 32 | DEF: 3 | EXP: 2 |
|---|---|---|---|

## GREEDY MOUSE

An inability to share led it to its battle with you. Teach it a lesson with a couple hits and hope that the little vermin leaves you a treat to snack on after the bout.

Peculiar Cheese (20% ) / Nut Bread (20%)

| HP: 86 | OFF: 47 | DEF: 16 | EXP: 35 |
|---|---|---|---|

## BEANLING

It may seem like a pushover since it runs from you, but this plant packs PK Fire α if you manage to fight it face-to-face.

| HP: 138 | OFF: 43 | DEF: 20 | EXP: 538 |
|---|---|---|---|

## SOOT DUMPLING

It only takes a few rounds of battle for this foe to blow away like dust in the wind, so your best bet to defeat this defensive fluffball is to string together some perfect combos. Their high experience yield is well-deserved.

| HP: 36 | OFF: 1 | DEF: 99 | EXP: 1000 |
|---|---|---|---|

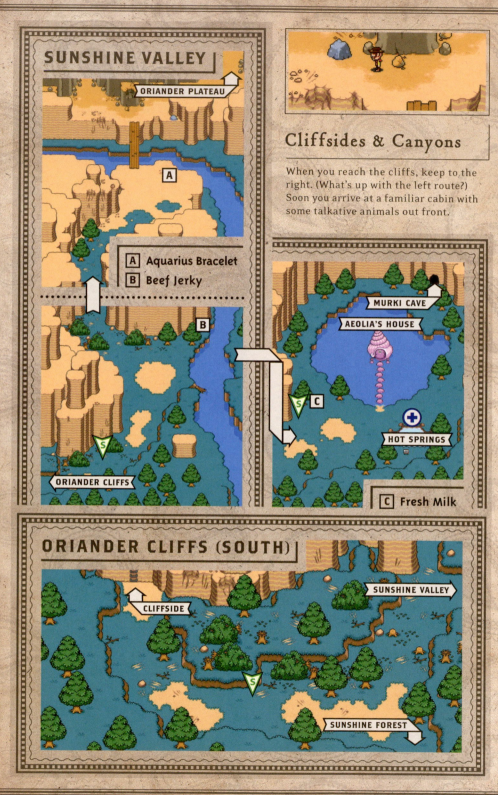

## SUNSHINE VALLEY

ORIANDER PLATEAU →

A

A Aquarius Bracelet
B Beef Jerky

B

S

← ORIANDER CLIFFS

## Cliffsides & Canyons

When you reach the cliffs, keep to the right. (What's up with the left route?) Soon you arrive at a familiar cabin with some talkative animals out front.

MURKI CAVE →
AEOLIA'S HOUSE →

S C

HOT SPRINGS →

C Fresh Milk

## ORIANDER CLIFFS (SOUTH)

← CLIFFSIDE

SUNSHINE VALLEY →

S

SUNSHINE FOREST →

## Smart Alec

Meeting up with Alec, you learn about his strange – but helpful-sounding – friends. Follow the directions of the arrow lizards, who hand you off to some helpful frogs.

## DIVINE BOVINE

You can get Fresh Milk from the cow near Aeolia's house. Be sure to drink it before it spoils!

## See the Shell?

In the clearing ahead looms a gigantic seashell house. If you've been listening to Alec, you will know to expect Magypsies, but... what's a Magypsy?

# ENEMIES

## SPUD BUG

While they may not look very challenging, they like to stick together in groups. If you find yourself against many of these bugs, use Flint's Swing skill to take them all out together.

Running Bomb (10%)

| HP: 80 | OFF: 47 | DEF: 10 | EXP: 24 |

## AGITATED BOAR

What a pig! These aggressive animals charge at anything they see, so try to maneuver around them while they make a beeline for where you were standing.

Beef Jerky (70%)

| HP: 133 | OFF: 58 | DEF: 25 | EXP: 62 |

## CRAG LIZARD

This petrified reptile has a stellar defense, so don't be shy about healing. Always Toughen Up first and then either try to Power Smash or Strengthen Up and attack.

Beef Jerky (20%)

| HP: 124 | OFF: 51 | DEF: 35 | EXP: 70 |

## WALKING BUSHIE

The experience you gain from defeating this helpful herb is far less useful than the healing it gives you if you don't hurt it in battle.

Antidote (10%)

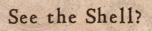

| HP: 108 | OFF: 45 | DEF: 22 | EXP: 8 |

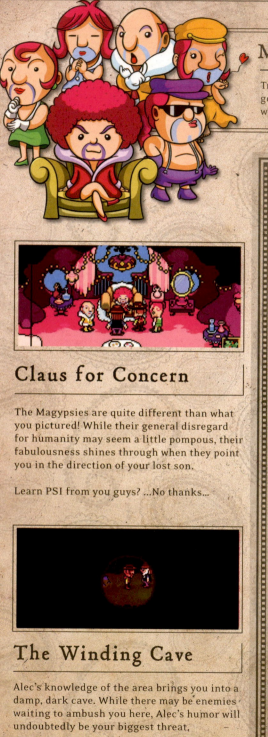

# MAGYPSIES

Transcending humanity and, more notably, gender, these 'unique' beings supposedly wield incredible powers.

## Claus for Concern

The Magypsies are quite different than what you pictured! While their general disregard for humanity may seem a little pompous, their fabulousness shines through when they point you in the direction of your lost son.

Learn PSI from you guys? ...No thanks...

## The Winding Cave

Alec's knowledge of the area brings you into a damp, dark cave. While there may be enemies waiting to ambush you here, Alec's humor will undoubtedly be your biggest threat.

**3** MURKI CAVE

ORIANDER CLIFFS (NORTH)

A Peculiar Cheese
B Beef Jerky
C Running Bomb

**2**

A

SUNSHINE VALLEY

**1**

B

C

## ORIANDER CLIFFS (NORTH)

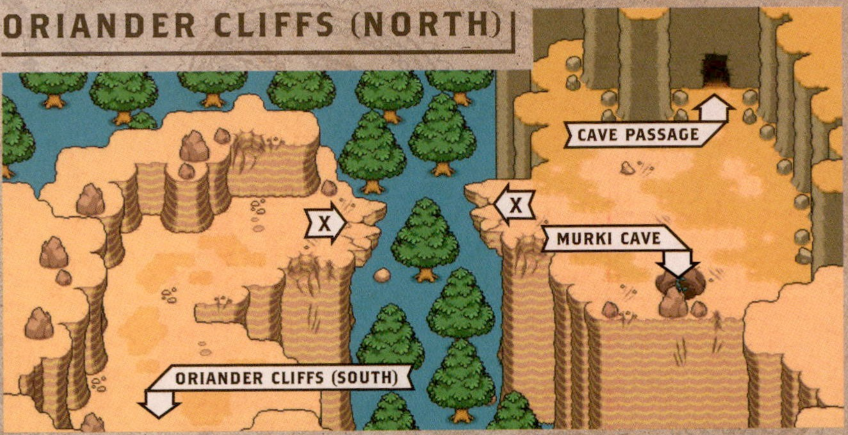

CAVE PASSAGE

X

X

MURKI CAVE

ORIANDER CLIFFS (SOUTH)

## CAVE PASSAGE

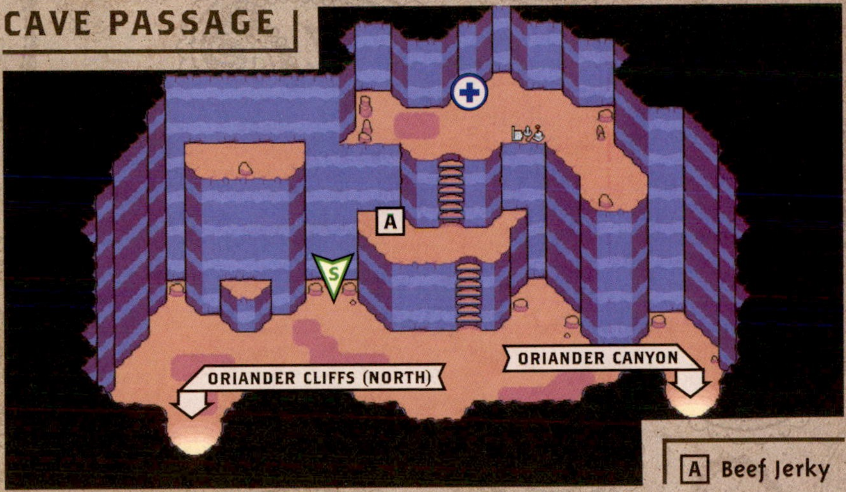

A

S

ORIANDER CLIFFS (NORTH)

ORIANDER CANYON

A Beef Jerky

## Suspicious Swine

Emerging from the Murki Cave, you come across a cavernous grotto whose highest plateau is littered with soldiers and strange junk. Chase off the Pigmasks and check out the strange machines.

## DRAGO PLATEAU

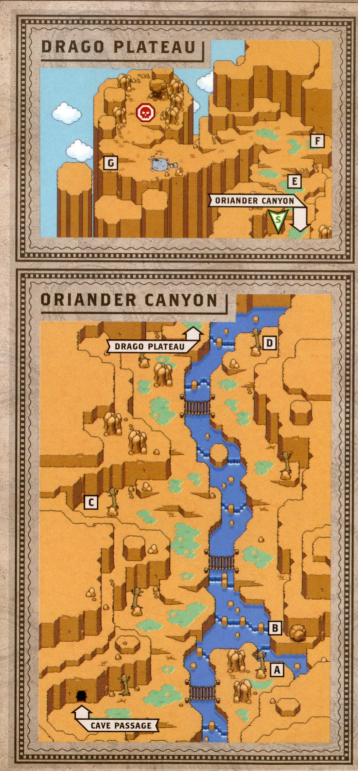

G

F

E

ORIANDER CANYON

S

## ORIANDER CANYON

DRAGO PLATEAU

D

C

B

A

CAVE PASSAGE

## A Step Further

Battle your way through the barren Canyon, careful to pick up as many healing items as possible on the way. Upon reaching the plateau, you'll find a young Drago toying with something dreadfully familiar.

## Trees with Bark & Bite

As you approach the foreboding wreckage of yet another animal experiment, keep your wits about you and avoid the trees, whose ambushes will sap your energy.

A  Sprinting Bomb

B  Beef Jerky

C  Fresh Lumber

D  Beef Jerky

E  Child's Shoe

F  Nut Bread

G  Beef Jerky

# BOSS WARNING!

## The Foe Emerges!

The sense of despair you feel as you come across Claus's second shoe is quickly replaced by dread and vengeance as the monster emerges from its lair.

# MECHA-DRAGO

- ❱ Use the Drago Fang to pierce its hide. Without the Fang, your attacks only do one HP damage.
- ❱ Drago's War Cry reduces Flint's offense one level while Flint's 'Strengthen Up' increases it one level. You always want it to be at a positive level, so be sure to Strengthen Up once at the beginning of the battle and then again every time Drago does his War Cry.
- ❱ Always keep your HP above 60, as every now and then Drago can shoot flames that burn you for 40+ damage.
- ❱ Flint's Power Smash can do 400+ HP of damage, depending on his offense level.
- ❱ Alec will heal you with herbs if your HP drops dangerously low (around 25 HP), but he's only got enough to save you three times! Each application will restore 20-30 HP.
- ❱ Mecha Drago's death throes are violent. Thanks to the rolling HP meter, you can minimize the injury. Flint must keep his HP above 40 or the final blow will do him in!

# ENEMIES

## TITANY

What exactly is this creature? You don't know, but what is clear is that it's unfriendly. You may want to Strengthen Up to better penetrate its outer shell.

**Running Bomb (10%)**

| HP: 119 | OFF: 50 | DEF: 30 | EXP: 63 |
|---|---|---|---|

## BALDING EAGLE

From the sky descends an avid avian! It might be tough to dodge their quick swoop from above, but the fight is well worth the jerky they often drop.

**Beef Jerky (70%)**

| HP: 80 | OFF: 53 | DEF: 16 | EXP: 68 |
|---|---|---|---|

## TREE

Fighting this lumbering foe is not recommended, as it contains a deadly mixture of chemicals that cause it to explode when defeated.

**Nut Bread (20%)**

| HP: 160 | OFF: 56 | DEF: 24 | EXP: 72 |
|---|---|---|---|

# MECHA DRAGO

## CHAPTER BOSS

From the wrecked terrain stomps a bionic Drago, the beast who has slain Flint's wife. This is the climactic, long-awaited battle.

| P: 724 | OFF: 60 | DEF: 34 | EXP: 486 |
|---|---|---|---|

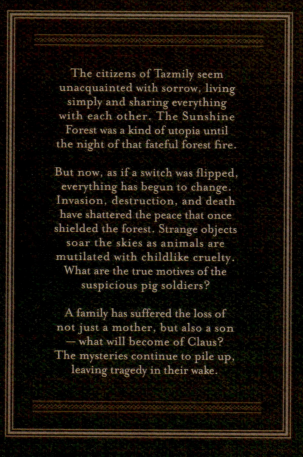

The citizens of Tazmily seem
unacquainted with sorrow, living
simply and sharing everything
with each other. The Sunshine
Forest was a kind of utopia until
the night of that fateful forest fire.

But now, as if a switch was flipped,
everything has begun to change.
Invasion, destruction, and death
have shattered the peace that once
shielded the forest. Strange objects
soar the skies as animals are
mutilated with childlike cruelty.
What are the true motives of the
suspicious pig soldiers?

A family has suffered the loss of
not just a mother, but also a son
— what will become of Claus?
The mysteries continue to pile up,
leaving tragedy in their wake.

# CHAPTER

**No. 2**

## THIEF ADVENTURE

# CHAPTER

# № 2

## PART I

### thick as thieves

*Wess has been training you in the fine art of thievery, but the training is over. Now is the time to test your skills. Your job is to break into Osohe Castle and retrieve a certain important item. Wess doesn't tell you what it is, just that it's very valuable and shines a little. Maybe.*

## MEMORY LAME

During your mission briefing, you can get a little background information on Duster and his dad by telling Wess 'No' when he asks if you're prepared to change the way you live. Wess does not seem very sure of his memory, though…

## At Sixes & Sevens

The Slightly-Less-Than-Seven Mystical Thief Tools. Is it really possible that Wess has forgotten how many Thief Tools there are? Surely a good memory is an important attribute for a thief? Maybe he's just trying to keep you on your toes.

**WALL STAPLES**
A climbing utility and can also briefly pin a foe down.

**SCARY MASK**
Scares your foe, lowering their offense.

**H. PENDULUM**
Sends foes to sleep, letting you hear their heartbeat.

**SMOKE BOMB**
Emits an acrid smoke, foes cry, lowering their accuracy.

**TICKLE STICK**
Tickles your foe, lowering their defense.

**SIREN BEETLE**
Makes foe stop and cover its ears, facing a different direction.

# CRASHING BOOM BANG

Before setting off on your quest, look behind the house for an explosive gift — a Thunder Bomb! Remember that it refills each time you visit the crossroads!

# INSIGNIFICANT TREE MESSAGES

Throughout the years, people have often carved messages into trees This is no different. It's nothing very significant…

## EAST TAZMILY

WESS'S HOUSE

TAZMILY SQUARE

CATTLE FARM

A Thunder Bomb
B Peculiar Cheese

## YADO YADO YADO

Yado Inn is crowded tonight. Some people are refugees from the fire, and others have stories to tell. Can you detect that whiff of unrequited love in the air, too?

**BETSY**

*A nosy blonde who knows all the local gossip*

**BOB**

*Likes mysteries and telling stories. Always up for a drink… or nine.*

## MARK MY MAP

Head towards Osohe Castle. On your way, have a chat with Mapson. He'll tell you of an interesting rumor and mark your map for you.

## THE NIGHTS ARE LONG

Lucas is finding it hard to sleep tonight…

## BUMP IN THE NIGHT

Exiting town, you bump into a strange man and his simian companion. What could they be doing in the middle of the night, and what's wrong with that monkey?

## CAPITAL IDEA

Butch is huddled in a corner, sorting through a bag of "money" that he traded for some pigs. He doesn't quite know what it's used for, but the traveler who gave it to him seemed to think it might be useful soon. Butch hides the money in the well, and you're the only witness, so don't go trying to take it!

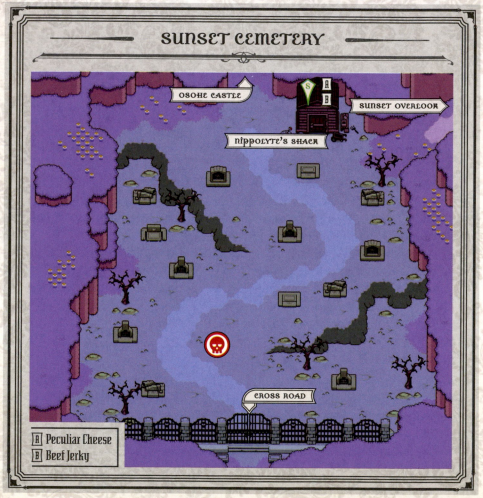

SUNSET CEMETERY

OSOHE CASTLE

SUNSET OVERLOOK

NIPPOLYTE'S SHACK

CROSS ROAD

A Peculiar Cheese
B Beef Jerky

## ROLLING DOWNHILL

In the dark, ominous shapes fall from an airship as it lumbers across the sky above the castle. What kind of surveillance or weaponry could it be unleashing? Unfazed, Duster heads straight for the castle via the graveyard.

## MINI-BOSS ENCOUNTER

### Graveyard Bash

Zombies are on the attack! These ghosts of the past are looking for a quick meal, but as long as you picked up a Thunder Bomb from behind your house you should have no problem sending them back from whence they came. Don't forget to run back home and replenish your thunder bomb stock afterwards!

## ⸗ enemies ⸗

### ZOMBIE MAN

The dead walk the earth — and they're hungry! And a little chatty. Zombies make up for being slow and weak by attacking in groups, so hit them with wall staples and focus your attacks on one at a time.

**Rotten Eclair (10%)**

| HP: 95 | OFF: 44 | DEF: 7 | EXP: 25 |
| --- | --- | --- | --- |

### ZOMBIE LADY

She's back from the dead and fighting fit! She's not a lot different from the Zombie Man, so use the same techniques to send her and her companions back to the grave.

**Rotten Eclair (10%)**

| HP: 87 | OFF: 44 | DEF: 7 | EXP: 25 |
| --- | --- | --- | --- |

## CARRY ON UP THE CASTLE

Once the zombies are all dispatched, head on up to the castle. Unfortunately the drawbridge is up, thereby preventing all entry. On your way back to the graveyard you'll receive an unexpected (and unsolicited) lesson in battle technique.

# Obey Your Ant

It kills this ant to see your lack of battle rhythm. Take his advice: pay attention to the rhythm of your enemies' movements and work towards a 16-hit combo!

## TUNNEL VISION

You could have sworn you watched Nippolyte enter his house, but he's nowhere to be found. Where could he be? His basement has some food (including one of your favorite types of cheese) and an... empty bookcase? Do a little redecorating and you'll find the gravedigger's creepy secret passage.

## STARING CONTEST

Outside of battle, the Spineless Lobsters will give you the ol' stink eye. Outstare them and you'll have an easy opening shot in battle.

### NIPPOLYTE

*Local grave digger and sower of agricultural abominations.*

### SPARROWS

*Chirpy little birds with a wealth of useful information.*

## OSOHE TUNNEL

OSOHE COURTYARD

A

NIPPOLYTE'S

Ⓐ Running Bomb
Ⓑ Nut Bread

## OSOHE COURTYARD

OSOHE GALLERY (3F)

OSOHE TUNNEL

## OH, SO, HEY—CASTLE TIME!

The tunnel leads to the castle courtyard where Nippolyte tends his culinary hobbies in secrecy. Nippolyte thinks you'd have to scale the walls if you wanted in the castle, and he's right—the front door won't budge. Check the discolored castle wall over by the tunnel.

## MYSTERY SOLVED

As you explore the castle balcony, watch your step. That air-ship's special delivery was not as threatening as you feared, but talk about vile.

## VENTURE INWARD

Head inside and make your way to the first floor. Beware of ghosts and their ghastly breath.

# enemies

## ZOMBIE DOG

*Don't let his winning smile fool you. He's not the toughest enemy around — his bark is worse than his bite. A few hits should be enough to tame him.*

**Nut Bread (70%)**

| HP: 115 | OFF: 42 | DEF: 5 | EXP: 29 |

## MOBILE GRAVE

*At night it's not just the dead that go walking. Stoneface here can be a tough customer, but a Thunder Bomb will help bring him down.*

**Running Bomb (10%)**

| HP: 158 | OFF: 63 | DEF: 26 | EXP: 60 |

## DETACHED LEECH

*Great leaping leeches! This sucker is fairly easy to over-power, but beware of large groups. There's safety in numbers, but not for you.*

**Edible Mushroom (70%)**

| HP: 61 | OFF: 33 | DEF: 5 | EXP: 21 |

## SPINELESS LOBSTER

*This crab may have a tough exterior, but he has his limitations. He can raise his offense, but only once, giving you the chance to nip in and leave him shellshocked.*

**Beef Jerky (20%)**

| HP: 80 | OFF: 42 | DEF: 24 | EXP: 40 |

# CHAPTER № 2

## PART 2

### Osohe Castle

*Osohe Castle is an abandoned mystery full of frightening spirits and impassable obstacles. That's never stopped you before, so perhaps it's time to blaze your own trail. That statue looks like a good starting place!*

## The Art of Osohe

The most interesting and dangerous aspect of the ancient Osohe Castle is the fascinating art packed into every room and hallway. Statues, paintings, and ancient weapons in various states of peril, decay, and enchantment fill the decrepit corridors.

## UNWANTED GIFTS

Don't be tempted to open the present at the bottom of the hole, as it contains an unpleasant surprise. If your curiosity gets the best of you, though, take heart—the present in the next room contains a little something to clear the air.

# Safety Warning

Every year dozens of people are injured in art-related accidents. Are you thinking about dashing into a heavy metal object? If so, follow these simple steps for a safe and happy art-wrecking experience:

## Dash—Don't Push!
*The greatest obstacle faced by young statue-crashers today, aside from the statues themselves, is the misconception that pushing is enough.*

## Left is Right!
*If you must dash into a priceless artifact, be sure to do it at a safe angle. Blindly dashing into an unwitting statue from the wrong direction could prove hazardous to more than just the artwork.*

## Leap Recklessly!
*Have you successfully ruined an ancient treasure? Not sure what to do next? Seasoned professionals agree that flinging oneself recklessly into the nearest hole is the best course of action.*

## NOW OPEN SESAME

Once you're in the entrance hall, you can throw open the castle doors. You can also shout your favorite incantation for dramatic effect.

### Oh-So-Ghost Busting

The halls and rooms of Osohe castle are filled with wandering spirits. Lucky for you it's easy to distinguish friendly ghosts from their less diplomatic cousins, since unfriendly ghosts tend to wander the hallways with bloodshot eyes. Watch out!

# Hotsprings of Nowhere

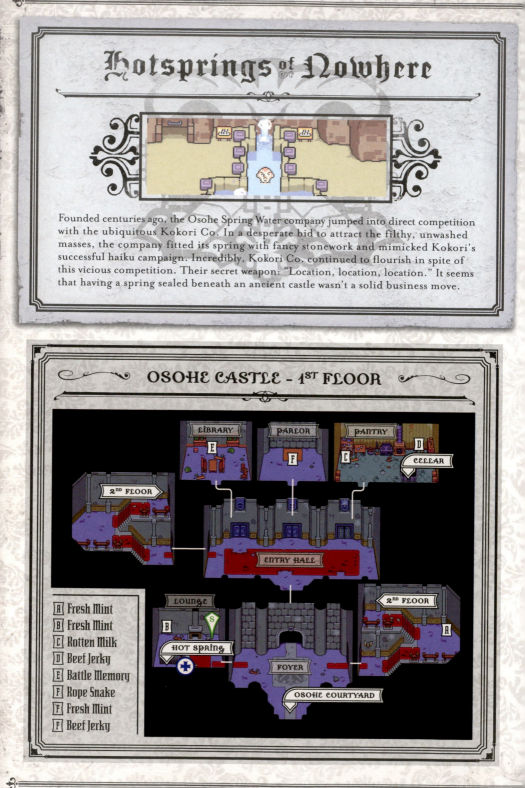

Founded centuries ago, the Osohe Spring Water company jumped into direct competition with the ubiquitous Kokori Co. In a desperate bid to attract the filthy, unwashed masses, the company fitted its spring with fancy stonework and mimicked Kokori's successful haiku campaign. Incredibly, Kokori Co. continued to flourish in spite of this vicious competition. Their secret weapon: "Location, location, location." It seems that having a spring sealed beneath an ancient castle wasn't a solid business move.

## OSOHE CASTLE – 1ST FLOOR

LIBRARY
E

PARLOR
F

PANTRY
C          D
CELLAR

2ND FLOOR

ENTRY HALL

LOUNGE
B      S

HOT SPRING

2ND FLOOR
A

FOYER

OSOHE COURTYARD

- A Fresh Mint
- B Fresh Mint
- C Rotten Milk
- D Beef Jerky
- E Battle Memory
- F Rope Snake
- F Fresh Mint
- F Beef Jerky

# Casper's
## ROT N' SWAP

Looking for an eclair on the cheap? Tired of paying retail prices for rotten food? Wander this mortal coil no longer, friends! Come on down to Casper's Wholesale Rot-N-Swap where you'll find the biggest selection of fresh mints, rotten food, and anthropomorphic plot devices in all of Nowhere! This week only we're having a special on Rope Snakes for just one eclair! We're practically giving them away, so hurry on down to the Ghost Bazaar because supplies are limited!

## CASTLE CELLAR

# enemies

### STINKY GHOST

*These spectres shouldn't be too difficult to dissipate. You can avoid their burping attacks by pinning them down with your wall staples.*

**Rotten Eclair (50%)**

| HP: 125 | OFF: 48 | DEF: 10 | EXP: 35 |

### ARACHNID!

*They'll try to trap you in their webs and may call for backup, but their defense is so low that they don't pose a real threat.*

**Fresh Mint (20%)**

| HP: 60 | OFF: 43 | DEF: 5 | EXP: 20 |

### BIG BRO

*These sad looking guys hang out in the castle cellar. They'd like to use psychic powers, but can't. In fact, they won't attack you at all, so you can't lose!*

**Nut Cookie (70%)**

| HP: 67 | OFF: 10 | DEF: 13 | EXP: 15 |

### BARREL MAN

*He's not a barrel of laughs and he's not very strong. Give him the old one-two and watch him roll away.*

**Nut Bread (70%)**

| HP: 100 | OFF: 50 | DEF: 18 | EXP: 32 |

# Memories are made of This

In the library west of the Ghost Bazaar is an important item you won't want to miss: the Battle Memory. You can use this special item to 'remember' the enemies you've already faced. They won't fight back, so take your time practicing combos, getting your timing right, and searching for vulnerabilities!

## CALL TO ARMS AND A LEG

Once you've got your Rope Snake, run to the library and check out the mysteriously empty books. (What's the point of a handsome book with no content?) Head upstairs via the door to the west, you'll find a hallway filled with ambulatory armor. The noise coming from the end of the hall could wake the dead...

**RISKY BUSINESS** You can avoid the Ghost Armor if you sprint straight down the middle of the hallway, but if you're running low on HP, don't risk it—take the chimney shortcut back to the hot spring and heal up first.

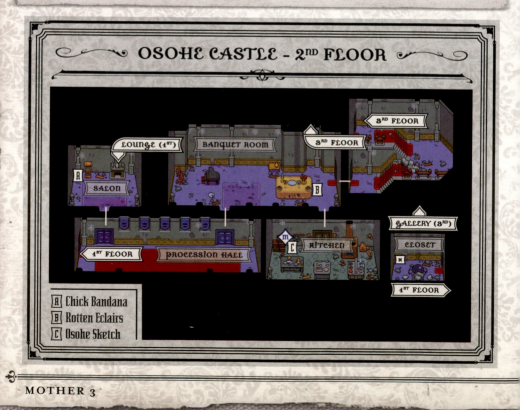

### OSOHE CASTLE - 2ND FLOOR

LOUNGE (1ST) — BANQUET ROOM — 3RD FLOOR — 3RD FLOOR

SALON — A

1ST FLOOR — PROCESSION HALL

B

KITCHEN — C

GALLERY (3RD)

CLOSET — x

1ST FLOOR

A Chick Bandana
B Rotten Eclairs
C Osohe Sketch

# TRAPS & CHIMNEYS

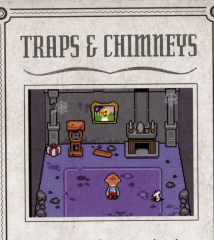

The mouse informs you that there is a secret chimney network! Check the fireplace to make your way back to the hot springs in the basement. In the corner of the room is the Chick Bandana, an important defense item that only Duster can equip. It's a trap—as soon as you spring for the present box, the painting flies off the wall and attacks! The Artsy Ghost uses very powerful PSI attacks, so Wall Staple him with reckless abandon.

## PARTY CRASHER

Osohe's party ghosts are all friendly, so take your time and get to know them. Visit the kitchen to see what's cooking and the ghost next to the present will give you some useful information: presents with blue ribbons contain maps! While you're there, watch out for the jar of preserves on the table— it's more potent than you might expect.

# ENEMIES

## GHOST ARMOR

These ghostly suits may look tough, but there's a chink in their armor. Use your Scary Mask and Tickle Stick to soften them up.

**Beef Jerky (20%)**

| HP: 141 | OFF: 47 | DEF: 30 | EXP: 72 |
|---|---|---|---|

## ARTSY GHOST

He may divide opinion, but his PSI Freeze leaves most critics cold. Tack him to the wall with some staples if you want to live!

**Peculiar Cheese (15%)**

| HP: 187 | OFF: 55 | DEF: 18 | EXP: 46 |
|---|---|---|---|

## VIOLENT ATTACK ROACH

They may be small, but they pack quite a punch. This can take a toll on your health if you're not careful.

**Nut Bread (10%)**

| HP: 88 | OFF: 55 | DEF: 11 | EXP: 40 |
|---|---|---|---|

## STRAWBERRY SLIME

This sludge is way past its sell-by date. Your pendulum, tickle stick, and scary mask will help, but if you have a Running Bomb, use it! Don't worry, you'll get it back.

**Sprinting Bomb (100%)**

| HP: 182 | OFF: 52 | DEF: 30 | EXP: 146 |
|---|---|---|---|

# A Party to Die For!

**WHAT ~** Ghost Party!
**WHERE ~** Osohe Castle, 2nd Floor
**WHEN ~** FOR-EV-ER!

Attempts at Digestion!
Shedding of Mortal Coils!
Formerly Live Entertainment!

## DON'T GET ATTACHED

You'll find that the stairs are impassable. Even though the maestro's song lays out the ground rules, that wall near the dining table looks more and more inviting. Check it out and don't forget to pick up the Aquarius Bracelet in the stairwell. Beware the southern-most giftbox—it's another sulfurous surprise!

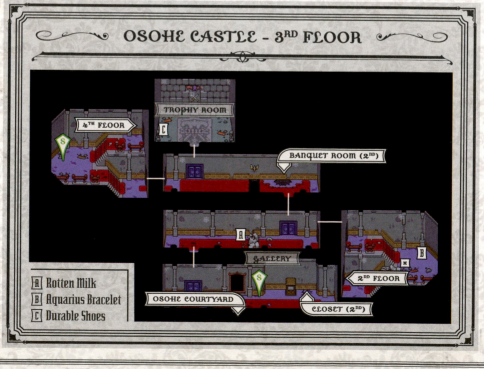

### OSOHE CASTLE - 3RD FLOOR

4TH FLOOR

TROPHY ROOM
C

BANQUET ROOM (2ND)

A
GALLERY

B
2ND FLOOR

OSOHE COURTYARD

CLOSET (2ND)

A Rotten Milk
B Aquarius Bracelet
C Durable Shoes

# I DO ECLAIR

If you need to stock up on real food, talk to the ghost on the right side of the dining table. He's cheeky but generous, as long as you answer his questions right. Keep talking to him to load up on Rotten Eclairs, then trade them for Beef Jerky with the ghost at the top of your staple ladder. You'll be glad you did!

## A Useful Friend

There's a gap blocking your way forward. Luckily, your pal the Rope Snake can help!

### ROPE SNAKE

*The best little Rope Snake in Tazmily. Full of confidence and likes to prove himself to others.*

# DURABILITY

Before fighting the Ghost Knight trio, be sure to open and equip the Durable Shoes on the left! They'll give you a nice offense boost. Don't forget to throw away your old shoes since you can't use or sell them.

# ᛖnemies

## CARPET MONSTER

*Never smile at this crocodile. He has a dangerous paralyzing attack, so watch out for that. With luck, you'll soon send him scurrying.*

**Beef Jerky (15%)**

| HP: 132 | OFF: 50 | DEF: 21 | EXP: 67 |

## GHOST SHIELD

*Don't be taken in by his toothy grin—although this chap isn't too aggressive, he has good defense. Send him looking for an orthodontist.*

**Rotten Milk (10%)**

| HP: 124 | OFF: 45 | DEF: 33 | EXP: 37 |

## GHOST SWORD

*He likes to slice and dice, but a few hits are enough to cut him down to size.*

**Peculiar Cheese (10%)**

| HP: 108 | OFF: 57 | DEF: 24 | EXP: 48 |

## GHOST KNIGHT

*A hardheaded ghost disliked by all the other ghosts in the castle. Keep your health up and lower his offense and defense frequently! Your thief tools (except for the smoke bomb) will come in quite handy.*

**Yogurt (70%)**

| HP: 200 | OFF: 68 | DEF: 36 | EXP: 180 |

# WELCOMING THE GHOST

A friendly ghost stands guard in front of a room with a formidable foe. Luckily, you've got two options for this battle. If you'd rather take it easy, you can attack each piece of the knight individually by approaching the shield or sword first. If you walk towards the armor first, though, it will team up with the sword/shield to become the Ghost Knight! Be warned that the armor is cursed—that's bad. You'll only have to fight one battle instead of three, which means less damage. That's good! However, it will be a more difficult battle—that's bad. But there's a 70% chance he'll drop a free Yogurt—that's good!

## Why Fight the Knight?

If the draw of a free yogurt isn't enough to lure you into a battle with the knight, you can at least look forward to a thank-you from the ghost outside the door.

## OSOHE CASTLE - 4TH FLOOR

## Dropping In

A strange girl appears and disappears in a flash of pink and purple. Grab the memento she drops and chase after her!

## Doors Galore

Watch out for the room with four doors — only the far right one will lead further into the castle, while the two middle doors hide unpleasant surprises. Beyond the fourth door, Mr. Passion is busy conducting his invisible orchestra. He invites you to listen to his classical interpretations, but be prepared to defend your honor if you decline his invitation!

## BOSS ENCOUNTER

## Artistic Passion

Composing music was his life, but if it's up to him, it's your career that will be cut short. As a musician he's quite emotional, so use your Smoke Bomb to reduce him to tears and decrease his accuracy. With that out of the way, lower his offense and defense a few times, and then start attacking him with any bomb you've picked up along the way.

# enemies

### ROCKIN' GHOST

*You can rock these chumps in a one-on-one battle, but if you're fighting two together there's a chance they'll get into a jousting match with each other.*

**Beef Jerky (15%)**

| HP: 152 | OFF: 54 | DEF: 24 | EXP: 68 |

### PSEUDOOR

*It's a trap! Luckily it will shut up after a few hits. After that, use your Tickle Stick to close this door for good.*

**Fresh Mint (15%)**

| HP: 215 | OFF: 58 | DEF: 27 | EXP: 76 |

### MR. PASSION

#### Mini Boss

*A melody of pain is ready to conduct your elegy. Make sure you're loaded up with beef jerky from the friendly ghosts. Use your thief tools and put your training to the test.*

| HP: 630 | OFF: 60 | DEF: 25 | EXP: 340 |

## SOFA LULLABY

After the poltergeist has been placated, that comfy-looking couch becomes a nice place for a nap.

## FROM TUNES TO SPITTOONS

Now that the music's over, you can find what you're looking for in the next room. It's a dance to a different spittoon. Remember, take a fire exit if you need to go downstairs quickly. Down the fireplace! Ker-PLUNK!

## BRIDGE TO NOWHERE

Once you're out of the castle, be sure to say goodbye to Nippolyte. He'll give you the key to the drawbridge, making your exit that much easier. Once outside the castle, head for home. There is an uneasy atmosphere in the town as many are talking about Hinawa and the creepy man staying at the Yado Inn.

## PIGGLY OH SO WIGGLY

The talkative pigs on Butch's farm are at it again. Speaking of Butch, he's starting to seem a little paranoid... Could it have something to do with the money-lending stranger who was lurking the other night?

### CAROLINE

*Angie's mom. Caring and maternal. Runs the local bakery.*

### ANGIE

*Young girl. Likes to copy her mom's cooking.*

## DOMESTIC DISPUTE

### DONA

*Lives with Bob down by Cerulean Beach. Was a good friend of Hinawa.*

Head back home to show Wess your find. He seems happy...but it doesn't last. Poor Duster's leg injury suddenly makes more sense! However, there's a more positive change of mood when Wess sees the pendant you picked up on the way. Head back to the castle, this time with Wess in tow.

# CHAPTER

# № 2

## PART 3

### Two of Thieves

*Wess, still bitter about your failure, joins you to ensure the mission gets done right. The enemy may already be on the move, so with the sun shining the mission has become more dangerous. What about this "valuable item" is so important?*

## B-B-BOMBASTIC!

As you set off for the castle, don't forget to pick up one of those useful Thunder Bombs! Might want to grab two if you can.

## THE GOOD WITH THE BAD

A cloud seems to be settling over the town. A forlorn Isaac wanders the village grousing about his lack of status and Bateau and Dona are down in the dumps. Even Scamp, a village elder, voices his fears for himself and the village.

### SCAMP

*Village elder with a nickname he earned as an ornery kid.*

### ALLE

*Scamp's spunky little grandaughter.*

### MYRNA

*Scamp's faithful bird that is constantly speaking as one of the family.*

## GOOD WESS, BAD WESS

Wess and Duster's father-son relationship is complicated, at best. Is Wess really so careless about his son's feelings and safety? He hardly even seems like a father…

## MONKEY BUSINESS

News of the stranger and his simian companion has spread around town, but it's not all good. Rumor has it that poor monkey is mistreated, and Betsy has found herself in the same situation as Butch—the clueless owner of a pile of money. What is that monkey man up to?

## RUMBLING IN THE DEEP

As you and Wess approach the castle, you hear an odd sound and the ground begins to shake. Is it an earthquake, or something more sinister? Strange tracks lead from a nearby tunnel to the castle. Could this be 'the enemy'?

## NIPPOLYTE'S OUT

In the castle grounds you find Nippolyte in some pain. He's been beaten up by some pig-looking guys who broke into the castle. Heed his warning and be sure you've got some health items and bombs before you go after the perps!

## HIRED GUN

As you enter the castle you are greeted by two Pigmasks. Rather than fighting you themselves, they bring a Clayman to life and send him to do the heavy lifting.

### MINI-BOSS ENCOUNTER

# Dirty Deeds

He's not light on his feet, but he is heavy handed. Throw a Smoke Bomb to make him cry, then use the Scary Mask and Tickle Stick respectively to lower his offense and defense. Wall staples will come in handy too, as will Wess's occasional assistance. Once the Clayman has received enough damage he'll crash down on top of you, leaving you flatter than a flounder. After this, it's fairly easy to finish him off. Just make sure to keep your health above 50!

## BACK TO THE DUST

With the Clayman defeated, the Pigmasks give the inanimate beast a final undignified kick and then scuttle away.

# MOVES OF THE MASTER

**SECRET THIEF ART TECHNIQUE:**

*Around 120 HP damage*

**THROW ONE OF DUSTER'S SOCKS:**

*Paralyze*

**THIEF ATTACK:**

*40-50 HP damage*

**SHARPLY SCOLD DUSTER:**

*No Effect*

**THROW A THUNDER BOMB:**

*40-50 HP damage*

## TO THE SPITTOON ROOM

Time to make your way back to the room where you found the Noble Spittoon. The Pigmask army have left sentries and wanton destruction in their wake, so step lightly.

# TOO MANY SPOOKS

On the way to the top floor, take a detour to the ghost's kitchen. The place is packed with spirits taking refuge from the Pigmasks. Even in hiding they're still a cheerful, curious, and chatty bunch.

# ENEMIES

## CLAYMAN

### Mini-Boss

This lump head has no choice but to attack. The work horse of the pigmasks, this creature is prone to falling over when overworked. Watch out for his unwieldy nature later in battle.

| HP: 879 | OFF: 72 | DEF: 23 | EXP: 200 |

## PIGMASK

They may be tough on the eye and the ear, but they're not too tough in battle. Look out for their defense-lowering beams and cowardly kicks.

**Bag of Pork Chips (50%)**

| HP: 160 | OFF: 55 | DEF: 20 | EXP: 61 |

## RECON MECH

This robot's not very good at his job, he just floats around and hopes you'll run into him. He's sneaky and can call for backup, so watch out. If you're lucky, you can get a Pencil Rocket for beating him!

**Pencil Rocket (3%)**

| HP: 90 | OFF: 50 | DEF: 35 | EXP: 65 |

## The Legend of the Osohe Jester

Long ago in the ancient Osohe castle dwelt a mischievous court jester who loved disorder. He incorporated the security door password ("Molewig") into his courtly songs, dug tunnels beneath the castle, and carelessly left the drawbridge keys lying about.

His coup de grace came when he modified the security system to respond to dance, rather than spoken word. Carving his likeness into the doors and the new "password" into the surrounding walls, the jester ensured that his joke would live on for generations. It wasn't long before a family of thieves discovered his myriad backdoors and secrets and began secretly infiltrating

## SHAKE IT, WESS

In the spittoon room, Wess tells you about the doorway and the "secret" way to gain entry. It won't be a secret for long if you keep taking peeks, though.

# Dustability

Despite his propensity for sleeping in and limping around, Duster can really move it when things get tense. From time to time he'll whip out some of the following footwork at the start of a battle:

➤ **Attack with blinding speed!** Sometimes an intense battle gives way to random 'feets' of strength! Duster will occasionally open up a battle with this swift kick.

➤ **Unleash a reverse kick with unfathomable speed!** Attacked from behind? It's not a problem when the guy with the bum leg can swing it like an axe.

➤ **Deftly flip behind the enemy!** Red swirls aren't always the end of the world. From time to time, Duster will execute a move so mind-blowing that the enemy is left scratching their head—giving you the opening shots instead!

## WHAT'S THE POINT

Seeing a large needle sticking out of the ground in the courtyard, Wess seems to remember that it provoked an unpleasant response from the old king.

### 4TH FLOOR (CONTINUED)

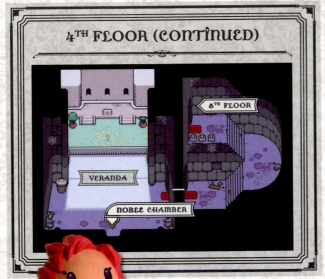

5TH FLOOR

VERANDA

NOBLE CHAMBER

## PRINCE OR PRINCESS?

In the next room you run into a familiar character— the girl who dropped the pendant—trapped on the landing. Wess frees her from the trap and, although he refers to her as royalty, she proves to be a wise cracking tomboy with attitude to spare. Some princess!

## KUMATORA    *A PSI powered, tactless princess.*

A mysterious young woman of PSI, tough as nails with a tongue just as sharp. Found and raised by the Magypsies, she is one character that doesn't take after her foster family's values. With a blunt way of addressing life and its circumstances, don't expect a royal courtesy call when she needs your help.

## GOT TO SWEAT IT OUT!

Discovering your potential can really take it out of you. You can't go running around the place while you're still sweating it, so you might want to avoid the brooms until you're nimble again!

# PSI Sigh

A rumor on the wind claims that Kumatora can use PSI, powerful psychic attacks that will give you a battle advantage. While you're dashing to the top of the castle get acquainted with your new attacks!

➤ **FIRE α** – Uses 6 PP and engulfs all enemies in flames. Very useful for battles with several foes. Occasionally you'll catch an enemy on fire, which deals continual damage for several turns.

➤ **FREEZE α** – Uses 5 PP and freezes a single enemy. A powerful and cost-effective attack which will sometimes leave your target unable to move.

➤ **THUNDER α** – Uses 7 PP and zaps a single enemy with lightning. Kumatora's most powerful PSI move, but also her most unreliable since it sometimes misfires. Occasionally you'll leave an enemy paralyzed.

➤ **LIFEUP α** – Uses 5 PP and restores around 60 HP to yourself or an ally.

## OSOHE CASTLE - 5ᵀᴴ - 7ᵀᴴ FLOOR

Ⓐ Flea Charm
Ⓑ Magic Gelatin

## Sweep 'em and Weep

As you near the top of the castle, beware of the brooms! They'll sweep you straight into that strange garbage can you saw in the foyer. They move in easy-to-avoid patterns.

## THE CASE FOR THE CAN

The brooms sometimes get a bad rap, but there's certainly something to be said for getting taken out with the trash. In addition to gaining valuable stair-climbing experience, winding up in the pail gives you a chance to run back to the sofa and rest your feet.

# ·enemies·

## LINGERING SPIRIT

There's no use crying over past sorrows, especially if they're not yours. Put a stop to the tears with a round of PK Freeze!

**Magic Gelatin (20%)**

| HP: 65 | OFF: 44 | DEF: 50 | EXP: 59 |
|--------|---------|---------|---------|

## OSOHE CAPE

Don't let this spooky cloak give you the cold shoulder. Kumatora's Fire and Freeze attacks are great, especially after he puts up his Shield.

**Peculiar Cheese (10%)**

| HP: 189 | OFF: 65 | DEF: 27 | EXP: 78 |
|---------|---------|---------|---------|

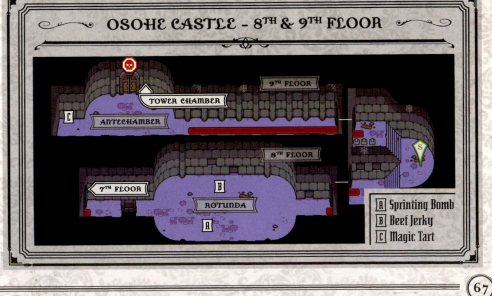

### OSOHE CASTLE – 8TH & 9TH FLOOR

9TH FLOOR

TOWER CHAMBER

ANTECHAMBER

C

8TH FLOOR

7TH FLOOR

B

ROTUNDA

A

S

| A | Sprinting Bomb |
| B | Beef Jerky |
| C | Magic Tart |

# SHIFTY INVENTORY

Kumatora can heal with PK Lifeup, but she may soon need to use her offensive PK full-time. Just in case, load Duster up with plenty of HP- and PP-restoring items. Danger lurks!

## THE HUMMINGBIRD EGG

At last you come upon the "certain important item," a surprisingly large Hummingbird Egg which supposedly contains the hope—or calamity—of the world. Wess and Kumatora seem to remember that it's important, but the details are a little fuzzy...

## EMERGENCY EXIT

The awe surrounding the Egg comes to an abrupt end when the Pigmasks start beating down the door, and Kumatora's take-charge attitude backfires when she unwittingly springs one of Wess's old snares. The castle's requisite trap door drops the trio down each floor of the castle (whose architecture suddenly makes sense), but... what's at the bottom?

## A WATERY GRAVE

You end up in an unpleasant dungeon flooded with water. Everyone, including the egg, seems to be unharmed, earning Duster a brief compliment. Unfortunately, this tender moment is interrupted by a dreadful shadow in the waters below...

## SLITHER N' SLIDE

Once the mystery host is gone you might think the turmoil was over, but no such luck. An opening appears in the pool and the trio get sucked down.

# BOSS ENCOUNTER

## Say it's Not So

Festive fuschia and full of smiles, this fearsome opponent is in its element, so don't hold back any of your healing items or bombs! Reduce him to tears with your Smoke Bomb to lower his accuracy and start repeatedly hitting him with Kumatora's PK Thunder attack. His biting and tail whipping attacks will deal a lot of damage, and if he manages to coil around you then you'll be paralyzed for a few turns. Once you've hurt him, the snake dives underwater, releasing a giant wave that will deal 50 HP of damage to everyone. Zap him with PK Thunder (which does more damage than when he's on the surface) and have Duster dole out healing items.

# Chapter Boss

## OH-SO-SNAKE

*This curious leviathan is more than a castle pet. Utilize the thief smoke bomb, use PK Thunder, and toss bombs before it throws a hissy fit.*

| HP: 1237 | OFF: 82 | DEF: 28 | EXP: 568 |

## WHERE'S DUSTER?

Wess and Kumatora are washed up on the riverbank and saved by Lighter and Fuel. Wess wakes up a little disoriented, though still capable of cursing his son. Kumatora, however, is keen to find Duster as soon as possible.

## SCAMP'S JUST WARMING UP

If you stop by and visit Scamp you'll see that he's feeling better about things, though he's not really giving many details. Run down to Matt's house for the full story.

## LOST AND ACCUSED

At the well, Butch is angry to find that his money is gone. People are still confused about the nature of money, but an enraged Butch continues to blame Duster, and by association, Wess. Kumatora steps into the fray, scaring Butch. Just as things seem like they could get out of hand, Flint arrives and calms everyone down by urging them to wait until Duster returns.

# CHAPTER № 2

The mysterious arrival of the Pigmasks seems to have marked a change in Tazmily and its people. Who amongst the villagers will find the strength to fight back against this evil foe? Kumatora and Wess have the right motives, if not the best attitudes. Even Flint has put aside his grief to help, but what has happened to Duster? And what business could that strange peddler and his monkey have in Tazmily?

CHAPTER

# NO. 3

THE SUSPICIOUS PEDDLER

# CHAPTER
# NO. 3
## PART 1
### DEATH DESERT

A massive aircraft descends from the sky and lands in a desolate desert. Pigmask soldiers–the same that have been wreaking havoc in Tazmily–pour out from the craft, but they aren't alone. The sinister Fassad emerges from the craft with Salsa and his girlfriend in tow.

## DON'T MONKEY AROUND

Fassad issues an ultimatum: do his bidding or risk losing your girlfriend! From here on out, you'll be following orders to ensure her safety. You can agree with everything he says in a timely manner to avoid a shocking punishment, although some of the zaps will be unavoidable.

P·KORP

# FASSAD
### A sinister stranger with ties to the Pork Army

This cruel stranger seems to be in a position of power in the Pigmask army. His brute strength isn't always used for evil, though: in battle you'll learn to rely on his attacks, which deal more damage than your 16-hit combos!

# SALSA
### A Brave Little Monkey

Salsa is on a mission to reunite with his girlfriend. His lack of strength in battle is compensated by his unique skills which can incapacitate enemies and boost your stats. He's also an exceptional dancer.

## SAMBA

Salsa's kidnapped girlfriend.

## JUST DESERTS

After the Pigmasks depart with your beloved, you must accompany Fassad as he makes his way through the desert. Take some time to build your strength and view all of Death Desert's interesting sights.

## BARREL O' FROG

The first save frog in Death Desert is sloshing around inside a barrel just south of the aircraft's landing spot. He'll kindly offer you some words of encouragement along with the option to save your progress.

## FOLLOW DIRECTIONS

Your first task is to prove your loyalty to Fassad. He will direct you to move in a certain way by pointing. Follow along by pressing the D-Pad in the corresponding direction. If you press a wrong direction, you'll get zapped until you get it right.

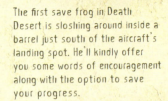

### DEATH DESERT (NORTH)

D

A

WAN SUM DUNG

DESERT VISTA

$

B

C

$

SOUTH DESERT

SOUTH DESERT

| A | BEEF JERKY |
| B | RUNNING BOMB |
| C | NUT BREAD |
| D | AQUARIUS BRACELET |

## WAN SUM DUNG'S
# DUNG EMPORIUM

Are you sick and tired of dung filling up your pockets? Do you wish there was some way to trade your stinky dung for valuable experience points? Wish no more, and come on down to:

*Cut out the middleman!* Wan Sum Dung is the only beetle around who can tell you what your pieces of dung are worth.

*Conveniently located* near the corner of Oasis and Palmtree!

*Trade your dung* for valuable experience points!

**DUNG EXP XCHNG**

| | |
|---|---|
| **REGULAR DUNG** | List price: 4.99 EXP, YOUR PRICE: 5 EXP! |
| **EXQUISITELY-AGED** | List price: 9.99 EXP, YOUR PRICE: 10 EXP! |
| **LEGNEDARY DUNG** | List price: 49.99 EXP, YOUR PRICE: 50 EXP!! |

A GUIDE TO BRAWN AND TECHNIQUES
# FIGHTING STYLE

## SALSA

Salsa is not the toughest of fighters, but he is quick on his feet and attacks early every round. Fassad will do most of the damage early on, but after gaining a few levels Salsa really begins to pack a punch.

### APOLOGIZE
Tell the enemy you're sorry and you'll sometimes stop them in their tracks, making them lose a few turns. The chance of success for Apologize varies for each enemy.

### MAKE LAUGH
Make your enemy laugh so hard they lose a few turns. Like Apologize, the chances of this working on an enemy vary.

### DANCE
Dance the round away to raise the offense, defense, or speed of a randomly selected member of your party. You also have a chance of lowering an enemy's stats. Dancing is Salsa's specialty!

### MONKEY MIMIC
You don't have to put up with an enemy onslaught. Give them a taste of their own medicine by using their own attacks against them. You'll retaliate with the same strength the enemy used against you. This is especially useful against multiple foes.

## WAN SUM DUNG

A shrewd insectpreneur in the waste management field.

# HOT SPRINGS? COOL OASIS!

The arid Death Desert is not a great place for hot springs, but luckily there's an oasis for the weary traveler. It will be clear and sparkling the first time you approach it, but once you start trading dung the water will carry a dung-like odor. No worries, though–the pond will still replenish your HP.

# ENEMIES

## DUNG BEETLE

It's easy to sneak up on a Dung Beetle because it will be too preoccupied diligently rolling its dung around. You won't gain much experience, but if you're "lucky" you'll get to keep the dung...

Dung (60%)

| HP: 43 | OFF: 15 | DEF: 2 | EXP: 2 |
|---|---|---|---|

## SAND LIZARD

Prevent its attacks by using your Make Laugh technique with 100% accuracy! It will eat any Dung Beetles that may enter the same battle with it, so focus on fighting the Sand Lizard if you encounter multiple foes.

Nut Bread (50%)

| HP: 76 | OFF: 19 | DEF: 6 | EXP: 10 |
|---|---|---|---|

## SARA-SARA SAHARA

Be careful of its status-affecting attacks. It will make you feel strange, which can cause you to attack yourself. Your best bet is to defend and let Fassad take care of the battle.

Ancient Banana (15%)

| HP: 88 | OFF: 26 | DEF: 4 | EXP: 15 |
|---|---|---|---|

# OH, BANANAS!

When you open your first gift box, you'll find Salsa's favorite food: a Luxury Banana! You won't get a chance to savor its sweet flavor, because Fassad quickly snatches it from you, gobbles it up, and discards the peel on the ground. If you dash over it, poor Salsa will fall face first into the sand.

| A | LUXURY BANANA |
| B | BUG SPRAY |
| C | BEEF JERKY |
| D | RUNNING BOMB |

**DEATH DESERT (SOUTH)**

## SAVE YOUR SAVER!

Up until now, all of the friendly frogs you've met have been faithfully saving your progress. It's time to return the favor by saving a dizzy frog swirling inside a Great Antlion's trap. This Great Antlion is practically identical to the others, except this one drops a useful piece of equipment: the Flea Charm. Salsa's regular attacks are useless, so try to make the Great Antlion laugh and let Fassad handle him. For an easy out, use the can of Bug Spray you found on the way in.

# WHAT A LOAD OF CRAP!

Nestled in a nook on the western edge of Death Desert is a stockpile of dung. Take a deep breath and carry as much as you can to Wan Sum Dung near the oasis for an Exp. boost. The area replenishes its supply once you leave.

## WE ARE PROUD TO PRESENT...

The only thing to do in the southern section of Death Desert is collect the many gift boxes scattered across the dunes. Once you're done with that, follow the dried cattle skeleton to the exit.

## BIOLOGY LESSON

Just above the frog in need of help is a sign with some interesting information. You'll learn a thing or two about frogs in the desert.

## HOW NOW DEAD COW?

Dead men may tell no tales, but dead cows don't mind a friendly chat. These bones recall the quiet life they once lived.

## BRACE YOURSELF!

Before approaching the creature guarding the domed building, be sure to grab the Aquarius Bracelet in the gift box to the northwest. It will give you a 5-point boost to your defense. Make sure you also equip the Flea Charm dropped by the Great Antlion—it's a very beneficial upgrade for a low-level monkey.

## ≫ MINI BOSS ≪

187

## CACTIED UP

Tougher than any enemy up to this point, the Cactus Wolf has four times the HP of the Great Antlion and higher stats to boot. If you still have any bombs, use them! While this wolf doesn't have any status-affecting skills, it's got some pretty tough attacks. Apologize and Make Laugh are pretty useless, so use Monkey Mimic once you're bombless.

# ENEMIES

## GREAT ANTLION

When a sand trap starts whirling in the desert, an antlion is lurking at its core. They can cause you to cry uncontrollably or lose a turn. Either use Monkey Mimic to inflict the most damage, or defend and let Fassad take care of the fight.

Beef Jerky (10%)   SAVE FROG: Flea Charm (100%)

| HP: 121 | OFF: 41 / 1 | DEF: 15 | EXP: 27 |

## CACTUS WOLF

This prickly scavenger is one that doesn't sit for strangers. Make sure to use your monkey mimic, bomb the beast, and let Fassad do the dirty work. If all goes well, it'll run off with its tail between its legs.

Beef Jerky (100%)

| HP: 468 | OFF: 43 / 1 | DEF: 20 | EXP: 143 |

# FASSAD'S FACULTIES

FASSAD COMMANDS A WIDE ARRAY OF BATTLE CAPABILITIES, BOTH GOOD AND BAD, FOR BETTER AND WORSE.

〉 **PLACE A FINGER ON THE PUNISHIZER BUTTON**   No effect.

〉 **SWITCH ON THE PUNISHIZER**   Removes confusion & deals 1 HP damage to Salsa.

〉 **ATTACK**   Standard attack, not bad for a big guy.

〉 **BUM RUSH**   Fairly powerful special attack.

〉 **THROW A BOMB**   Super-powerful bomb attack!

〉 **PEELING A BANANA**   No effect.

〉 **HIDE IN SALSA'S SHADOW**   Comedic effect only.

# PORK BEAN HOVERPOD
## SPEED & LUXURY!

There's no need to hoof it over long distances thanks to the mobile Pork Bean, the latest in luxury transport! Featuring patent leather seats and a powerful Pork-Grind Drive, this futuristic vehicle handles like a dream.

## 》 SINGLE ENTRY
Entering the Pork Bean is easy thanks to the automatic south-facing side door.

## 》 ONE-BUTTON OPERATION
No pedals, no levers, nothing but a single button for the Pork Bean's single speed. Just point in the direction you want to move and take off!

## 》 BRAKES
Press B once to brake and a second time to get out anywhere there's room to open the door.

## UNDERGROUND PASSAGE

DESERT DOME

UNDERGROUND TUNNEL

- A: BUG SPRAY
- B: UNDERGROUND MAP
- C: BEEF JERKY
- D: ANCIENT BANANA

# ENEMIES

## VIOLENT ATTACK ROACH

This familiar foe's tiny stature gives it the upper hand at catching you off guard. It has surprisingly high offense, so try Make Laugh or a can of Bug Spray if you don't think you're going to make it.

Nut Bread (10%)

| HP: 88 | OFF: 55 / DEF: 11 | EXP: 40 |

## HUGE PILLBUG

Avoid this guy altogether by running it over with the Pork Bean. If you approach one, it will roll up into a ball. Just press A next to it to initiate battle. HUGE Pillbugs are very easy to take out and give a nice amount of EXP.

Nut Bread (30%)

| HP: 60 | OFF: 35 / DEF: 20 | EXP: 30 |

## GOOEY GOO

You'll face not just one, but three of these creatures at once—a perfect opportunity for a Running Bomb. Incidentally, you'll find one in the nearby gift box. Use Make Laugh and let Fassad take care of the fighting. If you can kill off all but one and allow it to continue cloning, you can rack up a mountain of Exp.

Mosquito Charm (100%)

| HP: 92 | OFF: 35 / DEF: 12 | EXP: 82 |

## UNDERGROUND TUNNEL

DESERT DOME

SUNSET CEMETERY

CROSS ROAD

E {X5}

| | |
|---|---|
| A | NUT BREAD |
| B | CHICK BANDANA |
| C | BUG SPRAY |
| D | RUNNING BOMB |
| E | NUT |
| F | NUT BREAD |
| G | ROTTEN MILK |

## FAREWELL, DEATH DESERT

If you have any leftover dung, now is your last chance to bring it to Wan Sum Dung. When you're ready, approach the door of the domed building and press A to get Fassad to unlock it. Inside, an elevator will take you down to the Candrum Underpass where a Pork Bean is waiting to take you away. If you need to heal, use the Instant Revitalization Device to the left of the Pork Bean loading area.

## THE UNDERGROUND

The path to the east is a dead end, so hop aboard the Pork Bean and head west. While riding the Pork Bean you'll trample any enemies in your path, but if you need some experience, exit the vehicle and fight! Keep heading west through three long tunnels until you reach the Pork Bean parking space.

## A Chic Bandana

You can find some Bug Spray and a Running Bomb near your parking space. In the previous room with the tanks, you'll discover some Nut Bread, but more importantly you'll find a Chic Bandana for Salsa. A tempting stash of gift boxes lies just to the south, out of reach for the time being. Be sure to save your game before heading off to the next mini-boss fight near the escape ladder!

## CAUTION!

The signs insist that bomb-throwing is unacceptable, but some rules were made to be broken or blown up. Bomb with abandon!

## >> MINI BOSS <<

### Boogie Monsters

On your way out of the tunnel you'll come across some unpleasant little boogers. Fassad will handle most of the hard work as usual, but you can help out with Make Laugh.

### It Came from the Graveyard!

You'll exit the tunnel through a strange-looking grave in Tazmily's cemetery. If you have a need to re-enter the tunnel, check the tombstone. Fassad tells you to make your way to the Yado Inn. Head south, avoiding any emerging zombies and Mobile Graves you see along the way.

## SALSA ON RAILS

If you try to deviate from the path Fassad tells you to go, you'll get a nice little zap! Head directly for Yado to avoid unnecessary punishment. Hinawa's grave is one of the few tangents from the course you can take without repercussions. It looks like someone left some flowers.

# CHAPTER NO.3 PART 2

## HAPPINESS IS A WARM BOX

A stranger rises from the graveyard in the dead of night to book himself a room in the local saloon. Despite the suspicious circumstances surrounding his arrival, it seems that nobody's got something to hide except for him and his monkey.

## MONEY, THAT'S WHAT I WANT

When you enter the town of Tazmily, you'll notice Butch poring over the contents of a large sack. Farther into town you'll cross paths with Duster, who is on his way to Osohe Castle. You also get to see more of the events leading up to the mystery of the missing moolah—it turns out that Duster isn't the only one who sees where Butch hides his cash.

## HOW MUCH?

Talk to Jackie at the counter to get a room at the inn. Fassad will bow to show his appreciation for the generous accommodations. Follow his example pressing down on the D-pad to avoid getting shocked. You'll be left alone for the first time since joining up with Fassad in Death Desert, but don't think of it as your chance to escape. If you jet toward the exit, you'll get a shocking reminder to follow Fassad's lead. Head to your room (the middle door) to get some much deserved rest.

## OINK IN THE NIGHT

In the middle of the night, Fassad gets out of bed and heads outside. Follow him to eavesdrop on his plan and witness his devious theft.

## SNEAKY MONKEY

As soon as Fassad is off the radio, dash back to your sleeping spot! If you wander aimlessly you'll be caught and mercilessly punished. If you make it back to the room, hold perfectly still while Fassad is watching you—he's testing to see whether you're trying to escape!

## Awake In A Flash

Fassad's Punishizer doubles as an alarm clock, jolting you from one bad dream into another. He promises to set you free if you give your best performance today, so follow suit when he directs you.

## Happy Happy, Joy Joy

Fassad delivers a rousing speech on life, love, and happiness. He butters up the crowd with lavish praise and then strikes with a terrifying vision of impending doom. Towards the end of his performance you'll be asked to talk to everyone whose hand is boisterously raised (don't be afraid to talk to people with their hands lowered) in anticipation of a happiness-related delivery. Report back to Fassad to finish off your charade.

### BIFF
An impressionable but dubious young villager.

### REGGIE
An all-natural hippie who lives by his own way.

## Phony Fassad

Unexpected visitors are delaying Fassad's plans at the castle, so he gives you an arbitrary timeline for completing your next task alone: deliver the Happy Boxes from the cemetery to the four people whose names you just collected. Don't worry too much about delivering everything in a timely manner; you'll get the same result no matter how long it takes.

### PAUL
Calm, level-headed, and independent.

### LINDA
Loves surfing, even though she can't swim.

# WHAT A NUT

As Fassad suspected, Tazmily is full of people with a weakness for cute monkeys. Clear some room in your inventory and speak to the following people for a little treat!

- Betsy (Yado Inn) - Nut Bread
- Mike (Thomas's Bazaar) - Nut Cookie
- Caroline (Bakery) - Nut Bread

# MONKEY CHATTER

Every animal you meet along the way has something to say. Most humans cannot understand their lingo, but Salsa can easily converse with any critter that trots around Tazmily. Take the time to meet each one!

# WHEREFORE ART THOU?

Behind Pusher is an oil painting entitled Mt. Oriander in Summer. Now which one of those pixels corresponds with Alec's house?

## NICHOL

He and his sister often hang out in front of their father's store.

## RICHIE

A sweet young girl who can sympathize with beleaguered monkeys.

## JILL

A gossiping gal with a gargantuan smile.

## BRENDA

Her blunt words cut right to the point.

## LISA

Mother of Richie and Nichol and a gossip mainstay.

## MIKE

Village elder with poor hygiene and a constant case of the munchies.

# TAZMILY SQUARE

CROSS ROAD

CITY HALL

BAKERY

CERULEAN BEACH

EAST TAZMILY

BAZAAR

thomas bazaar

YADO

YADO

SOUTH SHORE

## PUSHER

Tazmily's self-important mayor.

## ELMORE

Pusher's posh house-wife. Leaves the work to Sebastian.

## SEBASTIAN

The first family's hardworking butler.

## NANA

She's either very quiet, or saving her words for just the right moment.

## NAN

The loving wife of Ed, and mother to Alle. She looks after Scamp and his Pet Bird.

## BATEAU

Lives by the beach with his doves and is prone to negative thoughts.

# CAVALRY CACHE

It seems that Fassad's late-night call brought the cavalry stomping through Cross Road, which means you finally get to raid that treasure trove of gift boxes you saw through the chainlink fence! Don't get too excited, though—it's just Nuts, Rotten Milk, and a Nut Bread. Oh, nuts!

## THE MARK OF HAPPINESS

Head to the cemetery and you'll spot Mapson paying his respects. Or, at least, that what it looks like—in reality he's thinking about his next strategic map-marking. Hand your map to him and then press the R Button to check it out.

## UNSPEEDY DELIVERY

The happy boxes are sitting outside the secret graveyard entrance, so check your map and start making deliveries in any order you choose. Unfortunately the boxes are pretty heavy, so you won't be able to dash.

# GROUND SHIPPING

Even though there were four people with their hands raised, there are only three circles on the map—this is because Abbot and Abbey live together.

P-KORP

## HAPPY BOX 1: ABBOT & ABBEY

Abbot and Abbey live in the first house to the left when entering Tazmily from the north. Since they live together, they'll only need one Happy Box. The extra box will automatically vanish from the cemetery.

## HAPPY BOX 2: BIFF

Head east of Tazmily and follow the path south to reach Biff, who is waiting outside eagerly anticipating his Happy Box. He's already starting to feel happy!

## Happy Box 3: Isaac

According to the stray dog in the town square, Isaac's house is at the entrance of the forest (the one with the antidotes). You may encounter some enemies in your path, but they don't pose any serious threat. Even if you lose, you'll regain consciousness near the hot spring—just a skip away from Isaac's house! Once the delivery is made, Isaac immediately puts the Happy Box (and its package) to work.

## P-KORP PRESENTS

# ❤ HAPPY BOX

**ERASE ALL THOSE WORRIES** Let the Happy Box's patented warble+strobe technology chase away all your discontent!

**ALWAYS-ON HANDS-FREE** Tired of working towards happiness? The Happy Box provides convenient 24/7 access!

**FREE DELIVERY SETUP** Obtaining everlasting happiness has never been cheaper or easier, sign up today!

The Happy Box makes the perfect gift! Do the right thing for your loved ones, give the gift of Happy Box. Created by master craftsmen at the friendly P Corporation, your Happy Box is guaranteed to bring many years of high-quality happiness.

## ...and a Dollar Short

Fassad is waiting for you back at the Yado Inn, chowing down on the banana he promised you and waiting to give you a zap instead. No matter how long it took you to deliver those Happy Boxes, you'll always arrive a minute late.

## Oh, So He's Leaving Again

Next on your to-do list is to follow Fassad to Osohe Castle, where he has some business to take care of. Head back to the cemetery, following the muddy tracks that lead to the castle grounds.

## WHAT DID YOU JUST SAY?

With Fassad back in your party, many of Tazmily's citizens have a change of heart. Pusher and Elmore, for example, wanted nothing to do with you. But when Fassad is present they'll gladly shake hands with a nasty little monkey for a chance to schmooze it up.

## THESE RUINS ARE RUINED

Tanks have smashed through the gates and torn up the garden along with the gardener. The Pigmasks in the foyer give Fassad the latest news: Duster and Wess are still keeping the swiney swindlers at bay, and they're headed to the top floor. Fassad's fury burns bright as he sends the soldiers to chase down the uninvited guests.

## HEBETUDINOUS HOGS

The Pigmask soldiers are a loyal bunch willing to risk their lives for their mission, but are any of them doing anything risky? Talk to every Pigmask you meet along the way and it becomes perfectly clear that these guys were not chosen for their brainpower.

## UP! UP! UP!

Climb up stairs and staples until you get to the gap in the hallway where Duster previously swung across with Rope Snake. There's no way a little monkey can make it across on his own. Your journey back to the first floor will be interrupted by a call: Duster and company have fallen out of reach and are in the basement.

## SPOOKS IN THE KITCHEN

For a haunted castle, Osohe seems to have a disturbing lack of spirits. As it turns out, the ghastly inhabitants haven't yet migrated; the Pigmasks have corralled them using the mysterious 'power of science.'

# Down! Down! Down!

Head back to the main hallway and enter the door on the far right (to the right of the former Ghost Bazaar). Deep in the basement, Fassad notices the door and orders you to learn the proper steps. Luckily it's engraved in the walls, so study all three panels and unleash your Funky Monkey Dance!

# Lever Out Of This

In the southwest corner of the basement lies a peculiar lever. Fassad forces you to pull it, unleashing a torrent that washes away Duster and co. along with the certain item Fassad has been after. There's nothing else you can do in Osohe Castle, so retire to your room back at the Yado Inn.

# ENEMIES

## CHEERY SKELETON

As his name suggests, this skeleton has a big funny bone. Make Laugh works every time, so let Fassad handle the rest.

Sprinting Bomb (10%)

| HP: 109 | OFF: 45 | DEF: 16 | EXP: 62 |
|---------|---------|---------|---------|

## LIL BIG BRO

That confused look on his face makes you wonder if he really wants to battle. Lighten the mood by making him laugh.

Beef Jerky (70%)

| HP: 138 | OFF: 47 | DEF: 20 | EXP: 85 |
|---------|---------|---------|---------|

OSOHE CELLAR

OSOHE CRYPT

OSOHE CRYPT

PANTRY 1ST FLR

OSOHE CELLAR

CELLAR PASSAGE

LEVER

A
X
B
D
C

| A | PISCES BRACELET |
| B | BEEF JERKY |
| C | ANCIENT BANANA |
| D | BEEF JERKY |

## OUT OF MY WAY!

As you exit Osohe Castle a pair of arguing Pigmasks are blocking the path with their tanks. Fassad's temper quickly empties the drawbridge. Continue south to Tazmily.

## MISSING MONEY + MISSING THIEF

Back in Tazmily, Butch has discovered his money is missing. He accuses the easiest target: Duster, who isn't around to defend himself. While your "master" cleverly spins the situation, Kumatora gives you a knowing look. Nothing gets past Fassad, though-can't you even look at someone without being punished?

## KUMATORA TO THE RESCUE

Later that night, while Fassad is fast asleep, you awake to Kumatora's voice. If you try to leave through the door or check on Fassad, he'll roll over on the remote and give you a zap. Check the window for your chance at freedom.

## RUUUUN!

Fassad and his cronies are on the attack! The path to Osohe Castle is blocked by the Pigmasks, so head west to the Sunshine Forest. Isaac isn't home to lend a hand, and Pig Tanks are barricading potential exits. After finding out that they're blocking every possible path, your only choice will be to backtrack and try to escape the way you came in: through the forest.

## WE'RE SURROUNDED!

Retracing your steps will lead you to an unfortunate scenario where Pigmasks surround your team. This time the tanks are loaded and on the offensive!

# »CHP. BOSS«

## NO WITHDRAWAL NO RETURN

The Pig Tank has an astounding amount of HP and an Offense that packs a powerful punch. There is only a slim chance of neutralizing this foe by making it laugh, and apologizing is useless. Monkey Mimic is useful for rebounding attacks, and Dancing may alter the stats in your favor. Kumatora should belt out her most powerful PK Thunder attacks. After the tank takes a good beating a soot-covered Pigmask driver will emerge. Finish him off without worry- the cannon is jammed, so his most powerful attack is no longer an issue.

# ENEMIES

## PIGMASK

Pigmasks pose no serious threat to your powerful party. Make them laugh and take them out with some PK skills.

Pork Chips (50%)

HP: 160 | OFF: 55 / DEF: 20 | EXP: 61

## RECON MECH

This machine's AI is susceptible to laughter. If you're really lucky, it'll leave behind a Pencil Rocket!

Pencil Rocket (3%)

HP: 90 | OFF: 50 / DEF: 35 | EXP: 65

## PIG TANK

Nowhere to run, nowhere to hide, the iron horse of the Pork Army is here. Use Monkey Mimic to rebound attacks and PK Thunder. Once the tank fumes up, send the pigmask squealing.

HP: 1782 | OFF: 74 / DEF: 21 | EXP: 624

## OH MY PORK!

The battle is over, but victory is hardly yours. Fassad appears with reinforcements, including another Pig Tank. Just when things look truly bleak, a hero emerges: Lucas, with Dragos for backup! The Drago exacts her revenge, dispatching the devious Pigmasks and sending Fassad flying.

## STORY TIME

Wess fills Lucas in on what's been going on, urging Lucas to protect Tazmily with his father. Kumatora and Salsa take off in search of Duster. What lies ahead for our adventurers?

Tazmily Village is now transforming
exactly according to the devious
peddler's plans. Only a handful of
citizens seem to realize that
things which were good and right
are now being systematically
tossed away, one after the other.

Although prosperity is increasing, an
eerie darkness seems to be growing
heavier over the village at the same time.

Within that darkness, however, a frail
young boy is beginning to grow
ever stronger. His family is torn apart,
but his resolve is strong.

The once-coddled Lucas stands ready
to repaint this tale of sadness with a
bright new color.

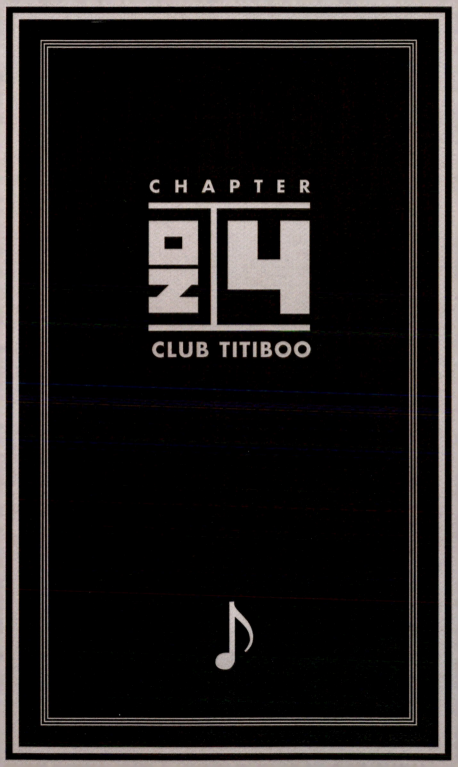

CHAPTER
No. 4

CLUB TITIBOO

# CHAPTER

## № 4

### PART ONE
**THE ADVENTURE BEGINS**

Three years have passed since the dark events which transpired in the Sunshine Forest. The small town of Tazmily has been transformed into a bustling suburb filled with fancy modern buildings and new modes of transportation. Fassad is still preaching in the converted town square, and there seems to be some kind of persistent lightning storm looming...

## A NEW BEGINNING

Lucas wakes from a recurring dream, padding solemnly through an empty house while memories of his mother fill his head. Flint only ever returns for a few hours of fitful sleep each night before the sun rises, leaving for the cliffs before dawn.

# CHANGING

Along with the town, Lucas has grown and changed. Memories of the past, however, still haunt him. It might be a good idea to visit Hinawa's grave, but be sure to change in front of the mirror first.

## ALIVE-STOCK

Flint's small ranch has certainly seen better days—charred livestock wander aimlessly around the remains of their stable. None of the animals seem fazed by this, for some reason. As you head toward town, Boney decides he's willing to take you for a walk.

# BONEY
## A FAITHFUL FRIEND

Boney has been by Lucas's side these past few years and is not about to leave him now. This friendly pup will help you fight anything that gets in your way. He can even use items too, despite not having opposable thumbs.

## TAZMILY VILLAGE
### TAZMILY SQUARE & SOUTH SHORE

CROSSROAD STATION

BAKERY

S

CERULEAN BEACH

EAST TAZMILY

STORE

YADO

A

LUCAS' HOUSE

S

A TRIVIA CARD #1

# DRAGON POWER!

A Save Frog near your house asks for your full attention—you can try to ignore him, but he's pretty persistent. And with good reason — there's a new currency system in place known as Dragon Power or DP for short. Lucas can now buy and sell items, and enemies will now drop DP. You can deposit and withdraw DP from Save Frogs as if they were little green ATMs. Welcome to the age of money!

# LIGHTNING HOUSE

**FOUNDED 4 YRS AGO**

Struck by lightning more than any other house on the island, 1 out of every 10 visitors to Lightning House has a chance of witnessing a strike in person!

*Weeknights from 8PM – 8AM*
*Admission must be paid in DP —NO BARTERING*
*No pet birds, umbrellas, or bronze sculptures, please*

*Come see the spectacle of the Nowhere Islands' most infamous & unlucky house:*

# TAZMILY

### TOUR PAMPHLET

**DEAR** *Valued Guest and Visitor*

Thank you for choosing Yado Inn, the latest in luxury suite lodging. Your patronage is important to us. During your stay in fabulous Tazmily, please carry one of these free Tourism Guides, graciously provided by the Mayor's Ontological Network of Entrepreneurs and Yeomen.

## DOLPHIN OSSICLES

You can find Dolphin Ossicles near the beaches. Come back later and more will appear. These are only good for selling at a low price (about 5 DP), but every little bit helps!

## METAPRESENTS

From time to time you will find a present holding nothing but a simple tune. Sit back and enjoy, because it only plays once. Sometimes the best gift is a fun memory.

## THUNDER BOMBS

Even though his house was seized and converted, old man Wess still manages to keep that secret box of Thunder Bombs stocked. Be sure to grab a few!

## MAGIC BUTTERFLIES

You can find a Magic Butterfly hiding in a vase on the first floor of Mayor Pusher's Mansion. It doesn't do much, but it's a nice way to relax.

## EH, OSOHE

The former party castle is full of crumbling suits of armor and tired ghosts. You can get a Rotten Eclair (to trade for Jerky at the top of the ladder!) and a Dolphin Ossicle from Li'l Ghosty if you answer his questions properly. Otherwise, it will just be awkward…

## NOT SO BAZAAR

Thomas's Bazaar has been redesigned and refurbished to accommodate all your modern needs! Remember to bring DP, as bartering is no longer accepted…

**PROVIDED BY THE NEW PORK TOURISM DEPARTMENT**

## URBAN RENEWAL

Tazmily Village no longer looks as rustic as it once did. The modernized buildings are surrounded by paved roads and every house has a Happy Box. Well, almost every house. Now is a good time for Lucas to explore and get up to speed with the latest village happenings.

**MAP**

# CERULEAN BEACH
### SUNSHINE-FILLED BEACHES OF WESTERN TAZMILY

POLICE STATION

TAZMILY SQUARE

Ⓐ BEACH MUSIC

# THE ADVENTURES OF
# DOORKNOB
# PART 2

Doorknob gleamed proudly as the medal of recognition was draped around its bronzed neck. In its first three years as a law enforcement knob, the brash young accessory had jailed dozens of shiftless punks, repeatedly placing itself in harm's way as bait for the department's various shakedowns and stings. Despite its decorated service, however, Doorknob longed to break free of the ranks of the law enforcement industry...

## TO BE CONTINUED...

# SUNSHINE & LIGHTNING

It seems that Lucas and Flint's house isn't the only place in town suffering from inexplicable sunny-day lightning strikes. The destruction of Alec's cabin forced him into the old folks' home, poor Reggie's tent has been reduced to ashes, and the list goes on. Stranger yet, the happier citizens don't seem to regard these as disasters...

## MAP

### CROSS ROAD STATION
THE FOREST GROTTO , SUNSET CEMETERY, & THE TRAIN STATION

SUNSHINE FOREST

ISAAC'S HOUSE

S  D

KOKORI SPRINGS

PRAYER SANCTUARY

OSOHE CASTLE

SUNSET OVERLOOK

B

C

TRAIN TUNNEL

TRAIN STATION

I

A

TAZMILY SQUARE

A  BEEF JERKY

B  BREAD ROLL

C  SPRINTING BOMB

D  BEEF JERKY

## PAYING RESPECTS

Flint is at Hinawa's grave paying his respects. When you speak to him, he suggests you do the same. Hinawa's grave triggers another flashback to happier times. When you're done reminiscing Flint will be gone…but where did he go?

## RIGHT ON TIME

It looks like a new train station was built over the old dirt crossroads. Go to the platform and witness a discussion between Bronson and Jackie. It seems Duster is still missing and that someone at "Club Titiboo" looks just like him. Perhaps you should tell Wess…

# THE TAZMILY CENTRAL

*Bringing You a Utopian View*

# MESSAGE BOARDS

Hey there, residents of Tazmily! Have you got something important to say but no one to hear you out? Got a job you want to advertise? A proclamation to announce on high? Then you're in luck, as the benevolent Mr. Fassad and his hardworking Pigmasks have created just the place for you! Stop on by the big board near Cross Road Station to read — or supply — the latest gossip from people like you!

P·KORP

*From forests to shores, mountains to fields, improve your world.*

# ITEM GUY
### YOUR FRIENDLY CART WANDERER

You will find an odd man with a covered wagon towards the left side of the road near the train station. Whenever you want to store an item, talk to this Item Guy and he will take care of it for you free of charge. What a nice guy!

I

## CARING FOR ITEMS LIKE A SISTER WOULD!

## CRAZY OLD MEN

Once back at the town square you'll witness a one-sided showdown between Fassad and Wess concerning the town's lightning problem. Eventually a Pigmask shows up to drag Wess back to the retirement home in the most undignified manner possible.

## VISITING HOURS

You'll find Wess upstairs in the middle room of his former house. Talk to him about the man at Club Titiboo who supposedly looks like Duster. Wess, who wants you to look into the matter, gives you a Carrier Pigeon to be released as a sign if it really is Duster.

# DON'T TELL
## THE GRANDKIDS

Mike is in the room across from Wess and is as generous as ever...as long as you make it clear that you came to see him, he'll be glad to give you a little spending money. He'll also have something to say about political correctness.

**MAP**

## EAST TAZMILY
### THE ELDERS HOME & TRAINING GROUNDS

ELDERS HOME

TAZMILY SQUARE

TRAINING GROUNDS

**A** THUNDER BOMB

# EXTRA ★ EXTRA!

The newspaper in the first floor of the retirement home is frequently updated with new headlines, so check back often!

# SHOP TILL YOU DROP!

If you want to buy some things from Thomas' Shop you will need much more DP than you currently have. Head to Sunshine Forest and fight some Slitherhens. When you feel you have doled out enough punishment, go and find a Save Frog to withdraw your DP. You can also find a Pisces Bracelet hidden behind a Grated Yammonster. Getting it now will save you some DP.

| | | | |
|---|---|---|---|
| Kid's Shirt | 100 DP | Antidote | 8 DP |
| Kid's Hat | 50 DP | Paper Fan | 12 DP |
| Pisces Bracelet | 160 DP | Alarm Cicada | 18 DP |
| Sprinting Bomb | 200 DP | | |

**SALE!**

## RESTLESS FOREST

With the Sunshine Forest all healed from the fire years ago, new creatures have taken up camp. Some of them have incredible amounts of Exp., if you can catch them...

# MUSICAL
## PRESENT-TATION

There is a present hidden near the river between the forest and Alec's house. Go behind the tree to find this musical wonder.

# ENEMIES

## SLITHERHEN

*Though this poultry-reptile combination is lacking a pair of poisonous chompers, it can gang up with other foes and become a nuisance. Watch out for its erratic movement patterns!*

**Fresh Egg (5%)**

| HP: 127 | OFF: 47 | DEF: 12 | EXP: 32 | DP: 17 |
|---|---|---|---|---|

## REALLY FLYING MOUSE

*No really, this mouse is flying. It might seem like one of your tougher foes at first, but the extra Exp. is a helpful boost.*

**Bread Roll (15%)**

| HP: 130 | OFF: 48 | DEF: 18 | EXP: 52 | DP: 26 |
|---|---|---|---|---|

# SUNSHINE FOREST

**THE GLEAMING WOODS OF TAZMILY AT THE BASE OF MT. ORIANDER**

E

ORIANDER CLIFFS

D

LIGHTER'S HOUSE

B

A

FOREST GROTTO

| | |
|---|---|
| A | PISCES BRACELET |
| B | PECULIAR CHEESE |
| C | BAKED YAM |
| D | SPRINTING BOMB |
| E | BREAD ROLL |

C

## HOP N' STOP BANKING

In keeping with the changing times, Save Frogs now double as little green ATMs. Remember: if you get your head handed to you in battle you'll lose half of whatever DP you have on hand, so don't run around with your pockets full of change!

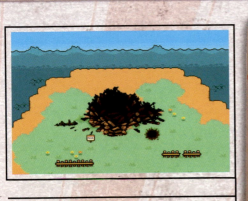

## LIGHT MIGHT BLIGHT

The unlucky houses in town aren't the only ones getting zapped by supernatural bolts of lightning. The debris from Alec's cabin scars the mountaintop like a black crater, and the thunder seems to have scared off all the livestock and wildlife. Lighter's newly-built cabin has been subject to bolt after bolt, though he remains stubborn as ever. Even poor old Nippolyte's shack has been blown to bits.

## INTO THE DARK TUNNEL

The only way to Club Titiboo is via the train. However, since it won't be arriving at all today your only course of action is to walk the rails. In doing so, Lucas will be stopped by a responsible citizen. After a short lecture on watching out for trains, he gives you the Railway Map. Into the very safe tunnel you go!

# ENEMIES

## GRATED YAMMONSTER

These starch-nemeses can use PK Freeze attacks, easily doing 150 damage in one round. Thankfully they like to stay in one place! It might be best to return when you're stronger.

*Magic Tart (5%)*

| HP: 387 | OFF: 94 | DEF: 43 | EXP: 422 | DP: 83 |

## BLACK BEANLING

### RARE!

This bean, possibly darkened by the forest fire a few years ago, is hard to come by. If you happen to see one, chase it down! It gives an extraordinary amount of Exp. but its super-powerful PK Fire power means you risk getting refried.

| HP: 377 | OFF: 50 | DEF: 25 | EXP: 16080 | DP: 0 |

## BIG SPUD BUG

They hang out in gangs of three and can be a real threat if you're weak. Luckily they're pretty slow, so battles are easy to avoid.

*Sprinting Bomb (3%)*

| HP: 280 | OFF: 88 | DEF: 20 | EXP: 159 | DP: 21 |

# CHAPTER NO. 4

## PART TWO
### THE TRAIN TO SUCCESS

## TRAVERSE THE TUNNEL

This long tunnel is more like a test of endurance for Lucas and Boney. There are many enemies in this area and they all want to tango, so stock up with as many of Caroline's bread rolls as you can afford before you leave. If you see a cluster of enemies (especially Slitherhens!) be sure to heal up before you enter battle!

# LOOK OUT!
## TRAINS AHEAD

Occasionally while walking on the tracks a train will come speeding by. Don't just stand there, jump! If you get cold feet and don't move, Lucas and Boney will be hit by the train and wake up all the way back in Tazmily Village. Pity that you didn't listen to your warning, fool!

## MAP

# TRAIN TUNNEL (WEST END)
#### THE WESTERN TRACKS OF THE TRAIN LINE

TUNNEL 1  B C
CROSS ROAD STATION
FOREST TRACKS

FOREST TRACKS
TUNNEL 1
A  TUNNEL 11

TUNNEL 11
BUTTERFLY SPRINGS
FOREST TRACKS

**A** BREAD ROLL
**B** SUPER BOMB
**C** LUXURY BANANA

# BUTTERFLY SPRINGS

**A REFRESHING SPOT ALONG THE BEATEN PATH**

HOT SPRINGS

TUNNEL II    TUNNEL III

## LEARNING PSI

Lucas will eventually come across a rocky valley filled with butterflies. Boney notices some womens' clothes lying on the ground next to a ladder. Soaking in the hot spring is Ionia the Magypsy. Speak to him and accept his offer to teach Lucas how to use PSI. Lucas will learn an immensely powerful attack named after his favorite thing. Try out your new powers by healing up with Lifeup α!

# MAGIC BUTTERFLIES

Until now magic butterflies were a neat anomaly. After learning PSI they will become important tools for your survival. When you catch one you'll recover a random amount of PP!

# ENEMIES

## RAMBLIN' MUSHROOM

These guys look somewhat familiar... Anyway, you will find them throughout the tunnel. If they mushroomize you, defend so you don't attack your own teammates.

**Edible Mushroom (60%)**

| HP: 178 | OFF: 43 | DEF: 16 | EXP: 29 | DP: 14 |

## SQUAWKING STICK

This cute little guy is no real bother, but it will call up its friends for help. Occasionally it will drop a great weapon for Lucas.

**Stick (15%) | Good Stick (5%)**

| HP: 160 | OFF: 49 | DEF: 20 | EXP: 25 | DP: 20 |

## MUTTSHROOM

Mush, boy! As the name implies, this pooch can spread its spores and make you feel funky. These dangerous dogs are slow enough to out-run, so conserve your healing supplies unless you're looking to level up.

**Doggy Biscuit (10%)**

| HP: 248 | OFF: 58 | DEF: 25 | EXP: 62 | DP: 40 |

## RECONSTRUCTED MOLE

As if a mole needed a more effective way to tear up a lawn. Don't let them gang up on you because those drills are powerful!

**Bread Roll (10%)**

| HP: 165 | OFF: 64 | DEF: 18 | EXP: 42 | DP: 33 |

## MAP

# TRAIN TUNNEL (EAST END)

### THE EASTERN TRACKS OF THE TRAIN LINE

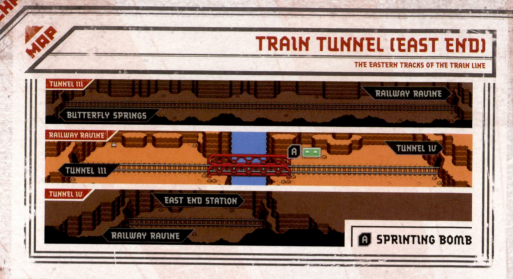

| | |
|---|---|
| TUNNEL III | RAILWAY RAVINE |
| BUTTERFLY SPRINGS | |
| RAILWAY RAVINE | TUNNEL IV |
| TUNNEL III | |
| TUNNEL IV | |
| EAST END STATION | |
| RAILWAY RAVINE | A SPRINTING BOMB |

# END OF THE LINE

Watch out for Cattlesnakes once you get to the station! You could take the train back to Tazmily Village for 50 DP... if you were a factory worker. As a non-employee, you are pretty much trapped by the 2500 DP price. Quite an employee discount! Follow the path towards the factory that everyone back in Tazmily Village keeps talking about.

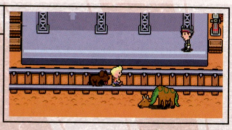

# STICKY

## » SQUEEZE «

Squawking Sticks near the train platform make it a tight squeeze! First heal up from battling in the tunnels. If you get in a fight, it could be a long one— the Sticks are faster than Boney and will try to call for backup. They can also use Lifeup, so come out swinging with your special PK attack.

## MAP

# EAST END TRAIN STATION

### THE EASTERN TRAIN TERMINUS AND THE FACTORY GATES

| | |
|---|---|
| | CLAYMAN FACTORY |
| TUNNEL IV | |
| A FLEA POWDER | |
| B BREAD ROLL | |

# ITEM GUY

The Item Guy from Tazmily has not only managed to stay ahead of you, but true to his name, he's toting all of the items you loaned him earlier. What dedication!

# MAGIC
## BUTTERFLY

A little southeast of the backhoe is a crate you can check for a relaxing surprise. Even amidst the machines of industry, beauty and magic still bloom.

# ENEMIES

## CATTLESNAKE

### WARNING!

*These chimeras might seem like easy targets, but defeating one requires serious physical and mental strength. Their HP is astronomical, and their offense is high enough to take you out in one hit if your level is too low.*

**Fresh Milk (50%)**

| HP: 786 | OFF: 90 | DEF: 50 | EXP: 536 | DP: 162 |
|---------|---------|---------|----------|---------|

## MAP
# CLAYMAN FACTORY GROUNDS
### P-KORP'S INDUSTRIAL CAMPUS

TITIBOO ROPEWAY

FACTORY COMPLEX

EAST END STATION

P-KORP

Ⓐ EYE DROPS

# TITIBOO ROPEWAY
TROLLEY TO CLUB TITIBOO AND THE FOREST WATERFALL

CLUB TITIBOO

ROPEWAY

CHIMERA LAB

CLAYMAN FACTORY

A FOREST MAP
B FIREWORKS

# THE CHIMERA LAB
AN AREA FILLED WITH HYBRID CREATURES

TITIBOO CLIFFSIDE

MURASAKI SPRINGS

CHIMERA LAB

TITIBOO ROPEWAY

P·KORP

## EXPLORE YOUR SURROUNDINGS

Your new surroundings can easily distract you from your goal of reaching Club Titiboo. Feel free to explore the area and open presents, but beware the powerful enemies lurking north of the factory!

# SHORTCUTS

The exclusive Club Titiboo is the sole domain of factory workers, but that won't stop some of the world's most determined clubbers…including old men who enjoy ogling the waitresses.

# ENEMIES

## PIGTUNIA

*A rather deadly variety of flower which is pretty boar-ing to look at. They can sprout sibling plants and make you cry, so take them out fast!*

*Flea Powder (10%)*

| HP: 352 | OFF: 96 | DEF: 48 | EXP: 182 | DP: 60 |

## BATANGUTAN

*Is it itching for a fight or itching from the fleas it carries? Either way, it's low offense and HP make it pretty easy to knock over.*

*Ancient Banana (15%), Luxury Banana (5%)*

| HP: 213 | OFF: 60 | DEF: 20 | EXP: 70 | DP: 50 |

## HOT SPRING
# WORKOUT

Skip the factory vending machine—there's a much cheaper way to simultaneously fill your inventory and gain experience! Go north of the factory and then head west, avoiding any enemies you come across. Just beyond the guarded Lab lies the super-strategic Murasaki Hot Spring!

**CHICK TRICK** A generous chicken stands near the sign, ready to offer you a free egg. Walk into the spring and it will become a "Hot Spring Egg" which replenishes a whopping 100 HP! Not only that, but once the egg is boiled you can go back for more. Repeat this trick until your inventory is filled.

**HOME BASE** With pockets full of nutritious boiled eggs, head out into the nearby forest and start fighting some of the weaker chimeras. Use the eggs to keep your health up, and when you're low on eggs or PP, head back to the spring to recharge and refill.

**SAFETY DANCE** Eventually you'll be powerful enough to tango with tough foes, including the vile Ostrelephant. Since Boney's attacks aren't very effective, have him guard (to keep his HP meter rolling slowly) and heal while Lucas uses PK attacks. Remember, the hot springs revive fallen party members!

## Club TITIBOO · TICKETS?

### TITIBOO CLIFFSIDE
#### A DEAD END BEHIND THE CHIMERA LAB

A MAGIC TART

CHIMERA LAB

## SORRY, EMPLOYEES ONLY

The only way to get to Club Titiboo is via the Ropeway, but don't get too excited about clubbing just yet—only employees of the factory can hitch a ride. With so many exclusive perks, it looks like it might be time to get a job…

---

# P-KORP PROUDLY INTRODUCES

# CLAYMAN ®

*Productive times demand a productive workforce. Today's laborer is experienced, smart, and determined to earn lots of money.*

| | |
|---|---|
| **! LIMITLESS DEDICATION** | Forged from the clay of the earth, Claymen® are industrial powerhouses. The P-KORP Clayman® quietly accepts any task, working to complete exhaustion. |
| **! ORGANIC *MUON* TECHNOLOGY** | Powering every P-KORP Clayman® is patented Multi-Use Orthostatic Neoplasm technology, which guarantees long life and dedicated service. |
| **! FINITELY RECHARGEABLE** | With industrial power supplies, each Clayman® can operate for days on end. Even in remote locations, recharging is simple thanks to the MCPs. |
| **! MOBILE CHARGE PRONGS** | For mobile charging, thrust the charging prongs deep into the Clayman® and give it a swift kick in the asphalt. |

P-KORP

## PRESENT-TATION
### IS EVERYTHING

Near the waterfall is yet another unusual present. Just sit back and enjoy a brief and unexpected treat!

## VENDING
### CLAYMAN FACTORY

| Fizzy Soda | 6 DP |
|---|---|
| Beef Jerky | 26 DP |
| Antidote | 8 DP |
| Paper Fan | 12 DP |
| Eye Drops | 10 DP |
| Flea Powder | 30 DP |

## PART-TIME JOB

Back at the factory, the Pigmask in charge is more than willing to hand out a job to a former holdout. The only signature he needs is…yours! After signing on the dotted line, Lucas is promptly sent to work. Boney's dogness makes him eligible for a special canine work program.

# ENEMIES

### DOGFISH

Chimera Lab experiments have turned this dog into man's worst friend. Watch out for its deadly PK Freeze attack! If you double back to where it leaps from its pond, you may be able to score an easy surprise attack.

**Doggy Biscuit (15%)** | **Doggy Jerky (10%)**

| HP: 368 | OFF: 102 | DEF: 42 | EXP: 322 | DP: 45 |
|---|---|---|---|---|

### TOP DOGFISH

#### RARE!
#### WARNING!

This rare chimera is ultra-powerful! As leader of the pack, it doesn't make many public appearances. If you can take it down you'll be rewarded with a huge amount of Exp., DP, and a valuable Meteotite.

**Meteotite (100%)**

| HP: 861 | OFF: 132 | DEF: 58 | EXP: 2032 | DP: 869 |
|---|---|---|---|---|

### OSTRELEPHANT

The odd roar/squawk they emit as they dash toward you is truly gut-wrenching. They may look silly, but their physical strength is something you'll always remember! Steer clear unless you've got plenty of PP and healing items.

**Beef Jerky (5%)**

| HP: 400 | OFF: 105 | DEF: 50 | EXP: 374 | DP: 75 |
|---|---|---|---|---|

## THE CLAY MINES

At the bottom of the ladder is the Pigmask in charge of the elevator shaft. Your job is to explore the mine and find tired-looking (and tired-sounding) Claymen. When you find one:

**1** *Push a tired Clayman all the way back to the Pigmask at the elevator.*

**2** *Talk to the Pigmask. He will lower the elevator and send the Clayman to the top.*

**3** *Go up the ladder and continue to push the pile of putty to the recharge room where Bud and Lou will handle the rest.*

### MAP

## FACTORY LEVEL
ENTRANCE, RECHARGE ROOM AND ELEVATOR

## WARNING! Energizing stations are for CLAYMEN® ONLY!

### MAP

## THE CLAY MINES
EXCAVATING MUD AND SLUDGE TO CREATE MORE CLAYMEN

⬆ ELEVATOR (FACTORY LEVEL)

🤖 # BROKEN CLAYMAN

## PAY DAY

Once you're finished charging the Claymen, talk to "Mr. Brown" (the blue Pigmask) to get your salary and a Ropeway ticket. Club Titiboo awaits -- it's finally time to find out who that Duster look-alike really is!

## SAVED: TWO

Before you take the Ropeway, you might consider running back to Tazmily for a nap. Just as you enter the tunnel, though, a stranger bravely plucks you from the clutches of impending doom! This ultra-dedicated public servant will do his best to keep you from making the mistake of your life—up to 5 times, at least. After that, he'll finally reveal a secret about his true identity.

## NICE VIEW

For 1 DP you can use the binoculars to check out the view. In the distance you can see an ominous tower that gives Boney the shivers.

## TIGHT SECURITY

You've finally reached the entrance to Club Titiboo, but there's a problem with the hired goons. They've had careful instructions about letting underage kids or dogs into the club. Just as things are about to get hairy, a good-looking waitress named Violet steps out and vouches for you.

## FIREWORKS

You'll find another once-in-a-lifetime present left by an anonymous pyrotechniac on the Ropeway bridge. ...Ah.

# CLUB TITIBOO (OUTSIDE)

CLIFFBOUND RESORT FOR EVERYDAY WORKERS.

CLUB TITIBOO

TITIBOO ROPEWAY (FOREST)

ROPEWAY

**A** FIREWORKS

## SKINHEAD

Professional bouncer with a keen nose for underage kids.

## NECKBEARD

Hired muscle who can smell a dog a mile away.

## ANOTHER SHADE OF KUMATORA

Safely inside the club, Violet reveals that she is... Kumatora! She'll explain everything later, but for now suggests that you find a seat for the DCMC show. Don't be afraid to do a little exploring first.

## NERDCHANDISE

If you talk to the bearded guy you can buy some high-quality fan-made merchandise, the best kind of merchandise there is! Don't buy the DCMC Pamphlet though. If you're patient, you're sure to score a free one sooner or later...

### DCMC MERCH

| | |
|---|---|
| DCMC Pamphlet | 100 DP |
| DCMC Shirt | 360 DP |
| DCMC Hat | 200 DP |
| DCMC Ring | 400 DP |
| Pickled Veggie Plate | 10 DP |

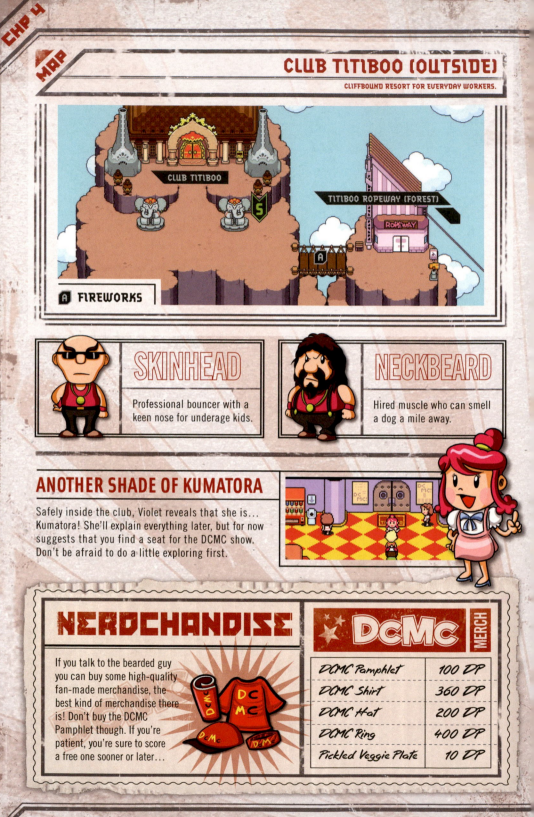

# Club TITIBOO

## CLUB TITIBOO (INSIDE)

### LOBBY, BATHROOMS, LOUNGE, AND MAIN THEATER

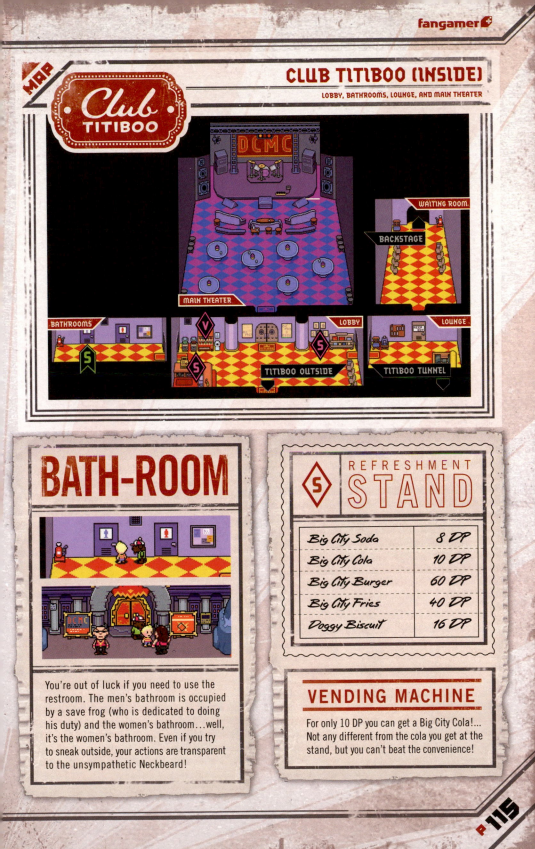

DCMC

WAITING ROOM

BACKSTAGE

MAIN THEATER

BATHROOMS

LOBBY

LOUNGE

TITIBOO OUTSIDE

TITIBOO TUNNEL

# BATH-ROOM

You're out of luck if you need to use the restroom. The men's bathroom is occupied by a save frog (who is dedicated to doing his duty) and the women's bathroom...well, it's the women's bathroom. Even if you try to sneak outside, your actions are transparent to the unsympathetic Neckbeard!

## REFRESHMENT STAND

| Big City Soda | 8 DP |
|---|---|
| Big City Cola | 10 DP |
| Big City Burger | 60 DP |
| Big City Fries | 40 DP |
| Doggy Biscuit | 16 DP |

## VENDING MACHINE

For only 10 DP you can get a Big City Cola!... Not any different from the cola you get at the stand, but you can't beat the convenience!

## SAY TONDA GOSSA TO DCMC

It looks like Lucas and Boney have missed the DCMC show! Luckily the encore is about to start. Do some mingling and talk to *everyone* in the room. After all that walking, Boney's dogs will be barking.

## PARDON
### ME & ME & ME

If you try to leave the theater someone will always bump into you, barring your exit. Even one of the DCMC band members shows up! If a waitress bumps into you and sees that you've got room in your inventory, she'll recognize her chance to sell you an overpriced item and apologize. If there's no room in your inventory, though, you'll just be another annoying kid getting in the way...

## SPIT-TAKE THOMAS

Violet offers to take your order, but a latecomer interrupts. Why, if it isn't Thomas! Violet tells you to meet her in the lobby after the show and that there is a lot to discuss. Don't worry about that now; the encore is about to start!

**DCMC**

**DESPERADO ★ CRASH ★ MAMBO ★ COMBO**

## SCORE SOME SWAG

On the way out of the theater after the encore you'll be offered a free DCMC Pamphlet. Take it even though it's not a great weapon—it could come in handy in the future!

## THE SECRET PASSAGE

Look for Violet towards the room on the right. Follow her down the ladder and into the underground passage. There are Slimy Slugs down here, but they won't be a problem. Follow the path south to find two presents containing a Salt Water Gun and a Made-You-Look. Go north and climb up the ladder at the end.

### MAP — TITIBOO TUNNEL

**A PASSAGEWAY UNDERNEATH THE THEATER**

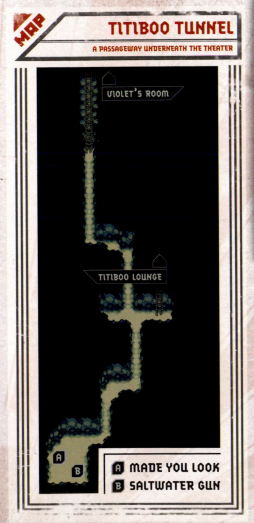

VIOLET'S ROOM

TITIBOO LOUNGE

**A** MADE YOU LOOK
**B** SALTWATER GUN

## ENEMIES

### SLIMY SLUG

These slimy mollusks aren't so tough without their shells. In fact, it's almost as if they have no defense at all. Mow 'em down with some combo attacks.

**Sprinting Bomb (5%)**

| HP: 167 | OFF: 64 | DEF: 8 | EXP: 38 | DP: 15 |

## VIOLET'S DIGS

The tunnel leads to a nice dressing room. Kumatora has already jumped in the shower and, when she's finished, insists you take one as well. Try saying 'No' and you'll get a reminder of how persistent and impatient she can be.

# CLUB TITIBOO (BACKSTAGE)

VIOLET'S ROOM AND THE BAND DRESSING ROOMS

WASHROOM

LUCKY'S ROOM

VIOLET'S ROOM

TITIBOO ATTIC

TITIBOO TUNNEL

BACKSTAGE HALL

WAITING ROOM

# SHOWER BREAKTIME

After your shower, the three adventurers put their heads together to reminisce and figure out what to do with their current situation. Kumatora knows that Lucky—the DCMC bassist—is really an amnesic Duster, but she's not sure how to break it to him. She asks you to talk some sense into him, opening up a hidden passage through the attic to Duster's room.

# CLUB TITIBOO (ATTIC)

THE CLUB'S STORAGE OF OLD INSTRUMENTS, MEMORABILIA & MORE

VIOLET'S ROOM

LUCKY'S ROOM

| A ATTIC MAP | D MAGIC TART | G NICE STUFF | J MAGIC GELATIN |
| B BUG SPRAY | E SPRINTING BOMB | H RICE STUFF | |
| C ANTIDOTE | F BIG CITY FRIES | I NICE RICE STUFF | |

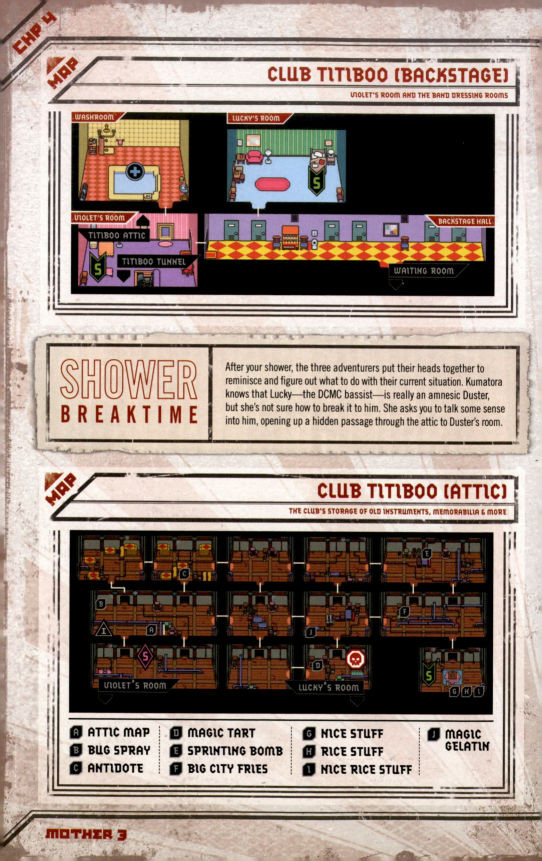

# STRATEGY
## A WELL-STOCKED ATTIC

You're about to run through a pretty grueling obstacle course filled with enemies. Surprisingly, this attic has everything you could ever want! Take some time to prepare for your journey:

**1** Save your game with the frog downstairs and grab all the DP you've got available.

**2** Talk to the Item Guy and give him your:
- **DCMC Pamphlet** (you won't need it now)
- **Saltwater guns** (useless against attic foes)
- **Unnecessary items** like Trivia Cards

**3** Pick up the **Attic Guide** from the blue present box

**4** Talk to the mouse. You'll need around 1000 DP (you can sell your Saltwater guns if you're low on cash) to purchase the following items, in order of importance:
- Upgrade Lucas to the **Better Stick**
- Buy one or more **Pencil Rockets** (you'll need them later!)
- Buy two or more **Antidotes** (to help conserve your PP)
- Buy two or more **Bug Sprays** (give these to Boney for one-hit KO's on spiders)
- Fill any and all remaining spaces in your inventory with **Bread Rolls**

# ENEMIES

### GREEDIER MOUSE

Chubby and greasy with dirty rat feet... A greedier mouse you will never meet... It drops a buffet of foods you can eat... Slice this guy's cheese for a chance at a treat!

**Bag of Big City Fries (30%)**
**Peculiar Cheese (50%)** | **Big City Burger (10%)**

| HP: 140 | OFF: 70 | DEF: 21 | EXP: 60 | DP: 35 |

### ARACHNID!!!!

### POISONOUS!

The extra emphasis really doesn't make these spiders much more intimidating, but they can still poison you. Always use your Antidotes first— Lucas needs to conserve his PP!

**Antidote (10%)**

| HP: 178 | OFF: 58 | DEF: 10 | EXP: 41 | DP: 18 |

### ELDER BATTY

Your mom told you to obey your elders, but she'd probably make an exception for these old bats. Watch your HP, as they can suck it away to heal themselves!

**Bug Spray (15%)**

| HP: 288 | OFF: 66 | DEF: 16 | EXP: 50 | DP: 31 |

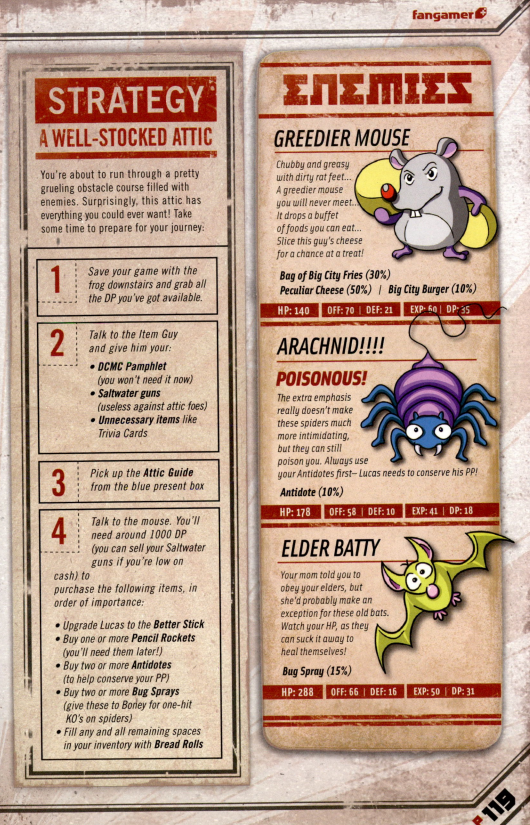

## MOUSE SHOP

| | |
|---|---|
| Better Stick | 500 DP |
| Bread Roll | 30 DP |
| Antidote | 8 DP |
| Anti-Paralysis | 14 DP |
| Sprinting Bomb | 200 DP |
| Pencil Rocket | 500 DP |
| Bug Spray | 100 DP |
| Made-You-Look | 50 DP |

## LIMEY RICE MICE

There is a small safe haven for mice in this attic. Speak to the limey old blokes at the table and you'll receive a Nut Bread, a Peculiar Cheese, and an earful of slang.

# RULES OF THE HIGH ROAD

If you pick up the Attic Guide near the Item Guy, you'll find the correct path through the attic marked in blue. Unless you're itching for a fight, follow it closely!

- - - - - - - - - - - - - - - - - - - - - - - - - - - - - - - -

Enemies in the attic respawn every time you move from room to room, so don't backtrack unless you have to. However, you can use this to your advantage. In some rooms enemies appear randomly, so if you enter/leave often enough you can actually make them disappear!

- - - - - - - - - - - - - - - - - - - - - - - - - - - - - - - -

*It's a long way through the attic, so conserve Lucas's PP whenever possible!*

- *Use antidotes to remove poison instead of PK Healing*
- *Use food items to restore HP instead of PK Lifeup*
- *Only use your special PK powers if you're facing a lot of enemies*

# RICE SURPRISE

There are three presents in this room (nice stuff, rice stuff, and nice rice stuff), and even though they'll all give you different messages, the effects of each box are the same:

- *Revive fallen party members*
- *Restore 50 HP to all members*
- *Restore 50 PP to Lucas*

Use them sparingly and remember: even if they say you're fully revitalized, they're only restoring some of your PP/HP, and they don't cure status effects either!

## GETTING TUNED UP

Before approaching the bass you need to ensure you're ready for a difficult battle! If your levels are low you'll get pulverized by these noisemakers

- *Restore your HP fully with food! If you're running very low on food, use PK Lifeup.*
- *Refill Lucas's PP with a Magic Tart/Gelatin*
- *Give Boney the following:*
  - *~ Pencil Rocket(s)*
  - *~ Bombs (unless Lucas is low on PP, if so you might want to let him keep a few)*
  - *~ High-yield healing items*

# CHP BOSS

# ENEMIES

## BATTLE OF THE BAD INSTRUMENTS

Lucas and Boney come across a hole in the attic which leads to Duster's room. However, the Jealous Bass and its cohorts are not happy about being left to warp in the attic!

- Lucas should use his special PK attack (or a rocket/bomb) as his opening attack
- Have Boney open the fight with the mighty Pencil Rocket (or a Sprinting Bomb)
- With the drum and guitar out of the way, dedicate Boney to bombing and healing while Lucas uses his special PK attack.

## STONE-SHEET-CLIPPERS!

You land in Duster's dressing room where the crisis is in full swing. Lucky says he hid the Hummingbird Egg at Unknown Valley but still does not remember who he really is. Resume his responsibilities as Duster or remain as the bassist for the ultra-popular DCMC? Unsure of what to do, the band decides that destiny must guide the way… via a game of Stone-Sheet-Clippers.

Play with each band member. They always throw the same hand and will even give you hints as to what they are going to throw. Even if you pick the wrong move, destiny always seems to get in the way! OJ, recognizing the designs of fate, tells you what to throw. After you beat him, the band wishes Duster goodbye.

### JEALOUS BASS

### CHAPTER BOSS!

While it has powerful attacks on its own, it can team up with its cohorts to make groovy group attacks that put the hurt on you. Stop the music by blasting him with your PK special and a bomb.

| HP: 978 | OFF: 58 | DEF: 25 | EXP: 1176 | DP: 624 |
|---------|---------|---------|-----------|---------|

### GENTLY WEEPING GUITAR

Looks like its capacitors still work after years in storage—take it out quickly or you'll be devastated by its double-strike electric blasts!

*Magic Gelatin (5%)*

| HP: 250 | OFF: 63 | DEF: 18 | EXP: 90 | DP: 52 |
|---------|---------|---------|---------|--------|

### BEATEN DRUM

This drum wants to beat on you. It can change the tempo and music in battle and string together its own combos. Show this dumb drum who's the bossa nova!

*Sprinting Bomb (3%)*

| HP: 312 | OFF: 70 | DEF: 30 | EXP: 86 | DP: 55 |
|---------|---------|---------|---------|--------|

As the newly-formed quartet leaves Club Titiboo they are stopped by a song from the stage—a goodbye from the DCMC to their Lucky friend. Once outside, Lucas completes his first mission, releasing the pigeon as a signal that Duster has finally been found. Onward to the Unknown Valley!

# CHAPTER

## NO. 5

### TOWER OF THUNDER

# CHAPTER NO. 5

## PART ONE

### THE EGG HUNT

An amnesic Duster returns to the group with vague memories of hiding the Egg of Light. Luckily he seems to remember his staple ladder move too! The newly accessible cliff, east of the Ropeway, opens a path leading deep into the Unknown Valley and hopefully to the Egg of Light.

## THE CAVE THAT HAS EVERYTHING

The small cave at the top of the cliff is quite accommodating. Inside you will find a hot spring, a Save Frog, and a mole selling some great items. Take advantage of this cavernous haven by upgrading everyone's gear.

## MOLE SHOP

| | |
|---|---|
| Better Stick | 500 DP |
| Durable Gloves | 300 DP |
| Sharp Shoes | 480 DP |
| Fly Charm | 350 DP |
| Sparrow Bandana | 200 DP |
| Azure Ribbon | 180 DP |
| Capricorn Bracelet | 600 DP |

# RETURN TO
# TAZMILY

After stocking up at the cave you might be tempted to jump straight into the next adventure, but it's worth your time to do a little backtracking first!

## Pick it Up
Head back to Club Titiboo's stage to see a little DCMC memorabilia.

## Swag Get
Get your hands on a DCMC Pamphlet, you'll need it soon!

## Day Job
You can continue working at the factory, earning 200 DP per shift.

## Egg Time
Ditch Duster and Kumatora's old food items and stock up on nutritious eggs!

# OSOHE
### REDUX

Osohe's resident maestro is back as Lord Passion! You won't be forgiven for thinking that his changes are all cosmetic, as he is a much more formidable foe.

Spend the first two rounds using Offense/Defense Down and Crying attacks, as well as Offense Up for Duster and Boney. With Passion weakened and crying, Boney and Duster can attack while Lucas and Kumatora use any of their PK skills.

When the music settles, so do the Mystical Shoes! These amazing kicks give a huge boost to almost all of Duster's stats. **This is your only chance to get them!**

# SIDE-BOSS

## Lord Passion

### SIDE-BOSS
Take down this passionate poltergeist with a mix of PSI and combos. Kumatora's PK Fire works well, while Duster's Scary Mask and Smoke Bomb will make the battle easier.

| HP: 2897 | OFF:82 DEF:43 | EXP:1086 DP:280 |
|---|---|---|

## THE FORGETFUL SON
# RETURNS

After silencing Lord Passion, make sure to visit Duster's old Dad, Wess. Do loving open arms await our reunited group?— Don't count on it.

### Family Reunion

You can take Duster back to see Wess, but don't expect him to get all teary-eyed. At least the trip was good for a Thunder Bomb...

### Pap's Paper

That weird newspaper in the old folks' home is still churning out strange headlines. After a quick read, return to scale the cliffs to the east of the Titiboo Ropeway!

## FOREST WATERFALL

VALLEY CAVE

A

TITIBOO ROPEWAY

A FIREWORKS

## UNKNOWN VALLEY – *West*

UNKNOWN VALLEY

S

+ S

FOREST WATERFALL

## NO SHIRT, NO SHOES, NO PROBLEM

During your trek through the forest, Boney will eventually become tired of walking on two legs and will remove his disguise to become a regular dog once more. Too bad, the hat looked nice.

## IT'S IN THE HOLE

Lucas and company come across a clearing in the forest with many large holes—mole holes, to be precise. You can jump down any of the holes and find yourself greeted with enemies, presents, and some friendly moles. If you'd like a shortcut, take the southwest hole to find a Save Frog and, more importantly, the exit.

## MOLE TUNNEL FACTS

Did you know that mole tunnels are more than just places to live? They also serve as traps to confuse and capture food. These tunnels can act as literal dungeons. And did you know that tunnels spanning over 100 meters are not all that uncommon? It's true! Next time you see a mole digging take a moment to watch this amazing process in action. You'll really dig it.

# ENEMIES

## Parental Kangashark

This overprotective mother is a formidable foe whose child can provide more than just moral support! Use PK Freeze to stop it cold.

**BEEF JERKY (10%)**

| HP: 289 | OFF:82 | DEF:24 | EXP:93 | DP:50 |

## Reconstructed Lion

Oh my pork it's a lion get in the Pork Bean! This nasty beast can use PK Fire, an attack that will quickly wear down your team, so dispatch of it quickly!

**SPRINTING BOMB (5%)**

| HP: 325 | OFF:88 | DEF:27 | EXP:96 | DP:62 |

## Mecha-Turtle

Sneaking up on this turtle is not such a good idea—strapped to the back of its shell is an array of weapons! Fight this reptile head on.

**SALTWATER GUN (3%)**

| HP: 400 | OFF:80 | DEF:40 | EXP:100 | DP:69 |

## UNKNOWN VALLEY : *Pot Hole Field & Thunder Basin*

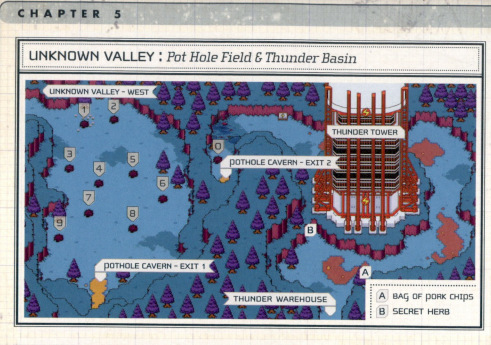

UNKNOWN VALLEY - WEST

1 2

3

5

4

6

7

8

9

0

THUNDER TOWER

POTHOLE CAVERN - EXIT 2

B

A

POTHOLE CAVERN - EXIT 1

THUNDER WAREHOUSE

| A | BAG OF PORK CHIPS |
| B | SECRET HERB |

## POTHOLE CAVERN

1 2

C

3

A

B

5

0

4

6

EXIT 2

7

THUNDER BASIN

8

9

EXIT 1

POTHOLE FIELD

| A | BEEF JERKY |
| B | PENCIL ROCKET |
| C | CAPRICORN BRACELET |

## SHOCKING DISCOVERY

Duster has hidden the Egg of Light in what appears to be a broken-down Clayman. As you approach the lifeless blob, it is suddenly brought to life by a stray bolt of lightning! Instead of a fight, you've got a chase on your hands. Follow him eastward and you'll find yourselves at the base of the Thunder Tower.

# TOWER OF
# LOVE & PEACE

**P·KORP**

FORM TLP1

### WELCOME VALUED GUESTS TO ~~THUNDER TOWER~~!

FRANCHISE STAMP HERE

TOWER OF LOVE & PEACE · SYNERGISTIC HAPPINESS

This structure is designed to house ~~P·KORP's machinery of indirect enforcement~~ *the hopes and dreams of mankind.*

This facility employs ~~steel-alloy conduction channeling~~ *synergistic happiness solutions* to stay on the cutting edge of technology!

In addition to our ~~robotic security~~ great atmosphere, we are proud of our ~~multi-purpose bathroom door hooks~~ *comprehensive joy-enhancement* protocols.

## BUTTERFLY
### PRESENT EFFECT

Near the Clayman Factory is a present containing a Magic Butterfly! If you've got plenty of PP already, heal your party before you open it.

### THUNDER WAREHOUSE GROUNDS

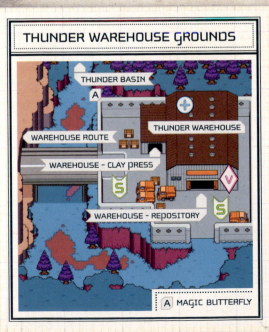

THUNDER BASIN · A · THUNDER WAREHOUSE · WAREHOUSE ROUTE · WAREHOUSE – CLAY PRESS · WAREHOUSE – REPOSITORY

A MAGIC BUTTERFLY

# VENDING

| | |
|---|---|
| Cup of Pork Noodles | 80 DP |
| Anti-Paralysis | 14 DP |
| Fresh Mint | 16 DP |
| Paper Fan | 12 DP |
| Recollection Bell | 20 DP |
| Eye Drops | 10 DP |
| Secret Herb | 600 DP |
| Better Stick | 500 DP |
| Durable Gloves | 300 DP |
| Sharp Shoes | 480 DP |
| Fly Charm | 350 DP |
| Sparrow Bandana | 200 DP |
| Azure Ribbon | 180 DP |
| Capricorn Bracelet | 600 DP |

## POINT OF NO RETURN

If you want to pick up a DCMC Pamphlet (or any other stuff from earlier), now's your last chance! When you enter the factory the two drivers from the Osohe mission will cross paths again, blocking your way back.

## MISTAKEN IDENTITY

Upon entering the factory, Lucas is mistaken for... the "Commander"? No time to question luck, there's a Clayman to track down. Shielded by your new costumes, venture into the belly of the Clayman Factory.

## THUNDER WAREHOUSE : *Repository & Clay Press*

WAREHOUSE GROUNDS

CLAYMAN

WAREHOUSE GROUNDS

Ⓐ MUSIC

0

# P·KORP DIY CLAY KIT
## CLAYMAN ®

**FOR KIDS!**

→ **FUN FOR ANY & ALL AGES!**
→ **THE MAGIC OF CREATION!**
→ **EASILY SELF-DISPOSING!**

### INGREDIENTS

**P·KORP**

Catalytic Acid-Bonding Agent (included)
Clay (1,800 kg, not included)
Electricity (1.21 gigawatts, not included)

FORM CM1

---

## JUST FRIENDS

Speak to the Pigmask in the first room on the far left. He will give Lucas a Secret Herb... strictly in a friend sense!

## GIFT OF GETTIN' FUNKY

Climb the ladder in the first room to find a present you can get down with.

## INSTANTANEOUS VITALITY

In the back room there is a nifty machine that will completely heal everyone's HP, PP, and status aliments.

---

## THE CHASE CONTINUES

You arrive just in time to watch the hot-footed Clayman being driven off in a garbage truck! Looks like he didn't receive the welcoming he thought his homecoming would bring—or perhaps this is just what he was programmed to do? Put your heels to the pavement and follow that truck!

# CHAPTER NO. 5

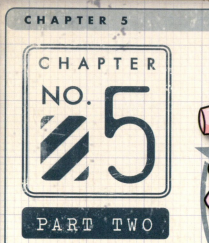

## PART TWO
### THE HIGHWAY

The chase is on for the mossy malfunctioning clay man. Engage with a high speed highway pursuit, but be careful of potential road hazards.

## SLIPPERY SLOPE

Once you enter the second tunnel you might consider healing up and giving Boney a DCMC Pamphlet, some bombs, and healing items. You never know where danger lurks!

### HIGHWAY : *Warehouse Route*

HIGHWAY SYSTEM

THUNDER WAREHOUSE

## RIGHT-OF-WAY

As "the Commander" you've got a free pass to run down the middle of the highway, but sticking to the sidewalk will help avoid awkward confrontations...

## COMPOUND PEELS

In pursuit of the garbage truck, Lucas's mistaken identity nets your group a free Pork Bean. Unfortunately, some slippery litter cuts your trip short. The Fierce Pork Trooper stops by to lend some roadside assistance, but his nose sees right through your party's charade.

### MINI-BOSS

## SPICY PORK

This is the same bulky fellow you met at Club Titiboo. You may remember that he's a huge DCMC fan, so it's time to put your merchandise to use!

### SUGGESTED OPENING ATTACKS:

**Lucas:** *Offense Up on Duster*
**Duster:** *Scary Mask*
**Kumatora:** *Offense Down*
**Boney:** *DCMC Item (Pamphlet)*

For the rest of the battle, have Boney heal and keep the Trooper distracted. Offense Down, Defense Down, and PK Fire will help wear him down while Duster uses combo attacks and Lucas hits with his special PK power.

### Wound-Up Road Hog

This road hog will often break his wind-up spring during his charge attack. If you're lucky, it will drop a valuable Secret Herb!

**SECRET HERB (10%)**

| HP: 420 | OFF: 98 | DEF: 36 | EXP: 150 | DP: 53 |

### Scrapped Robot

You've gotta feel bad for this robot. It can barely attack and can hardly keep its own parts together. Regular attacks are more than enough to scrap it.

**ANTI-PARALYSIS (15%)**

| HP: 332 | OFF: 79 | DEF: 20 | EXP: 82 | DP: 32 |

### Fierce Pork Trooper

## MINI-BOSS

He's the toughest Pigmask around, but this big guy has a not-so-secret soft spot for DCMC merchandise. Keep him distracted while you knock his offense/defense down.

**PICKLED VEGGIE PLATE (100%)**

| HP: 1758 | OFF: 125 | DEF: 46 | EXP: 1548 | DP: 620 |

## ON THE OPEN HIGHWAY

The Highway is pretty expansive, but luckily there's a handy map directly north of the crash site. There's lots to do out on the open road, but before you start exploring, head north to where there's a construction gap in the highway and talk to the mama mouse. She'll give you something to do while you're running around.

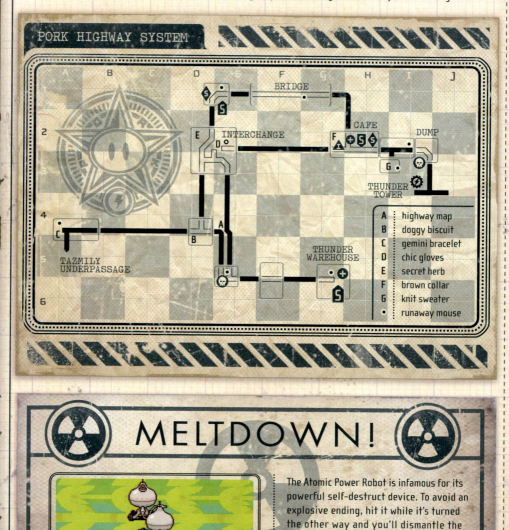

PORK HIGHWAY SYSTEM

BRIDGE

CAFE

DUMP

INTERCHANGE

THUNDER
TOWER

TAZMILY
UNDERPASSAGE

THUNDER
WAREHOUSE

| A | highway map |
|---|---|
| B | doggy biscuit |
| C | gemini bracelet |
| D | chic gloves |
| E | secret herb |
| F | brown collar |
| G | knit sweater |
| • | runaway mouse |

# MELTDOWN!

The Atomic Power Robot is infamous for its powerful self-destruct device. To avoid an explosive ending, hit it while it's turned the other way and you'll dismantle the explosive device.

# HAVE YOU SEEN US?

If you have any information pertaining to the whereabouts of any of these seven mice, do what's right... Tell them to get their butts home, pronto!

Last seen in the areas Noted by the map Dots, Refer to map on left

## REWARD

### SHIELD SNATCHER

# ENEMIES

## Road Block

These traffic enforcers will try Hypnosis Alpha on you, and if that doesn't work they'll call in reinforcements!

**FRESH MINT (20%)**

| HP: 333 | OFF:90 DEF:39 | EXP:108 DP:75 |
|---|---|---|

## Wobbly Robot

This robot may look like a pushover, but he is not like his broken brethren. He can emit an electro-magnetic pulse that will make you feel numb and leave you motionless!

**SECRET HERB (5%)**

| HP: 412 | OFF:93 DEF:28 | EXP:126 DP:64 |
|---|---|---|

## Atomic Power Robot

This refueling bot has deadly beams and an annoying capacity for recharging itself. Upon defeat, the machine will self-destruct! End the battle quickly to lessen the damage.

**BOMB (3%)**

| HP: 350 | OFF:64 DEF:26 | EXP:105 DP:68 |
|---|---|---|

# ROAD TRIP

If you keep following the road west, you'll find yourself all the way back at the Candrum Underpass. The graveyard has been sealed off, but if you check the nearby side tunnel you'll find a Luxury Banana and a Super Bomb, together worth more than 2500 DP!

# GETTING CHARGED

## PORK BEAN TRANSPORT RECHARGE

Having fun joy riding in the Pork Bean? If you want the good times to continue, you will need to recharge its battery **before you try to cross the bridge.** There is a recharge station in the scenic northeast section of the highway. Park on the Recharge Panel, step out, and turn on the nearby device. Once you hear the beep, stop the recharging process—if you don't, you'll be continuing your journey on foot.

# DANGEROUS STUFF SHOP

A Pigmask in this area sells some dangerous stuff that might come in handy. Don't come crying to him if you blow your hand off!

| | |
|---|---|
| Pencil Rocket | 500 DP |
| Bomb | 1000 DP |
| Super Bomb | 2000 DP |
| New Year's Eve Bomb | 3000 DP |
| Saltwater Gun | 400 DP |

# ONE DOG'S TRASH ♻

If you happen to have a Doggy Biscuit when you speak to the stray dog near the charging station, he'll beg for it. Unlike most dogs, he's got something for you in return! Where in the world could a stray dog have picked up a high explosive...?

# SOUVENIRS

| | |
|---|---|
| Handy Yo-Yo | 650 DP |
| Souvenir Dress | 1400 DP |
| Taurus Bracelet | 1200 DP |
| Bag of Pork Chips | 28 DP |
| Cup of Pork Noodles | 80 DP |
| Fresh Mint | 16 DP |
| Secret Herb | 600 DP |

## PIT STOP

Upon reaching the Parking Area you will see the garbage truck speed off into the east tunnel. Don't be so hasty in following it, there's still plenty of time to rest and take in the local color.

# ENEMIES

## Rhinocerocket

This speedy foe flies through the air with the greatest of ease and malice. When he attacks, he hits everyone in the party—twice! Take him down fast with your strongest attacks.

PENCIL ROCKET (10%)

| HP: 400 | OFF:80 DEF:27 | EXP:171 DP:178 |
|---|---|---|

## Bright Smile

### RARE!

This dazzling foe's appearances are as short as they are rare, so make the most of your time by using super-powerful attacks. Wipe the smile off its face and you'll get a huge cash reward.

| HP: 278 | OFF:67 DEF:30 | EXP:90 DP:2000 |
|---|---|---|

# VENDING MACHINES

As always, the Item Guy is one step ahead of you. Now might be a good time to get your belongings organized!

➡ Grab any Saltwater Guns you can get.

➡ Upgrade everyone's equipment at the vendor, and buy some overpriced food if you really need it.

➡ Sell your old collars, bracelets, and gloves, and then deposit your money with the Save Frog— you won't need it again anytime soon.

## HIGHWAY PITSTOP : *P Cafe & Charge Station*

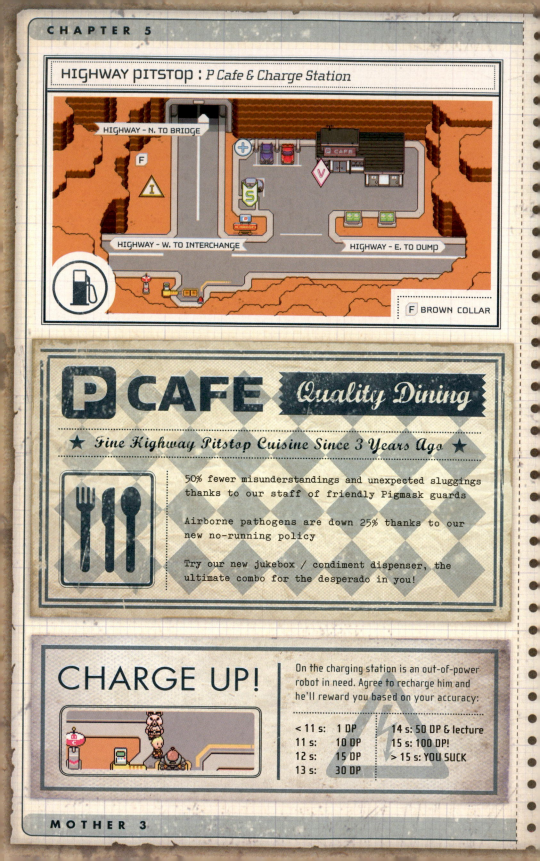

HIGHWAY – N. TO BRIDGE

HIGHWAY – W. TO INTERCHANGE

HIGHWAY – E. TO DUMP

F BROWN COLLAR

# P CAFE — *Quality Dining*

★ **Fine Highway Pitstop Cuisine Since 3 Years Ago** ★

50% fewer misunderstandings and unexpected sluggings thanks to our staff of friendly Pigmask guards

Airborne pathogens are down 25% thanks to our new no-running policy

Try our new jukebox / condiment dispenser, the ultimate combo for the desperado in you!

# CHARGE UP!

On the charging station is an out-of-power robot in need. Agree to recharge him and he'll reward you based on your accuracy:

|  |  |
|------|--------|
| < 11 s: | 1 DP |
| 11 s: | 10 DP |
| 12 s: | 15 DP |
| 13 s: | 30 DP |
| 14 s: | 50 DP & lecture |
| 15 s: | 100 DP! |
| > 15 s: | YOU SUCK |

# LEO-LEO THE LADIES MAN

In the east tunnel right near the Parking Area is Leo-Leo's lair. Speak to him a few times and he'll let you open a present. No matter what present you pick, you will always get a sweater with "LEO" knitted into it. Sure, this was a gift from a "girlfriend"... Even though it restores a few HP every round, its poor stats make it a good candidate for the Item Guy.

## END OF THE CHASE

You finally catch up to the garbage truck as it dumps the Clayman into its new home. Climbing down the ladder gets you one step closer to the Egg of Light, but it also gets you into a fight with the Forlorn Junk Heap!

## MINI-BOSS

### TAKE OUT THE
# TRASH

This guy is scrapping for a fight! To make things easier, give Boney the Shield Snatcher and have him use it in the first round while barraging with Offense/Defense Down.

**Attacks to Use:**
Lucas's special PK attack
Kumatora's PK Fire
Shield Snatcher
Explosive Items
Scary Mask / Tickle Stick

**Attacks to Avoid:**
Sniffing
PK Thunder
Saltwater Guns
Duster's Thief Techniques

## ENEMIES

### Forlorn Junk Heap

## MINI-BOSS

This junk heap can heal and increase its defenses by attaching pieces of trash to itself. It attacks by throwing trash around, sometimes hitting more than one target!

| HP: 1818 | OFF: 122 DEF: 45 | EXP: 2534 DP: 728 |
|---|---|---|

# CHAPTER NO. 5

## PART THREE

### THUNDER TOWER

## TO THE THUNDER TOWER

With the Forlorn Junk Heap permanently junked, Duster recovers the Egg of Light. After touching the egg he has a flashback and also recovers his memory! What luck! But you don't get to celebrate long as a Pig-mask arrives and once again mistakes Lucas for "the Commander."

## HIGHLY UNSUSPICIOUS

After a short elevator ride you'll find yourselves inside the not-so-well-guarded Thunder Tower. Use the various conveniences on this floor, grab the Tower Sketch from the present, and begin your journey to the top of the tower.

## ITEM GUY

The ubiquitous Item Guy is, as always, waiting with supplies and encouragement. You can grab or store that DCMC Pamphlet—even if you don't pick it up now, you can get another within the tower.

## REFRESH AND
# REVITALIZE

If you're weak and need to level up, blast away at some enemies with your PK attacks and head back to the lobby to heal up.

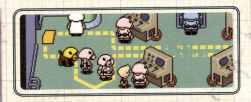

# VENDING

| | |
|---|---|
| Good Stick | 1500 DP |
| Rubber Boots | 1360 DP |
| Brown Collar | 1600 DP |
| Cup of Pork Noodles | 80 DP |
| Anti-Paralysis | 14 DP |
| Fresh Mint | 16 DP |
| Paper Fan | 12 DP |
| Secret Herb | 600 DP |

## THE PATH YOU CHOOSE

The first level of the Thunder Tower is one large ring. You can either follow the west path or north path as both will take you to the tower's Catfish Generator Room. There are three present boxes on this floor, so if you're a completionist you'll want to try both.

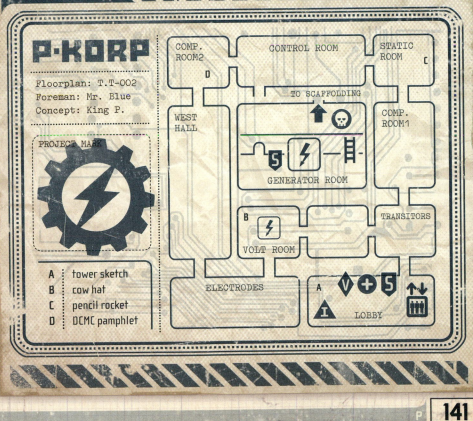

THUNDER TOWER

# P·KORP

Floorplan: T.T-002
Foreman: Mr. Blue
Concept: King P.

PROJECT MARK

| | |
|---|---|
| A | tower sketch |
| B | cow hat |
| C | pencil rocket |
| D | DCMC pamphlet |

COMP. ROOM2    D

CONTROL ROOM

STATIC ROOM    C

TO SCAFFOLDING

WEST HALL

COMP. ROOM1

GENERATOR ROOM

TRANSITORS

VOLT ROOM

ELECTRODES

LOBBY

## P-KORP

# ELECTRIC CATFISH

**MEGAZAPPOW SWIMMEOWATUS**

Class: Actinopterpigi
Order: Laziformes
Family: Malaporkidae

>> Electrogenic Genotype:
   Zzz (*heterozygous excessive*)
>> Desired Phenotype: Excitable
   w/ throughput of 1+ kZap
>> Notes: Due to the dominance of the
   excitabulus allele, many of the
   specimens are notably listless.
>> The single nucleotide polymorphism
   contributing to this condition has
   also, unfortunately, been tied to
   the emergence of the desired 1+ kZap
   phenotype. Pending further mutagenic
   labwork, the specimens will have to
   be manually encouraged to exercise
   their electrogenesis.

WARNING: DO NOT TEASE

## ✭ DcMc ✭

# DEVOTION

The Pork Trooper is the biggest DCMC fan in the world. Over the years he has collected tons of rare merch, including limited-edition fan club figurines and posters that aren't even on sale! And, like any self-respecting collector, he's got offsite backups in a secure storage facility.

## ◄ MINI-BOSS ►

### HANDLE WITH CARE:
# USE FISTS

A massive merchandise collection indicates that an obsessed fan lurks nearby. Sure enough, the Fierce Pork Trooper lies in wait, dressed for a fight. Like before, all you really have to do is whip out a DCMC item and you will have no problem taking him down.

## NOWHERE TO GO BUT UP

It looks like your cover is blown! Fassad arrives to unmask your deception and convey his vengeful intentions. Fassad and his minions are blocking the escape, so climbing up the tower is your only choice. Might as well get rid of these uniforms since they won't be doing any more good. Run up the many stairs to the top!

### TOWER SCAFFOLDING

PLAYROOM

GENERATOR ROOM

A

A TRIVIA CARD #2

# ENEMIES

## Whatever

These little guys aren't much of a threat. They'd rather give you a hug than a bruise, and you can even walk up to them without getting into a fight.

**MAGIC GELATIN (10%)**

| HP: 264 | OFF:80 DEF:25 | EXP:98 DP:12 |

## Minor Robot

These robots might look minor, but their bombs are not! Take them down with combos before they get the chance. Once their batteries die, they're helpless.

**BOMB (3%)**

| HP: 478 | OFF:98 DEF:38 | EXP:232 DP:60 |

## Battery Man

This little guy is pretty easy to handle, but if he's teamed up with a Minor Robot he'll sacrifice himself to restore the robot's charge!

**MAKE YOU-LOOK (15%)**

| HP: 300 | OFF:85 DEF:27 | EXP:165 DP:26 |

## Fierce Pork Trooper

This is the same guy, just tougher thanks to his combat suit. If you don't keep him distracted with merch, get ready to deal with his fists and powerful bum rush. Swag is more than just a good idea—its a necessity.

| HP: 2064 | OFF:159 DEF:59 | EXP:3286 DP:650 |

## THE PLAYROOM

It would appear that you have come across some kind of majestic playroom—certainly an odd amenity in such a dangerously industrial tower. There is plenty of action packed into this little room, so take your time here.

# ★★ THE PLAYROOM ★★

### LIL' MISS MARSHMALLOW

A robotic playroom maid with a deceptive name.

### SURPRISE!

You will find a surprise in the present box next to the guitar. Be warned—if you're not properly leveled up, this could be a very unpleasant surprise.

### THE JUKEBOX

This juke box plays some familiar music... Whoever this room was built for, they have a taste for the classics.

### DANGER FROG!

Warning! That innocuous-looking balloon frog could cause you some real heartache. Due to an unfortunate design error in the original game, saving with that frog could potentially leave your characters permanently stuck between the frog and the wall! You should take your chances and keep trucking until the next the Save Frog.

# VENDING

| | |
|---|---|
| Rubber Cape | 1200 DP |
| Cup of Pork Noodles | 80 DP |
| Luxury Banana | 500 DP |
| Anti-Paralysis | 14 DP |
| Paper Fan | 12 DP |
| Eye Drops | 10 DP |
| Secret Herb | 600 DP |
| Pencil Rocket | 500 DP |
| Made-You-Look | 5 DP |

# RUBBER CAPES

In the vending machine you can purchase some Rubber Capes that are strong against lightning. Since you're heading to the top of a tower that shoots lightning, it might be a good idea to invest in two or three of these. If you're low on money, the two major enemies in this room will both cough up some nice cash. Stock up on Pencil Rockets too, if you can afford them!

## THE PLAYROOM

ELECTRIC PLATFORMS

SCAFFOLDING

| A | SALTWATER GUN | C | SECRET HERB |
| B | MADE-YOU-LOOK | D | FRIEND'S YOYO |

# ENEMIES

## Screwloose

These guys like to call for help, but most of the time their pleas fall on deaf ears. If you dash past them, they usually won't be able to catch you.

FIZZY SODA (10%)

| HP: 350 | OFF:85 DEF:35 | EXP:180 DP:40 |

## Surprise Box

### WARNING

This little surprise loves to use PK Fire β, an attack that can easily devastate your party. You're in a room with a hot spring and a vending machine, so don't hold back.

| HP: 777 | OFF:80 DEF:40 | EXP:932 DP:777 |

## Lil' Miss Marshmallow

### SIDE-BOSS

The kid gloves are off! This metal maid's insane HP and Offense stats belie her kindly steel exterior, and "insane" won't be the half of it once you really make her mad.

| HP: 2300 | OFF:110 DEF:46 | EXP:2864 DP:824 |

For your trouble you'll get the **Friend's Yo-Yo** which Lucas, Duster, and Kumatora can all use. Wonder who it used to belong to?

# SIDE-BOSS

## S'MORE FUN

You can try to take the glass-enshrined **Friend's Yo-Yo** near the exit, but you'll have to do battle with the formidable Ms. Marshmallow. Her attacks start out powerful and then become ultra-powerful, so prepare for a long fight.

➡ You won't need your Rubber Capes for this battle, so don't equip them yet.

➡ Believe it or not, that knit sweater from Leo can help prevent KOs. Consider giving it to Lucas or Duster.

➡ Stick to the **Offense/Defense Down** strategy you've used for previous battles! It is especially important because of how long this battle is.

➡ Once Kumatora has diminished Marshmallow's stats, PK Thunder is her best attack.

➡ Feel free to make use of a Saltwater gun or two.

➡ Marshmallow's battle song uses offbeats. Tap along with the beat of the cymbal, not the bassline.

## IN NEED OF REPAIR

It looks like this part of the tower could use some repair work. These machines let off sparks which can actually attack you! Make sure you equip your Rubber Capes before you go dashing around.

## ELECTRIC PLATFORMS

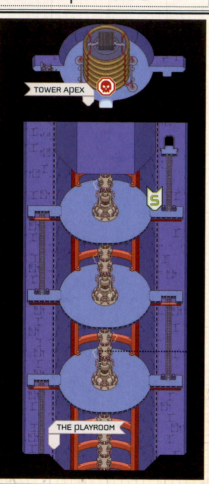

TOWER APEX

THE PLAYROOM

# SHOCKING
### E X P E R I E N C E

As you prepare to climb to the third level, Lucas gets struck by a stray bolt of lightning. Not only does he survive, he learns PK Flash! The sign didn't say anything about that.

# SHEEPISH

If you're a little nervous about running in front of the giant conductive coil, consider running behind it. You'll get a chance to meet the unexpectedly-meek guy with his finger on the trigger.

# RECHARGE

With danger looming on all sides and an uncertain fate atop the tower, it's time to prepare for a showdown! Give Boney the saltwater guns, heal your party, and get ready for 1.21 gigawatts of fun!

# CHP. BOSS

## SECURE THIS

As you walk through the generator room, you'll be stopped by a loud siren. Mr. Genetor, the security system robot, has spotted you!

While he's charged up, it's dangerous to hit Genetor directly-- not only will you find yourself unable to combo, but you'll receive an electric shock in return! Use the following attacks/items while he's up:

>> *Lucas's PK special*
>> *Scary Mask*
>> *Smoke Bomb*
>> *PK Freeze*
>> *Offense/Defense Down*
>> *Saltwater Guns*
>> *Explosives*

After he *stores electricity*, Genetor's next attack will knock himself (and any of your party members not wearing Rubber Coats) out of commission with a massive *Discharge Zap* attack. Heal up and start wailing on him with everything you've got as soon as he's down.

Eventually his generator will break, leaving him unable to defend or attack. Now's your chance for a full-on offensive!

# ENEMIES

## Short Circuit Zap!

Don't let his smile fool you! He can use PK Thunder θ, which can hit you twice. He can also use PK Flash, which can hit everyone with a status ailment -- or worse!

**MAGIC TART (5%)**

| HP: 300 | OFF:88 DEF:36 | EXP:265 DP:84 |

## Mr. Genetor

### CHAPTER BOSS

This mechanical monster likes to use a wide variety of physical and electrical attacks that can hit one or more of your party. If you physically attack him while he's charged, he'll counter with a small shock!

| HP: 3333 | OFF:120 DEF:55 | EXP:4389 DP:840 |

## NOWHERE TO GO BUT DOWN

Fassad finally "corners" you atop the Thunder Tower and announces his masterstroke: he plans to simultaneously eliminate the now-defunct Thunder Tower and take your party down with it. He falls victim to his own potassium-rich hubris, though, eliciting a brief flash of shock from Kumatora. With some help from Rope Snake the gang hijacks Fassad's ride, only to come face-to-face with a heartless masked man.

Lucas and his friends stare
down a massive, industrial enemy.
Common sense dictates that
they have no chance of success,
but even when the odds are
astronomical, a glimmer of hope
still remains.

Will this team of friends find
themselves separated once again?
As they fall from the flying ship,
a youthful, heartless, masked man
stares back at them.

# No. 6

## SUNFLOWER FIELDS

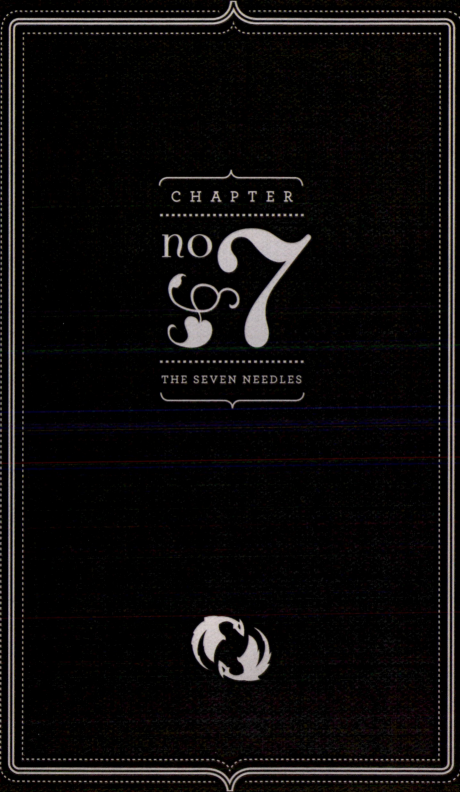

CHAPTER

no 7

THE SEVEN NEEDLES

Chapter 7

# CHAPTER

# no. 7

## PART I

### NEW DIRECTION

The Masked Man and the Pigmasks are planning something big enough that they couldn't risk any kind of interference. What could they be up to, and what happened to Duster and Kumatora?

## HAY IS FOR HORSES & RESCUE

Wess and Alec's impromptu haystacking session is interrupted when Lucas and Boney hurtle from the sky, their falls cushioned by the massive bales. They wake up in the retirement home as Alec discusses the dream which prompted his haystack.

## WHERE TO?

As you leave the retirement home, Alec asks about Duster and mentions that his Magypsy friends may be able to help you out.

## A STRANGER IN OUR MIDST

There's a commotion on the bridge outside the retirement home. Ionia, the strange being who helped you learn PSI, has been bound and gagged and the townspeople are too freaked out to help. Spitting out the gag, she explains that she was attacked and is concerned about Aeolia—time to go upriver!

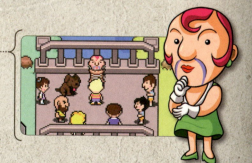

# Legend of the
# DOORKNOB
### Head East Young Doorknob

Doorknob rolled toward the station door, bidding a final farewell to his partner, the last man on the force. The department had undergone a massive "restructuring" provoked by the unprecedented growth of an adjacent precinct, and Doorknob had unexpectedly gotten his wish: his walking papers. He had hardly gotten out the door when he was plucked from the earth—surely an opportunistic ex-con seeking revenge—and violently catapulted heavenward, into the east.

## BACK IN TOWN!

You can take the rowing team up on their offer to head straight to Aeolia's "house," but it won't hurt to see what's new around town first. You're sure to get some looks for having a tied up Magypsy bouncing in tow behind you—even Mapson is thrown off guard!

## OH, THAT OLD THING?

If you've got that horrifying Knit Sweater, you might get a kick out of taking it to the scenic spot near the beach. There's a pretty lady there who seems like Leo-Leo's type…

# ★ NEW PORK CITY ★

### Glamorous, Modern, & Expensive

Tired of the boring country life? Want to experience the lights, the excitement, and the fun of the big city? Come to New Pork City today! Worried about leaving family and friends behind? Take the first step and the weaker citizens will follow in your wake, guaranteed! Nobody can resist the call of the big city — nobody.

SIGN UP NOW

Biff  Isaac
butch  MATT
~~Nichol~~ :)

# A BOAT TRIP

Paddel and Rowe finally have a real boat and they are really itching to use it. They're more than willing to give you a lift upstream. Why buy a boat and not use it, you know? You can still go the long way through the woods if you like, but these boys will save you a lot of time.

# Aeolia

A calm, practical sort of Magypsy with a taste for rose hip tea, Aeolia guards the Needle in Osohe's courtyard. She hosts an occasional Magypsy tea party, and her hot-pink 'fro makes her stand out from the other Magypsies—relatively, at least.

### FORESHADOWING LIGHTS!

As Ionia finishes straightening herself out and putting her face on, the ground begins to shake and the sun is blotted out by dark clouds... What happened? And what's wrong with Aeolia?

### A MAGYPSY TRICK

Aeolia reveals a passage to Osohe castle that will lead you to the needle that she is bound to.

## *The Practical*
# MAGYPSY'S MEMENTO

After Aeolia announces that her Needle has been removed, she asks you to investigate and... disappears? She leaves behind an invaluable memento (a razor and lipstick) which will automatically revive the character who carries it if they're struck unconscious during battle.

## OSOHE CATACOMBS

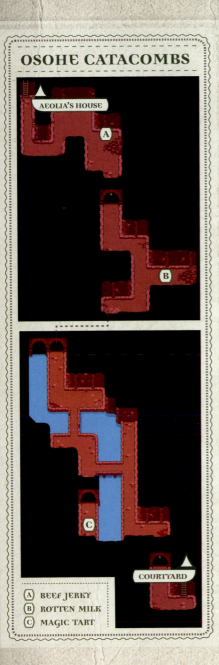

- (A) BEEF JERKY
- (B) ROTTEN MILK
- (C) MAGIC TART

# • ENEMIES •

## CLEOCATRA

This pretty kitty is well-preserved and will use Lifeup β to stay that way. They can be troublesome in packs, so focus on one at a time.

SECRET HERB (10%)

| HP: 312 | OFF:89 DEF:36 | EXP:285 DP:45 |
| --- | --- | --- |

## OSOHE COURTYARD

## WHO PULLED THE PLUG?

In the center of the courtyard lies a gaping hole where that mysterious "Needle" previously protruded. Just as Aeolia said, it's been taken! ...But by whom? Ionia muses about the possibility of a heartless person.

## LOST & FOUND

Someone dropped their transceiver in the courtyard. Answering it, Lucas learns that getting to the next Needle involves the Chimera Lab and... monkeys? The guy on the other end doesn't elaborate, but he gives you directions to the Chimera Lab.

# LEDER'S BELL

From time to time during your adventure you may find yourself suddenly entranced by some dulcet tones. Your nerves calm as a little tune fills your head, reminding you of home. For some reason, it sounds an awful lot like the bell that old Leder (who is still mysteriously absent...) used to ring. Stop to evaluate your progress and, if you're feeling tired, maybe find a place to relax and take a break. Take off your shoes, save your game, brush your teeth, do your business, and hit the hay. You have earned it, and your dad won't have to be so worried!

# The Needles

The Nowhere Islands are protected by an immeasurable power which rests beneath them: The Dragon. It is the size of all the islands combined, a dark, massive, dormant beast whose limitless power cannot be controlled. For that reason, a race of ancient Magypsies lodged seven "Needles" (one per Magypsy) into the Dragon, forcing it to sleep.

Since then, the Magypsies have been tasked with guarding the Needles. There are stories of a "chosen one" capable of pulling the Needles, someone capable of using a special PK power that not even the Magypsies can use. This person will come in a time of crisis to wake the Dragon by pulling the Needles, and the Dragon will obey the wishes of their heart, whether good or evil, even if it leads to the destruction of the world.

When a Needle is pulled, the Magypsy tasked with guarding it ceases to exist. It is not death, but simply the end of a nearly ageless existence. How romantic!

# CHAPTER no 7

## PART II

### THE CHIMERA LAB

Following his stunning revelation, Ionia (literally) takes off as Lucas and Boney prepare for the race of their life. Can they reach the needles first? Do they even stand a chance? Lucas must hurry to the Chimera Lab!

## OSOHE CRYPT

PANTRY – 1ST FLOOR

OSOHE COURTYARD

A  PISCES BRACELET
B  BEEF JERKY
C  ANCIENT BANANA
D  BEEF JERKY

## OSOHE CASTLE EXPOSED!

After taking the secret passage from the courtyard, you arrive in the underground passage to Osohe's waterway. Now that you've completely explored every crevice of Osohe Castle, it's just a boring old castle with no secrets—or parties.

# WHICH NEEDLE *Goes When?*

You can actually acquire many of the Needles in whichever order you wish. Some may be more difficult to get than others at the moment, but feel free to explore and experiment!

## A PROUD FATHER'S MEMENTO

On the way to the train station, Boney drags Lucas to Hinawa's grave. Nippolyte is there with a gift Flint wanted to give Lucas. It's a dirty old badge, but who knows? It might bring you luck!

# THE TAZMILY RAIL

## *Faster, Safer, & More Fun than Walking*

**NEW RATES**

**50 DP** per passenger for standard fare

**200 DP** Special! Ride the Green Train, a colorful & musical new experience!

*Now even you can experience the joy of riding a train!*

# SUBJECT: FACTORY DOWNSIZING

TO: *Mr. Brown*
FROM: *Mr. Black*

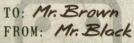
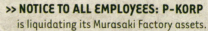

>> **NOTICE TO ALL EMPLOYEES: P-KORP** is liquidating its Murasaki Factory assets.

>> Full-time employees are welcome to reapply at the New Pork City plant.

>> Part-time employees needed at the nearby top-secret lab. No physicals required. Insurance not offered.

## THE SEALED DOOR

You can't get through the door north of the lake yet. Apparently there's some sort of trick to it. Those engraved figures look familiar, but what's on the other side?

## HOT SPRING *Eggs*

That generous chicken is still hanging out near the Murasaki Hot Spring. Eat or sell all your weaker foods and stock up on eggs again! You can also make a little money by letting the Fresh Eggs hatch and selling them when they grow into Chickens.

## THROUGH THE FRONT DOOR

Some monkeys have escaped in the lab and are causing a huge commotion. This is your chance to slip in!

# • ENEMIES •

## BRO TEAM

These guys are much tougher when they work together, serving as a valuable lesson to siblings everywhere. Use Flash to make them cry or just avoid them altogether.

NUT COOKIE (50%) | BEEF JERKY (30%)

| HP: 380 | OFF: 104 DEF: 45 | EXP: 447 DP: 70 |

## SQUAWKING BOOMSTICK

These upgraded birds will blow up if you give them a chance, so avoid them. If you can't avoid a battle, knock them out quickly with everything you've got!

BOMB (10%)

| HP: 400 | OFF: 80 DEF: 37 | EXP: 240 DP: 150 |

## HORSANTULA

These creepy horses sometimes hit multiple times in the same turn, and their bites are poisonous! They also have an overabundance of eyes, all of which can cry, so keep that in mind.

ANTIDOTE (10%)

| HP: 458 | OFF: 116 DEF: 57 | EXP: 352 DP: 67 |

## EINSWINE

Einswine won't pick a fight, but watch out: their strong PSI can easily overwhelm you. Take them out quickly or deplete their PP.

MAGIC TART (10%)

| HP: 387 | OFF: 94 DEF: 43 | EXP: 422 DP: 83 |

# THE CHIMERA LAB

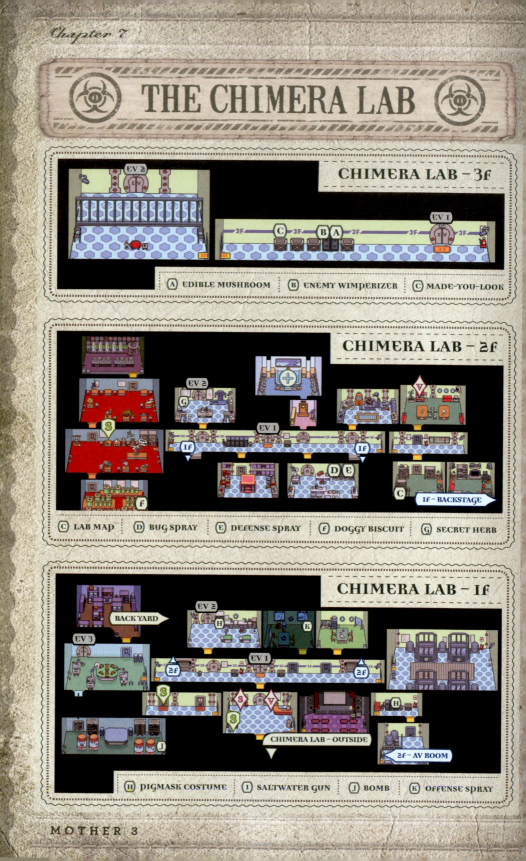

## CHIMERA LAB – 3f

- (A) EDIBLE MUSHROOM
- (B) ENEMY WIMPERIZER
- (C) MADE-YOU-LOOK

## CHIMERA LAB – 2f

- (C) LAB MAP
- (D) BUG SPRAY
- (E) DEFENSE SPRAY
- (F) DOGGY BISCUIT
- (G) SECRET HERB

## CHIMERA LAB – 1f

- (H) PIGMASK COSTUME
- (I) SALTWATER GUN
- (J) BOMB
- (K) OFFENSE SPRAY

# ARMCHAIR CHEMIST

There's a researcher in the lobby of the Chimera Lab who's willing to sell you some interesting medicines that you can't buy anywhere else. They're a little pricey, but they can be worth the cost in the right situation.

## CHEMIST'S WARES

| | |
|---|---|
| OFFENSE SPRAY | 1000 DP |
| DEFENSE SPRAY | 1000 DP |
| ENEMY BUFFERIZER | 800 DP |
| ENEMY WIMPERIZER | 1200 DP |

## *The Better* BLACK BEANLING TRICK

**1** Purchase a few Enemy Bufferizers from the Chemist in the Chimera Lab lobby.

**2** Hunt down a Black Beanling in the Sunshine Forest area south of Lighter's house (this is the hard part—stay persistent).

**3** Use the Enemy Bufferizer on the Black Beanling during battle and defeat it!

### NEED LEVELS?

This trick doubles the already insane amount of experience the Black Beanling leaves. If you're low on money, though, don't worry about it yet—there's sure to be a freebie in the lab.

## LAB VEND

| | |
|---|---|
| VERY GOOD STICK | 2000 DP |
| CUP OF PORK NOODLES | 80 DP |
| PORK STEW | 120 DP |
| ANTIDOTE | 80 DP |
| EYEDROPS | 10 DP |
| ANTI-PARALYSIS | 14 DP |
| FRESH MINT | 16 DP |
| SECRET HERB | 600 DP |

### DON'T FORGET TO SNORT

If you sneak in through the theater room, you'll find an open locker with some Pigmask helmets. Disguised, Lucas and Boney can run around the Chimera Lab freely. However, once you put the disguise on you won't be able to leave the lab, so make sure you're prepared!

## *Incognito* EXPLORATION

It's obvious that these Pigmasks aren't up to the task, so there's no rush to find the monkey. The lab is a fascinating and horrifying facility filled with questions and answers.

# THE DRAGO PURGE

The Dragos all seem to have disappeared following Hinawa's death. Some may have gone into hiding, but it seems that many met their fate in this lab. The Pigmask army may sometimes seem bumbling and incompetent, but malice seems to permeate the higher ranks.

## QUIT MONKEYING AROUND!

When you're done exploring, you can find the monkeys hiding out in the brain room north of the Ossuary (the skeleton room). Don't forget to speak to a Save Frog first! As soon as you confront the familiar-looking simians, they scamper away.

## MINI·BOSS

### SIGH... BORG!

As you reenter the ossuary you come face-to-face with a very metal, very mean-looking lion chimera. It's a tough fight and the result is the same regardless of whether you win or lose, but there's always pride in succeeding!

The Almost-Mecha Lion is immensely powerful, and its only exploitable weakness is a vulnerability to crying. So have Lucas use the following attacks while Boney keeps all healed:

- ➤ PK Flash
- ➤ PSI Counter
- ➤ Defense Up
- ➤ Offense Up
- ➤ Thunder Bombs
- ➤ Combos

## · ENEMIES ·

### ALMOST MECHA-LION

#### MINI-BOSS

This almost beast is capable of biting, scratching, breathing fire, and stabbing with a poisonous tail—in other words, it's an ultimate chimera! Or is it?...

| HP: 1684 | OFF: 126 DEF: 60 | EXP: 4560 DP: 848 |

### ESCAPING CHIMERAS!

Win or lose, the Almost Mecha-Lion won't give up. Luckily, your diversion gave the Pigmasks time to bring in backup. However, there's another chimera loose: a big red one that has everyone sweating bullets. In their panic they've forgotten everything, but your task is still clear: find those monkeys!

## MEMORANDUM: EMERGENCY ⚠️

**FROM:** *Mr. Black*
**TO:** *Dr. Andonuts*

Containment Protocol Memo: In the event that the Ultimate Chimera escapes, it is vital that all lab personnel follow protocol. Commit these steps to memory, habit, or even instinct:

| | |
|---|---|
| *SEAL ALL EXITS* | If it escaped a small cage, seal it in a bigger cage. |
| *DO NOT ENGAGE* | You have been warned. |
| *IF ENGAGED, RUN!* | Or hide. Or play dead. |
| *FEIGN IGNORANCE!* | If it escapes the lab...pretend like nothing happened. |
| *DESTROY ALL FILES* | Burn this message! For insurance purposes, we are obligated to disavow all knowledge of the UC. |

DO NOT COPY/REPRODUCE THIS MESSAGE ON BULLETIN BOARDS, WHITEBOARDS, T-SHIRTS, ETC!

# MUSICAL TERRORS

While the Ultimate Chimera is stalking about, listen carefully.
If you hear Pigmasks screaming in the distance you're safe.
If you hear music, you're the one who will be screaming soon,
so get out of there before it's game over!

## OCCUPIED

A scientist is hiding in a trash can in the
hallway. If you talk to him you find out that
he's doing research here against his will,
though he's too frightened to say anything
more at the moment.

# Dr. Andonuts

*"I'm being forced to conduct various sorts of research by a certain man."*
Dr. Andonuts is a brilliant scientist currently working in the field of
chimera development. He doesn't like having his creations used for evil,
but it seems he has no choice in the matter. Hiding in a trash can
might not seem brave, but you can't deny that it's the smart thing to do.

## CHIMERA LAB – B1f

(J) PORK STEW

## TAILING THE MONKEY

The monkeys have fled to the basement, which you couldn't access before. The elevator you need is on the first floor in the far western room. In the basement, you learn that not only was the monkey responsible for freeing the Ultimate Chimera, but—that monkey is Salsa! Doesn't he remember you?

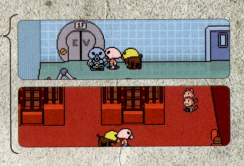

# THE ULTIMATE
# SHOWDOWN

When you corner the monkeys (in the far east room on the 1st floor), the Ultimate Chimera follows and corners you. Dr. Andonuts arrives to explain how to defeat the monster right as it launches its first attack, sending Lucas and Boney's helmet disguises flying. Salsa, recognizing Lucas, springs into action!

# LAB
# MONKEY HIJINKS

With the threat neutralized, why not do a little exploring with your new friend? There are new experiences to be had now that the lab is calm, and Salsa can reach shelves that you couldn't before.

167

## STONE COLD SKILLS

Once you follow Samba to the sealed door northeast of the Lab, Salsa will demonstrate his door-opening abilities. Shake it left or right—his other tricks won't do the trick!

## POOL PROBLEM

Enter the Magypsy house and you'll find Doria and — surprise — Kumatora! Say hello and follow them outside to find out what's gone on. Doria will suggest you head back to the lab for help reaching the Needle.

# Doria

In spite of her motorcycle-gang appearance, Doria is one of the friendliest Magypsies. He cares for Kumatora after her fall and has been protecting the Needle of the twin pools.

## ~ AT LARGE ~

When you get back to the lab, you'll see a clear path of destruction where the Ultimate Chimera made its escape. It's in the wild—time to forget about it!

## CLEANUP CREW

If you head back into the lab you'll see that the clean-up crew arrived while you were out. They've got captains and sentries patrolling the grounds, so it will be much more difficult to get around!

## VIEWING ROOM

The third floor of the Chimera Lab seems to be some kind of sparse, semi-luxurious viewing room for the head honcho to evaluate new chimeras. And on the other side of the glass stalks some kind of metallic abomination!

## FOREST SANCTUARY

DORIA'S HOUSE

S

CHIMERA LAB – LAKE

## CHIMERIFFIC?!

Dr. Andonuts, fresh from the pail, wants to help out with your quest by offering a little help from the same science that was about to make you into the ultimate meal. The candidates line up for inspection. They're all pretty curious… can they really help with your pool problem?

## · ENEMIES ·

### NICE POSER

This third-floor triangular terror won't do much to hurt you beyond status effects. Don't bother using PSI on him, he's immune!

SECRET HERB (15%)

| HP: 280 | OFF:50 DEF:50 | EXP:300 DP:50 |

### PIGMASK CAPTAIN

You might want to take this Pigmask seriously. His gun is pretty strong and he can take quite a few hits. DCMC goods might distract him, but you should focus on taking him out quick.

PORK NOODLES (10%)

| HP: 453 | OFF:121 DEF:52 | EXP:854 DP:150 |

### ZOMBIDILLO

These sickly roller rats can be found in the depths of the Chimera Lab basement. They're too weak to really be a major issue.

ROTTEN MILK (5%)

| HP: 372 | OFF:108 DEF:37 | EXP:522 DP:47 |

### SECURITY ROBOT

Security Robots provide efficient automated security services, but as usual electricity is all it takes to send them crashing to the ground.

PENCIL ROCKET (5%)

| HP: 300 | OFF:90 DEF:67 | EXP:480 DP:100 |

fangamer

169

## LAST DANCE

Before you start picking out chimeras to solve your pump problems, you should get ready to say goodbye to little Salsa. Don't forget to clear out his inventory, but try not to be too callous about it—he's a very sentimental monkey.

# CONSCRIPT-A-CHIMERA!

Got a problem? There's a chimera to solve it! Put our practical-use chimeras to work for fast, easy results! Check out the newest line of chimeras straight from Dr. Andonuts's secret stash!

### THE DRYGUY!

The latest model of Dryer Chimeras! Utilizes a jet engine! X-TREME! Dries anything in moments, even the thickest afros and mullets!

### BUCKET BROS.

Combining Clayman tech with cutting edge dough wizardry! They work exceptionally hard! There's no "i" in Bucket Brothers!

### MR. PUMP

It's Ho-Hum Technology! Extraordinarily ordinary! Serves but one purpose! Best to forget about this one.

## THE EXCITABLE MAGYPSY

Once the Pump Chimera makes its humble exit, Lucas can finally pull the Needle. Everyone gathers to watch as Lucas takes hold of the Needle and rips it from the earth, triggering a massive quake. Doria begins to fade away, handing Lucas her memento (if your inventory is full, check inside her house later). With Kumatora back, it's time to move onward to the next Needle!

# CHAPTER

## no 7

### PART III

#### HOLES TO HEIGHTS

---

## So Speak's
# THE SQUEEKZ

You might encounter a rodent as you head away from the pond. Teach him a lesson and you'll learn that he's not just any wannabe—he's the father of those scattered highway mice! Getting walloped can change a mouse's priorities.

## EYE OF THE CRICKET

As you head toward the Ropeway, you'll run into an old rival. For three long years he has been training for a rematch, and he won't let a simple 'No' stop him from achieving his goal. To the Cricket Dome!

# · ENEMIES ·

## THE SQUEEKZ

### MINI-BOSS

'Eyyyyy! He may act street-savvy, but a single round of combat is probably enough to send him back to the highway.

| HP: 320 | OFF:78 DEF:41 | EXP:157 DP:23 |
| --- | --- | --- |

## THE BLIND LEAD THE BLONDE

After the battle, the mole cricket elder decides to help you out. He doesn't know anything about the Needles or the Dragon, but he suggests you pass through the mole cricket tunnel anyway. Who knows what you'll find on the other side?

## O'BROTHER

When Lucas decides to conquer the mole cricket hole, the champion lends you his little brother to lead you back if you get lost. The depths of the hole are a confusing maze, so he might come in handy!

## DOUBTFUL
### ~ Sincerity ~

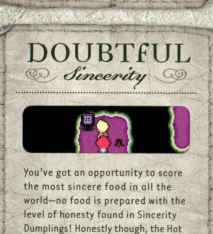

You've got an opportunity to score the most sincere food in all the world—no food is prepared with the level of honesty found in Sincerity Dumplings! Honestly though, the Hot Spring Eggs are a much better deal.

## THE MOLE CRICKET HOLE

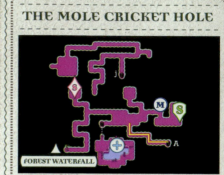

FOREST WATERFALL

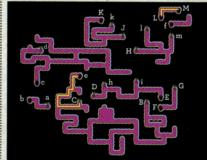

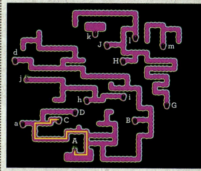

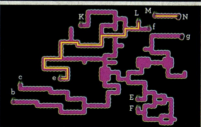

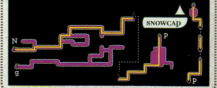

SNOWCAP

## YOU HAVE TO TAKE TURNS

The tunnel paths are sinuous, but there's a secret: turn at every chance. It's not the fastest way, but it will get you through. No enemies to worry about, so take your time. If lost, use the Mole Cricket's Brother to start again. Use the yellow path on the map (left).

## SLIPPERY SLOPES

Beyond the mole cricket tunnels is a snow-covered mountainside. The path is fraught with dangerous battles with wolves and yetis, but that's beginning to seem like the usual.

### EXTREMELY CONVENIENT STORE

Nearing the top, a mole cricket will catch up with you. He's decided to travel and sell the junk he picks up along the way. Don't be surprised if you see his entrepreneurial buddies popping up in all sorts of places now!

### CRICKET SHOP

| | |
|---|---|
| Sincerity Dumplings | 100 DP |
| Heavy Sweater | 1000 DP |
| Bantam Charm | 540 DP |
| Bear Cap | 720 DP |
| White Ribbon | 520 DP |
| Cancer Bracelet | 1000 DP |
| Double Jerky | 240 DP |
| Flea Powder | 30 DP |
| Secret Herb | 600 DP |

## • ENEMIES •

## TEN-YETI

These happy snowmen will throw anything at you—even nearby Chilly Dogs! Just remember that they cry easily and their fur is flammable.

LUXURY BANANA (15%)

| HP: 653 | OFF:112 DEF:47 | EXP:633 DP:85 |
|---|---|---|

## CHILLY DOG

These doggies shine like diamonds, but they're just imitations. They can freeze you and howl for help if you don't take them out quickly. Melt them with fire and they'll slink away.

SECRET HERB (10%)

| HP: 337 | OFF:108 DEF:40 | EXP:505 DP:68 |
|---|---|---|

## FROSTED BUN
### RARE!

While on Snowcap Mt., you might see what looks like a white rock. That's a Frosted Bun, a timid but rare creature. Its freezing attacks hurt, so melt it with PK Fire.

MAGIC TART (10%)

| HP: 522 | OFF:95 DEF:38 | EXP:1800 DP:300 |
|---|---|---|

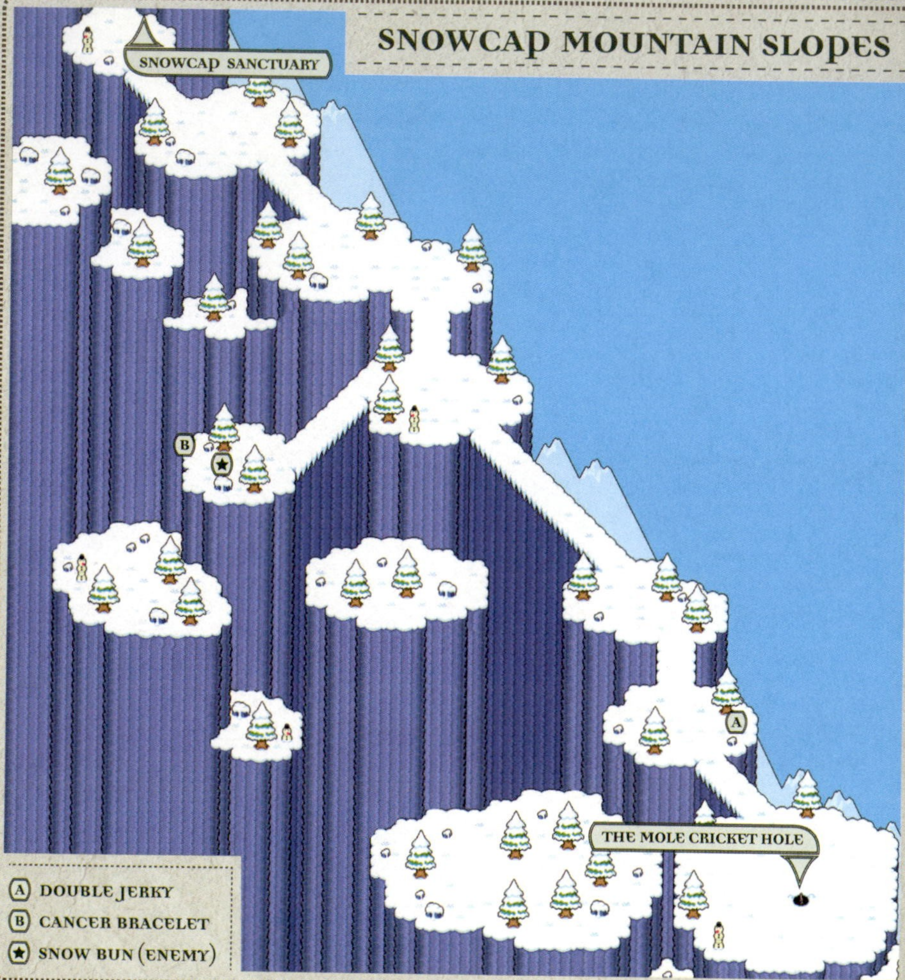

## SNOWCAP MOUNTAIN SLOPES

SNOWCAP SANCTUARY

B

A

THE MOLE CRICKET HOLE

(A) **DOUBLE JERKY**
(B) **CANCER BRACELET**
(★) **SNOW BUN (ENEMY)**

## UNEXPECTED VISITORS

At the top of the mountain you'll find Lydia tending to her snow bunnies. She invites you in from the cold. It seems she didn't expect to see you any more than you expected to find her!

# Lydia

Lydia is surprisingly warm-hearted given her cold environment. Extending her care to all corners of the mountaintop, she tends to rabbits and creates talkative snowmen to liven up the environment. She even lends her prized fluffy bed to a sick Pigmask lost on Snowcap Mountain.

# PREPARATIONS

Before progressing any more, get your inventory spruced up. Heal up in the hot spring, update your weapons, and give Boney plenty of PP- and HP-restoring items!

## AN OMINOUS SOUND

Lydia explains his misgivings and dutifully opens the door to the next Needle. Before exiting though, the sound of invaders fills the air. Rushing outside, the party finally confronts the Masked Man aside a freshly-pulled Needle! After a brief glare at Lucas he flies off, leaving an irate ape in his wake.

## NEEDLE·BOSS

# COLD STEEL

The Steel Mechorilla is good at one thing: dealing physical damage in spades. Luckily this kind of straightforward battle is easily fought with the right PSI.

**Lucas:** *Start off with a Defense Up Ω, and maybe even a second time. Next, it'd be wise to set up Counters, first with the weakest of the party. Next, focus on using your new PK special.*

**Kumatora:** *Cast her strongest PK Freeze every round, pausing only to heal. PK Thunder is effective too, but only the first two times; the third shot will fry the ape's circuits and send him into a rage!*

**Boney:** *Can't compete with Lucas and Kumatora's damage output, so use him to keep everyone healthy and ready to fight.*

## SNOWCAP SANCTUARY

SNOWCAP SUMMIT

LYDIA'S HOUSE

SNOWCAP MT. - SLOPES

## ·ENEMIES·

# STEEL MECHORILLA

## NEEDLE BOSS

The Steel Mechorilla's metal fists and fierce kicks make him a physical powerhouse. He'll bring down your offense sometimes, but that won't matter much since you won't be needing physical attacks anyway.

| HP: 2860 | OFF:164 DEF:68 | EXP:9432 | DP:710 |

175

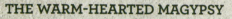

## THE WARM-HEARTED MAGYPSY

With the Needle pulled, Lydia's time is short. She tells Lucas that he must be the one to pull the remaining Needles. Leaving her memento behind, she asks you to check on the Pigmask she saved before you depart from the mountain.

## Of Rabbits & PIGMASKS

You're in for a bit of a surprise when you check on the wounded Pigmask: his helmet is off, and he's just a normal, chubby guy. In fact, without the helmet, he even seems to have feelings—try to dash and you'll get a stern lecture about rabbit safety! Don't forget to check out his helmet before you leave to reveal a further mystery. Can Pigmasks really be good in spite of their wicked ways?

## THE FRIENDLY SKIES

Technically you could fight your way back down the mountain and muddle your way through the mole cricket complex again, but why would you want to? Lydia has provided a perfectly reasonable exit, so follow her advice and head to the top of the mountain.

## CAN'T KEEP IT BOTTLED UP!

Your improvised vehicle conveniently comes to a stop in the Tazmily graveyard, where you'll have no choice but to notice a lively message in a bottle. Follow its lead down below and you'll find yourself faced with a truly perplexing piece of furniture.

# CHAPTER
# no. 7

## PART IV
## MISTER WHO?

---

## *Small town* BLUES

If you head back to Tazmily, you might notice that the townspeople seem to be flocking en masse to "the big city." Some houses are simply empty, Abbey and Abbot are packing, and even the old lady at the retirement home is already gone. It seems like Tazmily might be destined to become a ghost town...

---

## ZOOM ZOOM!

→ Runs. ZOOM!   → HorseyPower!
→ Seats AND Seats   → Coffee Holder

---

## *Family* REUNION

The Squeekz is back home with his family. With a role model like him, it's no wonder his children tended to wander off.

## TAKING THE SLOW ROAD

When you reach the Thunder Tower it is (of course) closed, but the tunnel to the east has been opened. The newly-opened highway seems to lead to a dead end, but there's a passageway that can be reached on foot...

## OCCUPATION IN THE VALLEY

Emerging from the tunnel, you find yourself in a valley filled with strange buildings and even stranger folk—the Mr. Saturn from the Chimera Lab projector room! The village has already been annexed by the Pigmasks, but these bizarre creatures don't deserve the terrors being visited upon them by the invaders.

## THE LAST PIECE OF THE PUZZLE!

Duster is being held in the northeast house! Once you free him, Mr. Saturn reveals that he knows the next Needle is located north, in the fiery mountain beyond the village. Go quickly, before the Pigmasks get there! You might want to pick up a few Flame Pendants from the shop, just in case.

## MR. SATURN

Members of a curious race—all named "Mr. Saturn"—who talk and act as strange as they look. In addition to being resourceful and creative, they are gentle and pacifistic creatures with a penchant for invention.

## SATURN VALLEY

GOVA SANCTUARY

G

I

SATURN SPRINGS

B

UNFINISHED ZONE

H

f

E D C

B

S

S

A

(A) FART
(B) GOOD KID'S SHIRT
(C) STRAWBERRY TOFU
(D) SILVER DRAGONFLY
(E) FART
(F) BLACK COLLAR
(G) FART
(H) CUP OF LIFENOODLES

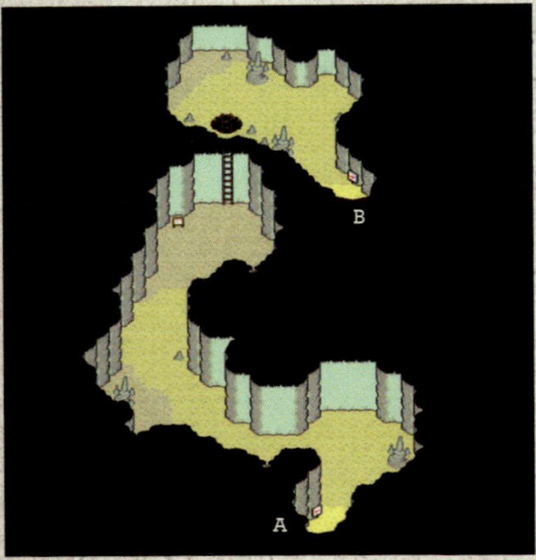

B

A

# ◆ ENEMIES ◆

## NAUGHTY MUSHROOM

These seemingly arrogant tunnel fungi can't be trusted. If you're cornered by a gang of them, burn them up with PK Fire before they start spreading their spores.

BREAD ROLL (15%)

HP: 361 | OFF:98 DEF:48 | EXP:486 DP:102

## FILTHY ATTACK ROACH

These roaches are not only more resilient than mole crickets, but they're also the undisputed champions of the inter-species insectoid martial arts tournaments.

PAPER FAN (10%)

HP: 335 | OFF:118 DEF:40 | EXP:450 DP:92

## FRIGHTBOT

Machines mostly used to scare impressionable Saturns with terrifying tales. These bots can't bite, but they can take a beating. Take out their Pigmask companions first.

HP: 700 | OFF:68 DEF:60 | EXP:360 DP:150

## PIGMASK MAJOR

These higher-ranking Pigmasks are tough! Their guns pack a punch, and sometimes they'll try to stick a time bomb on you. Use PK Fire and your PK special power.

HOT DOG SUSHI (10%)

HP: 721 | OFF:147 DEF:75 | EXP:2788 DP:300

## SHOP SATURN! BOING! ZOOM!

| | | | | | | |
|---|---|---|---|---|---|---|
| FUNNY STICK | 2400 DP | THUNDER PENDANT | 1500 DP | WHITE CROISSANT | 40 DP |
| SEVOLG | 1200 DP | BOING RIBBON | 780 DP | STRAWBERRY TOFU | 180 DP |
| BAREFOOT SHOES | 1520 DP | RAIL BANDANA | 940 DP | LUCKY RICE | 126 DP |
| FLAME PENDANT | 1500 DP | LEO BRACELET | 1600 DP | LOTTO MEAL | 104 DP |
| ICE PENDANT | 1500 DP | HONEY SHOWER | 300 DP | DOGGY JERKY | 54 DP |
| | | ATTACK ATTRACTOR | 400 DP | SECRET HERB | 600 DP |
| | | | | CUP OF LIFENOODLES | 1780 DP |

# EXPLODING DOG TRICK

In the southernmost hut in the valley you'll find a few entrepreneurial Saturns who sell some outrageously great wares. The Flame Pendants, in particular, are something you should invest in. There's no such thing as a free lunch, so consider this great trick for raising lots of cash:

1. *Sell all the useless junk in your inventory like cheap status-clearing items and old charms/weapons, then buy as much Doggy Jerky as you can hold.*

2. *Run all the way back to the highway's scenic overlook and talk to the dog. He'll take every biscuit you've got and give you a bomb in exchange.*

3. *Talk to a vendor and sell most (or all) of your bombs—they fetch a whopping 500 DP each! Talk about explosive returns!*

## SCALING DIFFICULTY

The northern path to the volcano is a dead end! Check the soft spot in the cliff and then talk to the nearby Mr. Saturn, who will summon his ladder-loving friends. Once you're up they'll tumble apart, so make sure you've got everything you need before you visit the northern cliff - there's no going back!

## *Mapful* UNDANDY

One of the Saturns in the totem pole house will give you a map if you talk to him. Of course, a map is merely a reflection of the cartographer...

# Phrygia

Phrygia claims to be the most serious and detail-oriented of the Magypsies. He lives near a volcano and has a taste for Chamomile Tea, which makes him restful—so restful, in fact, that Phrygia is fine with the idea of ceasing to exist, as long as he's allowed to sleep through it.

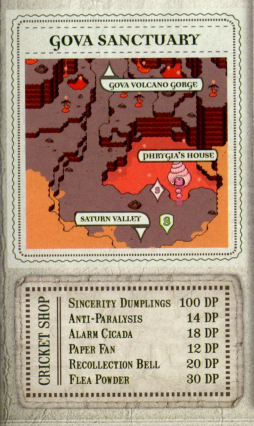

## SLEEPING BEAUTY ROCKS

Heading north you'll come across the quiet abode of Phrygia, the sleeping Magypsy. A note beside her says that the boulders blocking the way to the volcano need some Encouraging Words. The smaller boulders just need a little direction. Talk to the horizontiboulder, then the vertiboulder, then the two horizontiboulders again. Piece of cake.

### GOVA SANCTUARY

GOVA VOLCANO GORGE

PHRYGIA'S HOUSE

SATURN VALLEY

| CRICKET SHOP | | |
|---|---|---|
| SINCERITY DUMPLINGS | 100 DP |
| ANTI-PARALYSIS | 14 DP |
| ALARM CICADA | 18 DP |
| PAPER FAN | 12 DP |
| RECOLLECTION BELL | 20 DP |
| FLEA POWDER | 30 DP |

# ENEMIES

## SKY TITANY

An aerial subspecies of the earthbound Titany which utilizes Hypnosis and physical attacks. Its battle rhythm is the only difficult thing about it.

SALTWATER GUN (5%)

HP: 486 | OFF:121 DEF:70 | EXP:946 DP:245

## MRS. LAVA

Ice this old flame as soon as possible. Otherwise, her PK Fire γ will quickly sap your party's HP. Of course, if you brought along some Flame Pendants you won't have too much trouble.

METEOTITE (5%)

HP: 461 | OFF:108 DEF:58 | EXP:837 DP:484

## PYREFLY

These little buggers have to gang up on you to be a real threat. They can breathe fire and hurt the whole party, but they're only a real problem when they swarm.

ALARM CICADA (10%)

HP: 302 | OFF:108 DEF:50 | EXP:544 DP:163

## GENERAL GOSSIP

Heading north, you'll come across a pair of Pigmasks talking about Fassad—and how he's "changed!" How could he have possibly survived the fall from Thunder Tower, much less become louder and meaner?

## *There she* FLOWS

Be careful where you walk inside the crater, as Mrs. Lavas love to erupt onto unsuspecting passers-by. It may be safer to dash so you can avoid any fiery surprises.

## ~ A HEALTHFUL ~ HAVEN

The westernmost cave is a getaway from the threats that lurk in the crater. No enemies live there and you can usually find a Magic Butterfly to help restore some PP. Heal everyone in your party and then exit/enter the cave repeatedly to restore your PP in full!

## GOVA VOLCANO GORGE

GOVA VOLCANO CRATER

C

B

A

GOVA SANCTUARY

(A) PENCIL ROCKET
(B) DOUBLE JERKY
(C) CUP OF LIFENOODLES

## MAGMATTACK

Don't underestimate the power of the Magman! Even with Flame Pendants, this enemy will knock you for a loop, especially when flanked by Pyreflies (which it can spawn at will). Use Kumatora's PK Freeze β to take Magman down first, then handle the other enemies.

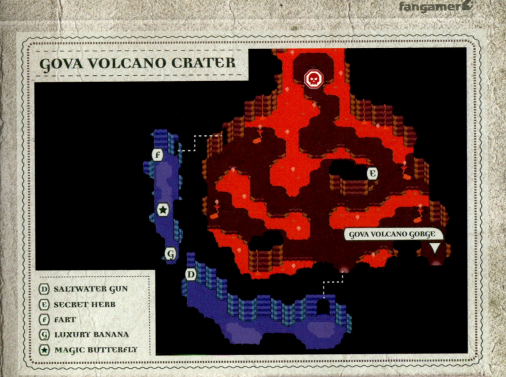

## GOVA VOLCANO CRATER

GOVA VOLCANO GORGE

(D) SALTWATER GUN
(E) SECRET HERB
(F) FART
(G) LUXURY BANANA
(★) MAGIC BUTTERFLY

---

## *Heal* THOSE BURNS

While heading north in the volcano, you'll pass a present box and a Mrs. Lava. As soon as you finish that battle, it's time to heal up and get your items rearranged!

- ➤ Take a moment to get everyone up to 100% health with PSI Lifeup. Once that's done, restore as much PP as you can to Lucas and Kumatora—they'll soon need every last point.

- ➤ Give Boney the Shield Snatcher and a good supply of both HP- and PP-restoring items. Fill the rest of his inventory with explosives.

- ➤ Give Duster any Saltwater Guns you have, as well as your remaining healing items.

---

## · ENEMIES ·

### MAGMAN

The Magman is the toughest creature in the volcano. He has high HP and defense, can hurt everyone at once, and can produce Pyreflies at will. Freeze him first—and fast!

DOUBLE JERKY (20%)

| HP: 594 | OFF:135 | DEF:72 | EXP:1194 | DP:278 |

### SCAMPERIN' MUSHROOM

Compared to the other enemies in the volcano, these guys are nothing. Just watch out for their spores.

HOT SPRING EGG (10%)

| HP: 386 | OFF:102 | DEF:55 | EXP:543 | DP:143 |

# RAUCOUS REVENGE

As you finally get the Needle in your sights, an eerily musical, robotic voice fills the air. A mechanically-enhanced Fassad hovers down, promising revenge for his humiliation on Thunder Tower. Don't let his ridiculous-looking "upgrades" fool you – he means business!

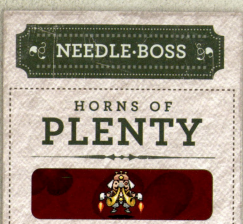

## NEEDLE·BOSS

### HORNS OF
# PLENTY

Get ready to lock horns with the new and improved Fassad! Not only does he have a wide array of offensive and defensive moves at his disposal, but he loves shields and can take multiple turns each round. When his HP gets low, Fassad will start scarfing Luxury Bananas. You've got him on the ropes, so keep going!

**Early Strategies:** Use these in the first few rounds of battle to help level the playing field.

- ➤ *Lucas: Defense/Offense Up Ω, Shield Ω*
- ➤ *Kumatora: Offense/Defense Down*
- ➤ *Duster: Smoke Bomb, Tickle Stick, Scary Mask*
- ➤ *Boney: Honey Shower, Shield Snatcher*

**Attack Strategies:** With Fassad's defenses cracked, it's time to start doing some damage!

- ➤ *Lucas: Combo Attacks, PK Love β*
- ➤ *Kumatora: PK Thunder β*
- ➤ *Duster: Combos, offense items*
- ➤ *Boney: Offense items, Shield Snatcher*

## I NEEDLE LITTLE GUIDANCE!

After his defeat, a humiliated Fassad flies off, swearing his future vengeance. Lucas steps up to pull the Needle and learns a new PK power! Phrygia, fading fast yet still detail-oriented, appears to reveal the location of the remaining Needles. Remember to heal yourself for the return journey through the volcano. Danger still lurks!

## CORPOREAL LADDER

When you return to the cliff, you're greeted by some Mr. Saturns who were kind enough to construct a less-squishy ladder for your return. Relax in the nearby hot springs to wash away your "exhaust." You've earned it!

## A BOMB-ABLE BLOCKADE

A familiar sound hums through the air as a Pigmask pilot ship makes a short stop with a goal of stopping you short. Go to the tunnel to survey the damage—looks like you won't be leaving anytime soon. Duster will suggest a chat with the Mr. Saturn in the totem hut.

## A BIRD-BRAINED IDEA

The answer to your dilemma seems so simple to the Mr. Saturns: fish for some birds and fly out! Could it really be that simple? The only way to find out is to try it! The Saturns have their own unique way of "fishing," but since you've got opposable thumbs you might try just walking up to one slowly and grabbing it.

## THE DIRTY BADGE OF COURAGE

After you hand over your bird, you'll be invited to take another dip in the Hot Springs, where you'll be offered an unexpectedly refreshing drink. Let your mind wander as the Mr. Saturns assemble their idea. After some time, a lone Saturn asks for your Courage Badge. He takes it with a promise to clean it up!

## HOPE ON THE ROPE

The Mr. Saturns' handiwork is as incredible as their speed! With this cage, you'll be able to fly—probably? Before you start your journey, however, an old friend once again offers his assistance in a cord-ial fashion.

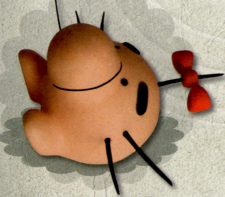

## • ENEMIES •

### NEW FASSAD

### NEEDLE BOSS

This remade nuisance is ready to rock. His attacks include powerful charges, a wide variety of bombs and beams, and a re-deployable shield.

**LUXURY BANANA (100%)**

| HP: 3182 | OFF:164 | DEF:78 | EXP:11121 | DP:1200 |

185

# SHEER DETERMINATION

The Rope Snake is bound and determined to get back in the game. You can accept his offer without question, but you'll be regaled with anecdotes of the moody reptile's preparation if you continuously turn down his offer. Surely such a proud, hardworking snake can be trusted with a second chance?

# INVENTOR'S DIGEST

This month's issue of Inventor's Digest takes a deeper look into the ingenious creation of the CageFlight flying apparatus. Created by Mr. Saturn, a creature who is continuously proving the Inventor's Digest motto: "It takes a uniquer thinker to create under restraint!" Mr. Saturn has used his stunning intellect to weigh the setbacks, sum the factors, and carry the one, resulting in this aerodynamic retro-wonder!

## ENERGY
The CageFlight brilliantly harnesses its energy from the pre-installed flock of birds. If you're following along at home, you'll want to backorder issue 64 for information on how to catch your own flock with a Fishing Poloon.

## PROPULSION
Using natural wind energy and the deflection of air pockets from other birds in the flock, a series of micro-vortices are created, propelling the CageFlight skyward!

## CONSTRUCTION
A lightweight iron alloy cage holds the flock safely in place. The only major oversight noted by our reviewer: no safety device to ensure that any reptiles, humans, or walnut-crackers attached to the bottom of the cage stay put.

## MAKE A SPLASH

After holding on for as long as he can, the Rope Snake gives way—luckily over a body of water! Your party washes up on Tazmily's western shore with a severely depressed reptile in tow.

## BEAN AROUND THE BLOCK

Head back to where you found the Saturn Table and you'll find a Pork Bean remodeled in the image of the beings who probably designed it. Zoom! Saturn Valley's entrance is repaired, but not much else is different there.

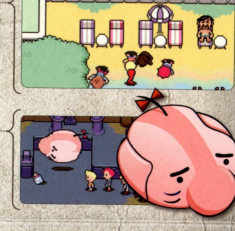

# CHAPTER
# no. 7

## PART V
### LOWS TO HIGHS

## SO MUCH TO SEA!

By 'talking' to the sea, you'll be able to walk your way into its depths. What a beautiful reef! You're not here to snorkel, as you'll quickly remember when you spot the Pigmasks patrolling the seafloor.

### Don't Hold Your BREATH

During your maritime excursion, you'll need regular doses of oxygen. The good news: P-KORP is way ahead of you. The bad news: P-KORP is completely unconcerned with your comfort. The creepy mermen robots scattered about the depths serve as oxygen tanks, refilling your lungs with precious air. Watch your meter and be sure to fill up when you can!

## · ENEMIES ·

### NAVY SQUEAL

These aqua-based Pigmasks show no new battle tactics and usually travel solo. They're also so severely underpaid that they might just vacate the bout on a whim.

PORK STEW (10%)

| HP: 563 | OFF:115 DEF:70 | EXP:774 DP:118 |
| --- | --- | --- |

# CERULEAN SEA fLOOR

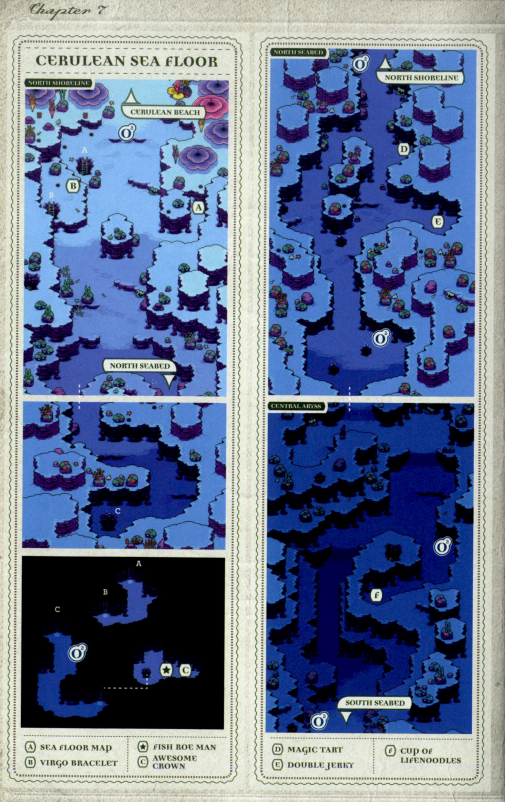

NORTH SHORELINE

CERULEAN BEACH

O²

A

B

B

A

NORTH SEABED

C

A

B

C

O²

★

C

NORTH SEABED

O²

NORTH SHORELINE

D

E

O²

CENTRAL ABYSS

O²

f

SOUTH SEABED

O²

| | | | |
|---|---|---|---|
| **A** SEA fLOOR MAP | **★** fISH ROE MAN | **D** MAGIC TART | **f** CUP Of LIfENOODLES |
| **B** VIRGO BRACELET | **C** AWESOME CROWN | **E** DOUBLE JERKY | |

## ROE NO!

During your meandering, you may come across a walking delicacy which is anything but delicate. Fish Roe Man packs a powerful punch and has a huge amount of HP. The reward for taking him down is one of the best pieces of headgear Lucas will come across.

## SHELL SHOCK

Roaming the lonely sea is a sad hermit crab who lost his shell. If you happen to find its golden shell later on, return it to the crushed crustacean for a nice reward!

### DON'T MISS THE MACHINES

The huge number of holes in the South Seabed can be confusing. Head left (west) to find an Oxygen Machine, then use that as 'home base' to explore the other holes.

# • ENEMIES •

### FISH ROE MAN

For a pile of unfertilized eggs, this thing is a well-developed fighter. It can launch attacks to hit 3 party members for pretty huge damage. Give it a little freezer burn with PK Freeze.

| HP: 1856 | OFF: 168 DEF: 65 | EXP: 943 DP: 200 |

### CAREFREE JELLYFISH

They're so carefree you can easily walk up to their backs and get an easy green swirl. Watch out for their stinging tentacles, as you may end up paralyzed.

ANTI-PARALYSIS (20%)

| HP: 485 | OFF: 111 DEF: 50 | EXP: 579 DP: 86 |

### ROOOUND FISH

You'll find more sphere than fear around these fish. Duster's Hypno-Pendulum can easily make all of their eyes shut. Make 'em sleep with the fishes before they can PK Freeze B!

MAGIC GELATIN (5%)

| HP: 531 | OFF: 123 DEF: 64 | EXP: 720 DP: 93 |

### ROCK LOBSTER

You may find yourself in a pinch with these cool crustaceans. Their stylish defenses are rock-solid, so hit them with PK Thunder or Freeze.

GIANT ABALONE STEAK (10%)

| HP: 589 | OFF: 172 DEF: 100 | EXP: 865 DP: 148 |

## CERULEAN SEA FLOOR

SOUTH SEABED

CENTRAL ABYSS

E

D F

G

H

$O^2$

SOUTH SHORELINE

---

D E

$O^2$

G

H

F G

J

H

I K

Ⓖ MAGIC TART     Ⓙ MAGIC PUDDING

Ⓗ HERMIT SHELL     Ⓚ TRIVIA CARD #3

Ⓘ BOMB

SOUTH SHORELINE

SOUTH SEABED

L

$O^2$

S

M

$O^2$

TANETANE ISLAND

Ⓛ MAGIC PUDDING     Ⓜ MAGIC TART

## BEWARE THE TIDES OF ED

As you near the shore of Tanetane, you'll meet a scuba diving Frog who opts to save your game. Danger lurks, so you should consider healing up and rearranging your inventory. Make sure to grab the present box east of the O2 Machine before diving into the current of Master Eddy.

# MINI·BOSS — ENEMIES

## CARRIED AWAY

Master Eddy might look like a pushover, but his whirlpool attacks will do some pretty serious damage to everyone in your party. On top of that, he can attack twice each round, which means it will be important to cripple him quickly.

**Early attacks:**
- **Lucas:** Shield Ω, Defense Up Ω
- **Kumatora:** Offense/Defense Down α
- **Duster:** Smoke Bomb, Combos
- **Boney:** Explosives, Honey Shower

**Later Strategies:**
With Eddy's attacks weakened
- **Lucas:** Offense Up Ω, combos
- **Kumatora:** PK Thunder β
- **Duster:** Combos
- **Boney:** Healing items (keep everyone above 100 HP!)

When he's about to go down, Master Eddy will summon one final whirlpool. This knock-out-punch is so tough that it carries away all of your HP —and your items! Don't worry, though, even if everyone in your party gets knocked out by this rogue wave, you'll still make it to Tanetane.

## MASTER EDDY
### MINI-BOSS

Master Eddy musters many malicious maelstroms! His whirlpools will ebb away your HP, but you can strike back with PK Thunder and explosives. You might not last long without a shield, though...

HP: 2568 | OFF:127 DEF:81 | EXP:0 DP:721

### AWASH AGAIN

As the tsunami calms to a ripple, you find yourself once more on hot beach sand. Without your items or health, things look mighty grim! How will you cope?

### EMERGEN-SEA GUIDELINES

With only your equipped items, no PP, and 1 HP each, the circumstances are dire! Even a Save Frog in the middle of being digested takes a moment to remind you that you're in quite a pickle. If only you could find some food...

Fangamer

## LESSON: MYCOLOGY BIOLOGY

You've undoubtedly seen many types of mushrooms growing in the woods, around mountains, or on the shores of forsaken tropical islands, but have you ever wondered which ones are safe to eat? Here's a handy list of what to look for in edible fungi:

### LIFE
*Obviously you don't want to eat something which appears to have died already. This is also true for undead mushrooms.*

### IDENTIFICATION
*It takes a pro to safely identify poisonous shrooms, but it's not hard to spot some of them. If your mushroom has a mouth and is capable of speaking its own name, keep looking!*

### SIZE
*As a rule of thumb, mushrooms should be no more than a few inches tall at most. Once they're the size of a full-grown man, they become unwieldy.*

### SIDE-EFFECTS
*While some fungi are okay to eat, some may induce unexpected side effects including dizziness, vomiting, and hand-to-hand combat.*

## CRAAAZY, MAN

Well, you've certainly regained all of your HP and PP, but how will you regain your senses? There's nowhere to move but forward, so tread into the depths of the wild Tanetane Island and look for a cure. Your first obstacle is optional, but can you really resist the temptation to see what he's doing here?

## FAUX FAMILY

You'll meet many familiar faces along your journey. The things they'll say and do run the gamut from weird to mean to downright terrifying. Avoid them if you can, as these aren't just mere hallucinations: they're enemies in disguise!

## WAIL MAIL

Isn't it strange that there are postboxes on a deserted island? You can peek into them without risking harm. Physical harm, at least.

## MINI·BOSS

### COMFORTABLY EERIE

You might be excited to see Flint again, but his harsh words will quickly spoil your enthusiasm. The being will appear as a disembodied smile when you enter battle, but after a few whacks it will reveal its true form: the Zombieshroom!

Don't be afraid to go all-out. The mushrooms you ate can fully restore you if you go back for a second helping, so feel free to use your most powerful PSI!

The undead mushroom will frequently unleash a barrage of poisonous spores upon your entire party. It might not be worth your time healing the condition, so just fight through it.

## ·EMIES·

### ZOMBIESHROOM

#### MINI·BOSS

This towering toadstool is not a fun guy. Its spore attacks can poison you, but you can fight back with PK Fire and numbness-inducing attacks.

| HP: 2489 | OFF:151 DEF:65 | EXP:6336 DP:780 |

### EERIE SMILE

This foe won't show it's true face until its HP is low. You can usually figure out which enemy it really is from its battle actions, or by relying on Boney's nose.

| HP: ???? | OFF:??? DEF:??? | EXP:??? DP:??? |

### TANETANE ISLAND SHORE

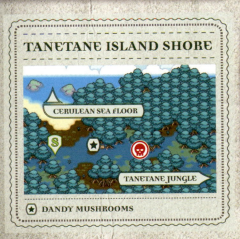

CERULEAN SEA FLOOR

TANETANE JUNGLE

★ DANDY MUSHROOMS

### LITTER-ALLY

By exploring deep into the foliage, you'll find many trash cans tucked into the corners of the island. While it's hard to be certain about anything in this state of mind, rest assured that your treasures are true.

### ~ A BATH FOR THE WASTED ~

Ahh, a deluxe bath! Who cares if it's in the middle of the jungle, those restorative waters are just what you need to feel 100% again! Say, aren't you coming in, Boney?

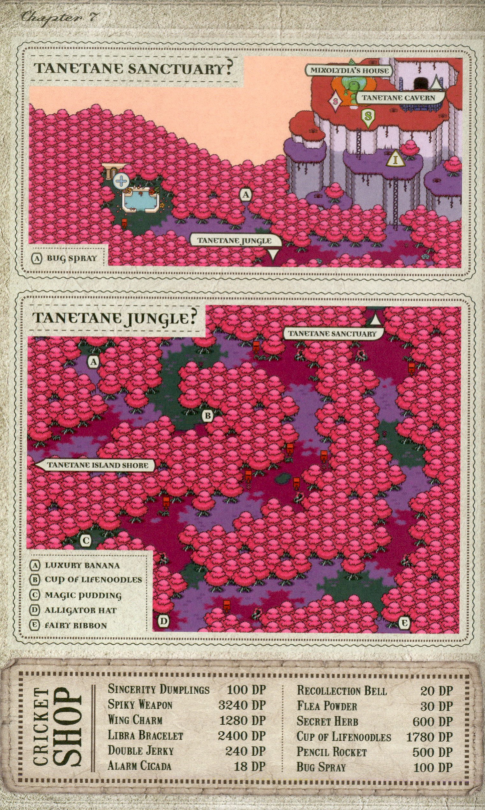

## TANETANE SANCTUARY?

MIXOLYDIA'S HOUSE

TANETANE CAVERN

TANETANE CAVERN

A

TANETANE JUNGLE

Ⓐ BUG SPRAY

## TANETANE JUNGLE?

TANETANE SANCTUARY

A

B

TANETANE ISLAND SHORE

C

D

E

Ⓐ LUXURY BANANA
Ⓑ CUP OF LIFENOODLES
Ⓒ MAGIC PUDDING
Ⓓ ALLIGATOR HAT
Ⓔ FAIRY RIBBON

## CRICKET SHOP

| | | | | |
|---|---|---|---|---|
| SINCERITY DUMPLINGS | 100 DP | | RECOLLECTION BELL | 20 DP |
| SPIKY WEAPON | 3240 DP | | FLEA POWDER | 30 DP |
| WING CHARM | 1280 DP | | SECRET HERB | 600 DP |
| LIBRA BRACELET | 2400 DP | | CUP OF LIFENOODLES | 1780 DP |
| DOUBLE JERKY | 240 DP | | PENCIL ROCKET | 500 DP |
| ALARM CICADA | 18 DP | | BUG SPRAY | 100 DP |

## SEE SHELLS

Atop a cliff jutting out of the jungle sits a familiar Magypsy dwelling. It may not be polite to visit while you're tripping, but there's no time for pleasantries. The resident Magypsy complains nonsensically about some kind of stench, but she really shouldn't be talking: she's pretty much the only person so far who is benefitting from the shrooms.

### COMB AGAIN?

After a brief chat with Mixolydia, you learn the resting place of her Needle. Furthermore, her assistant Ocho will return all the items you lost after your bout with Master Eddy! If you need more room for your items, you'll be glad to know that bizarro-Pusher was actually the Item Guy.

# ENEMIES

## MONKALRUS

You must stay on tusk if you want to triumph over this ape. He hits hard and can spread fleas, so try to take him out fast. Perhaps you'll get lucky and find the powerful gloves he drops!

LUXURY BANANA (15%) | MYSTICAL GLOVES (3%)

HP: 668 | OFF:168 DEF:80 | EXP:1071 DP:273

## ANCIENT DRAGONFLY

As the name and appearance imply, this insect can breathe fire at you. Luckily its HP and Defense are so low that a couple decent combos can knock it out of the canopy.

BEEF JERKY (15%)

HP: 402 | OFF:118 DEF:55 | EXP:612 DP:98

## TITANIAN

A rock-hard defense makes these bugs tough to squash. Watch out for its frequent use of Hypnosis and use PK Freeze or Bug Spray to kill it quickly.

SECRET HERB (10%)

HP: 450 | OFF:135 DEF:110 | EXP:1005 DP:325

# Mixolydia

Mixolydia (or Missy, as she nicknames herself) is the friendly Magypsy of Tanetane Island. She's become one with her island, familiarizing herself with all of its flora and fauna. Unlike the other Magypsies, she's secured her precious Needle.

## DIPS IN THE DIP

With your senses returned to normal, you should consider revisiting the jungle. You may find that things drastically differ from what they seemed to be!

### TANETANE CAVERN

TANETANE BLUFFS

TANETANE SANCTUARY

### TANETANE BLUFFS

TANETANE CAVERN

Ⓐ MUSIC
Ⓑ VIGOR STICK
Ⓒ SWALLOW BANDANA

## SHORT SPELUNKING

Mixolydia warned you that her Needle was well-guarded, which might explain why it's so easy to get to. After a quick trek through a cavern, you'll emerge on a windy, winding network of paths. You may want to avoid the foes here to conserve your strength for the real threat!

## ENOUGH POWER TO BARRIER ALIVE

At the end of the perilous cliffs are three odd purple statues encircling the Needle. How tough can these violet beings be? Before you get too close, be sure to heal up!

## NEEDLE·BOSS

## BATTLE OF THE
# BARRIERS

Although there are three of them you need only focus on these odd figures as a whole. Their elemental weakness varies depending on which character calls out their pose.

- **Barrier Man:** *Immune to Freeze/Thunder, Weak against Fire*
- **Barrier Gal:** *Immune to Fire/Thunder, Weak against Freeze*
- **Barrier Dude:** *Immune to Fire/Freeze, Weak against Thunder*

**Lucas:** *PSI Counter on every member of your party and keep it strong, then use your special PK γ.*
**Kumatora:** *Defense Down α will keep the Trio busy reboosting. In the meantime, use whichever PK attack they're vulnerable to.*
**Duster:** *Use combos and, when appropriate, the Tickle Stick.*
**Boney:** *Start off with the Shield Snatcher, then use explosives and Honey Showers.*

Toward the end the Trio will concentrate, which means PK Starstorm is coming. Heal and get those PSI Counters reinforced!

## · ENEMIES ·

## UNWELCOME GUST

These swirling goons love pelting unassuming travelers with rough winds. If you must fight them, use PK Thunder.

MAGIC PUDDING (5%)

| HP: 598 | OFF: 145 | DEF: 64 | EXP: 1456 | DP: 281 |
| --- | --- | --- | --- | --- |

# BARRIER TRIO

## NEEDLE BOSS

This PSI-wielding threesome starts out with a shield and is only susceptible to one of Kumatora's PK attacks, depending on who calls the pose. PK special is always a safe bet.

| HP: 4000 | OFF: 145 | DEF: 121 | EXP: 12346 | DP: 1538 |
| --- | --- | --- | --- | --- |

## THUNDEROUS APPLAUSE

With the Barrier Trio safely out of the way, the needle is vulnerable—perhaps too vulnerable. Pigmask ships land, rolling out a red carpet for none other than the Masked Man. Before you can say anything, he summons a massive bolt of lightning, ending your valiant effort to pull Mixolydia's Needle.

## RUDE AWAKENING

Mixolydia wakes you from your stupor with disappointing news: the Masked Man's empty heart now stops the gap where her Needle stood. Thoughtful as ever, she gives you a gift to take to Ionia.

## 🙦 HOW LOVELY! HOW THOUGHTFUL! 🙥

Your return trip won't be easy, as your HP/PP is drained from battle. If you make a stop at Mixolydia's house, you'll find it filled with magic butterflies. Travel back to the shore where you washed up and you'll find Ocho, who offers you a ride back to town.

## NATIONWIDE CLEARANCE

Upon reaching the beach once more, you'll notice a distinct lack of townspeople. Vacant houses line the once-bustling town of Tazmily. Where did everyone go?

Just south of the Sheriff's Office, Alec informs you that nearly the entire town has up and moved to the big city. The future for your hometown looks bleak, but there's no time for hand-wringing—you've got to make your way to Ionia!

### ∽ Steadfast ∽
## STRANGERS

Very few people still remain in Tazmily. Thomas is still tending to his shop, at Cross Road Station Lighter and Fuel are debating what to do, outside the old folks' home Wess wonders what the evacuation portends, and Mayor Pusher gloomily looks over his dying burg from the middle of Town Square. Even the Pigmasks have moved out of their training facility. The handful of others in town find sadness in the emptiness that remains ...mostly.

# CHAPTER

## no 7

### PART VI
### LEAVING HOME

## SEE YOU NEXT FALL

Make your way north through the forest and, not too far from the ruins of Alec's cabin, you'll find the ant-free entrance to Argilla Pass. A nearby sign tells you to watch your step, but nothing can stop you now! Just put one foot in front of itself...erm, that's not right...

## NOW YOU'RE IN A PICKLE

When you stumbled across Argilla Pass, Ionia's Jar of Yummy Pickles went flying. Boney's enhanced sense of smell can locate it.

## ARGILLA PASS

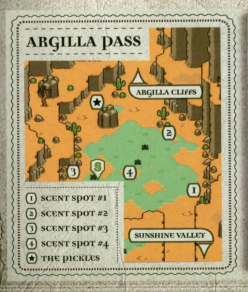

ARGILLA CLIFFS

SUNSHINE VALLEY

1. SCENT SPOT #1
2. SCENT SPOT #2
3. SCENT SPOT #3
4. SCENT SPOT #4
★ THE PICKLES

## ·ENEMIES·

### BLUE BALDING EAGLE

They're not especially threatening, but they do have pretty sharp talons. These birdbrains move quickly and often bring nearby Tender Loving Trees into battle with them.

DOUBLE JERKY (15%)

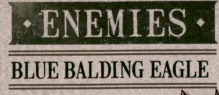

| HP: 568 | OFF:156 DEF:66 | EXP:1714 DP:158 |

# PICKLE SURPRISE!

Argilla Pass is like a wishing well, filled with valuable (and not-so-valuable) items dropped by travelers. Boney can sniff out and return items to Lucas to identify, and depending on your luck, you might end up with some useful stuff!

| HARD THING | SMALL THING | SOFT THING | DELICIOUS |
|---|---|---|---|
| Made-You-Look | Pumice Charm | Fresh Mint | Rotten Eclair, Nut Bread |
| Enemy Bufferizer | Heavy Charm | Recollection Bell | Peculiar Cheese |
| (Rare) Super Bomb | (Rare) Thud Charm | (Rare) Secret Herb. | (Rare) King Burger |

As soon as you find the "sour-looking thing" in the northern area you'll have to continue moving, so grab everything else first. If anything, you'll want to pick up the Thud Charm, which helps protect the wearer from all status effects!

## CRICKET SHOP

| | | | |
|---|---|---|---|
| SINCERITY DUMPLINGS | 100 DP | GRILLED FISH | 150 DP |
| CLEVER STICK | 3980 DP | GRILLED CHICKEN | 300 DP |
| STRONG GLOVES | 2690 DP | ANTI-PARALYSIS | 14 DP |
| NON-SLIP SHOES | 3660 DP | ALARM CICADA | 18 DP |
| OTTER HAT | 1620 DP | SECRET HERB | 600 DP |
| CROW BANDANA | 1520 DP | CUP OF LIFENOODLES | 1780 DP |
| PUMICE CHARM | 1540 DP | | |

## ARGILLA CLIFFS

OUTLAND DUNGEON

ARGILLA HOT SPRINGS

ARGILLA PASS

★ MYSTERY METAL MONKEY (ENEMY)

## BRANCHING OUT

North of the stumbling grounds is a fork in the road. To the left lies the Argilla Pass Hot Springs, a nice place to recover and stock up on items; to the right is the path up to the Outland Dungeon. While scaling the cliffs, beware of the flora and fauna! Even the trees themselves seem to want to stop your progress.

## OUTLANDISH EXPLORATION

There are many paths in the Outland Dungeon. While the most direct route is east then south, you can pick up some helpful equipment if you fully explore the cave. Battles are right around the corner, however, exploding Cuddle Bomb sentries and many unseen foes pop up in the worst places!

### DEPRESSING MATTERS
### *At Hand*

Deep in the dungeon dwells the most self-loathing and hopeless enemy in existence: Negative Man. This sorry sap spends more time in battle self deprecating than actually fighting. Take your time here learning how to combo with his battle music — it'll help in future fights.

# ◆ ENEMIES ◆

## TENDER LOVING TREE

Like their earlier counterparts, these trees explode when defeated. They also have status-draining vacuum attacks and PK Brainshock, and those innocent-looking birds can call down a Blue Balding Eagle.

**FRESH EGG (20%)**

| HP: 686 | OFF:133 | DEF:84 | EXP:2022 | DP:200 |
|---------|---------|--------|----------|--------|

## MYSTERY METAL MONKEY

### RARE!

You can usually get a free round of attacks on these shy simians. Their speed and defense are top-notch, so you'll need to string together a good combo to damage them well. If they get an attack in, they pack PK Fire. Use PK Thunder to short-circuit them permanently.

**MADE-YOU-LOOK (20%)**

| HP: 12 | OFF:120 | DEF:255 | EXP:GOOD | DP:120 |
|--------|---------|---------|----------|--------|

## NEGATIVE MAN

### SIDE BOSS?

This pathetic excuse for an enemy isn't a threat unless you're easily depressed. He'll drone on and on about his uselessness, but he is good for one thing: the occasional Meteotite drop!

**BAKED YAM (10%) | METEOTITE (2%)**

| HP: 2238 | OFF:1 | DEF:85 | EXP:3 | DP:50 |
|----------|-------|--------|-------|-------|

Fangamer

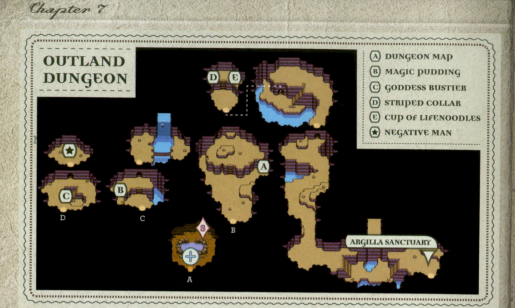

## OUTLAND DUNGEON

(A) DUNGEON MAP
(B) MAGIC PUDDING
(C) GODDESS BUSTIER
(D) STRIPED COLLAR
(E) CUP OF LIFENOODLES
(★) NEGATIVE MAN

ARGILLA SANCTUARY

## A WHELK-COMING SIGHT

Clear through the Heftyheads and you'll find yourself back in the sunlight. To the north is a mysterious temple, guarded by stiff vines. You won't be able to move them, so head back to Ionia's house to meet the fair Magypsy.

# Ionia

Ionia, Alec's friend and the guardian of the sixth Needle, is the most supportive and helpful of the Magypsies, constantly offering insight and teaching you valuable skills. A true queen of the group!

## THE LAST MEAL

Inside, Ionia greets you cheerfully despite knowing that 'the time' has come. She happily accepts Mixolydia's gift and takes a moment to reflect on the personal growth of each member in your party. With a calm and brave demeanor, she hands over a treasure that will grant you access to her Needle in Chupichupyoi Temple.

## CHUPICHUPYOI CRICKET SHOP

| | |
|---|---|
| SINCERITY DUMPLINGS | 100 DP |
| GRILLED CHICKEN | 300 DP |
| SECRET HERB | 600 DP |
| CUP OF LIFENOODLES | 1780 DP |
| SPRINTING BOMB | 200 DP |
| PENCIL ROCKET | 500 DP |

## CHUPICHUPYOI TEMPLE

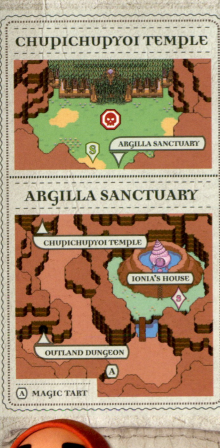

ARGILLA SANCTUARY

## ARGILLA SANCTUARY

CHUPICHUPYOI TEMPLE

IONIA'S HOUSE

OUTLAND DUNGEON

Ⓐ MAGIC TART

## SECRET SATURN

On your way to the temple, an unexpected guest from the opposite side of the continent stops you to return your dad's old Courage Badge, now polished to shine. Upon further inspection, you realize that it's the Franklin Badge, a legendary relic said to reflect lightning attacks. What a treasure!

# ◆ ENEMIES ◆

## MECHA-MOLE!

The bright red light atop their heads can signal other moles to aid in battle, so take them out before you're facing a squadron!

BOMB (3%)

| HP: 564 | OFF: 142 | DEF: 72 | EXP: 1590 | DP: 115 |
|---|---|---|---|---|

## CUDDLE BOMB

After latching onto someone, it counts down and explodes. Keep your cool and try to follow its accelerating battle rhythm, use a blast of PK Freeze, or just flee and save yourself the trouble.

SUPER BOMB (5%)

| HP: 884 | OFF: 150 | DEF: 120 | EXP: 1890 | DP: 162 |
|---|---|---|---|---|

## STICKY SLUG

They cling to the ceiling and rain down on unsuspecting adventurers. If they group up, use a dose of PK Fire to clean out the area or just slug 'em one by one.

SALTWATER GUN (5%)

| HP: 368 | OFF: 138 | DEF: 45 | EXP: 936 | DP: 74 |
|---|---|---|---|---|

## HEFTYHEAD

Traveling alone, these guys can wreak havoc with nasty noggin attacks. PK Freeze will help you avoid their awkward rhythm. If you're lucky you'll find one of Lucas's best weapons, but try not to get your head handed to you!

MYSTICAL STICK (3%)

| HP: 1864 | OFF: 172 | DEF: 88 | EXP: 2863 | DP: 312 |
|---|---|---|---|---|

fangamer

## ❧ SECRET REST ☙

If you take the time to talk to Ionia before tackling the temple, he'll let you take a quick nap to recharge your batteries. Don't miss this opportunity as you're sure to face resistance from the Pork Army!

# The Grind

With the second-to-last Needle at stake, the Pork Army is going to bear down with full force. With this in mind it's very important that Lucas is at Level 50, where he will learn his most useful recovery skill: Lifeup Ω. The best way to do this is to battle with the Heftyheads!

➡ Head into the nearby cave
➡ Fight the Heftyheads using your most powerful PK attacks
➡ Rest at Ionia's
➡ Repeat!

## THUNDEROUS APPLAUSE

A troop of Pigmasks has formed at the temple entrance, struggling hopelessly to break through the vines. The Masked Man has little patience, however, and tries to force his way in himself. Your sudden arrival diverts their aggressions – towards you!

## FACE-OFF WITH THE MASKED MAN

His soldiers cast aside, the Masked Man himself approaches you once more. Unsheathing his sword emotionlessly, he summons a bolt of lightning and gets an unexpected taste of the Franklin Badge! Gritting his teeth, he pounces onto you and your party.

## RETREAT, RETREAT!

Your victory scares away the troops, and the Masked Man concedes defeat by flying away. With your threats all taken care of, all that's left is to use the Waters of Time on the vines barring your entrance to the temple.

## THE PEAK OF PK

As you approach the Needle, Ionia enters the temple. As a last-minute gift, she bestows a powerful PSI ability to Kumatora. When all things are ready, you must pull the Needle to even the score against the Masked Man— and to learn your final PK attack!

## NEEDLE BOSS

# MAN IN THE METAL MASK

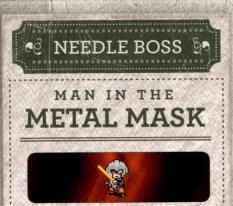

The Masked Man is undoubtedly the toughest foe you've faced up to this point. His special PK attack is enough to quickly sap the strongest of fighters.

- Fix the fight! The Masked Man has supremely powerful attacks, so have Lucas raise everyone's Defense while Duster and Kumatora lower his offense. Boney should use the Shield Snatcher to get rid of the shield he starts with.
- Don't cast shields of your own. This foe has a Shield Killer that he'll always use right before letting loose a $\gamma$-level PK special.

**Lucas:** Defense/Offense Up Ω at least twice each! If you're going to end this fight quickly, you'll need all the stat boosts you can get. Lifeup Ω immediately after the Masked Man attacks with his PK special, and whenever the party is struggling. Special PK attack $\gamma$ when possible.

**Kumatora:** Offense/Defense Down, but focus on Defense to make your party's attacks more effective. Afterwards Kumatora should focus on combos instead of offensive PSI, but if PSI is necessary, PK Freeze is best.

**Duster:** Scary Mask/Tickle Stick are great even though they won't always work. Combos from Duster will go a long way toward wearing down the Masked Man, especially once your stats are boosted by Lucas.

**Boney:** Shield Snatcher to get rid of the Masked Man's physical shield. Healing items to keep individuals alive between Lucas's Lifeup Ω spells. Combos/Explosives until the cows come home.

# ·ENEMIES·

## PIGMASK COLONEL

You might need the Shield Snatcher for the first round, and maybe later if he uses his shield device. PK Freeze and Bombs are effective against him, and while he can really put up a fight, don't waste your PP. There's a bigger battle coming right after this!

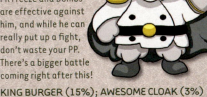

KING BURGER (15%); AWESOME CLOAK (3%)

| HP: 895 | OFF:168 | DEF:100 | EXP:3910 | DP:500 |

# MASKED MAN

### NEEDLE BOSS

His elemental defenses are tight, so raising your offense and going all-out physically may be your best bet.

You're definitely going to need Lifeup Ω, and if Kumatora has learned it, PK Ground will make your life much easier.

| HP: 5000 | OFF:165 | DEF:120 | EXP:15474 | DP:1321 |

### GUIDANCE & DISTURBANCE

With her power fading fast, Ionia tells you to seek out the missing Magypsy, Locria. Her Needle is the final obstacle holding the Dark Dragon asleep! As she fades away, odd music fills the air outside the temple...

CHAPTER
no. 7

And so with the last of the known
Magypsies gone, Lucas and his
friends are left alone to face their
final task. Locria, the last of
the Magypsies, is approaching her
Needle, which means that the Pork
Army is close behind. Whose heart
will be passed onto the dragon?
What kind of wishes will it fulfill?

CHAPTER

NO. 8

ALL THINGS...

# CHAPTER NO 8

## PART ONE
### BRAVE NEW PORK

## ALL EXPENSES PAID

Lucas and his friends emerge from the temple to find...
a limousine? It seems that their activities have finally
attracted the attention of the elusive Master Porky, the
Pig King himself, who has invited them to New Pork City.
WARNING! Once you get in, you can't go back to Tazmily!

### KING P LIMO

 ## SMALL TALK

New Pork City is a short trip when you're in a flying limousine,
so if you want to get the full limousine experience talk with
the chauffeur first. Once he gets tired of your distractions,
you're free to roam about the cab at your leisure.

## PSEUDOLUXURIOUS

Make your way around the opulent limousine
and you'll quickly realize that something is amiss.
You can't play any of the games or drink anything.
Even the champagne tower is just... a painting?

# NEW PORK CITY

PORKY'S TOWER

FOOD SHOP

PORKY

GAME ARCADE

THEATER

LIMO PORT

# ★ NEW PORK CITY ★

## TOWARDS A BETTER TOMORROW

I♡NP

P-KORP BUREAU OF
ENFORCEMENT & TOURISM

Welcome to fabulous New Pork City!
This glittering empire is the shining
jewel of the Nowhere Islands.

▶ Enjoy local cuisine served by beautiful women
  at Beauty & Tasty. By reservation only.
▶ Kill some time with your pals at our critically
  acclaimed Game Arcade, featuring authentic scuff
  marks, sticky quarters, and unfortunate odors!
▶ Take time to visit the King Statue, an extravagant
  landmark commemorating the divine righteous-
  ness of our great leader.

## MAY THE PORK BE WITH YOU!

## CITY MAP

On your way out of the limo, the chauffeur gives you a wonderfully-detailed map of the bustling metropolis and bids you a temporary farewell. What makes him so sure he'll see you again?

# BEAUTY &TASTY

| | |
|---|---|
| King Burger | 1700 DP |
| Beefsteak | 2000 DP |
| Pasta with a Past | 1400 DP |
| Favorite Pizza | 1560 DP |
| Rich Kid Stew | 1000 DP |
| Rich Parfait | 1300 DP |

## REUNION

The former residents of Tazmily have come to New Pork City ahead of Lucas. There's no telling who you'll bump into next, but one thing is certain: your arrival has been anticipated.

# CASINO★TIME!

The Sanchez brothers and their friend run the loosest slots in town. In fact, they're the only slots in town. It's just 1 DP per spin, and if you hit the jackpot, you could walk away with some great prizes!

SEVENS: MAGIC TART
LIMES: BIG CITY SODA
LEMONS: CHICK
BARS: BAG OF PORK CHIPS

# BEHIND THE SCENES

For some reason, the women who staff New Pork City's various establishments (the real ones, at least) don't like it when you walk up behind them. You're not staring at their hips, are you?

100 NP

## VENDORIFFIC

You can find explosives and overpriced food elsewhere, but you'll want to save your money for the unassuming Piggy Vend in front of Master Porky's massive tower—it's got vital upgrades for pretty much everybody.

| | |
|---|---|
| Master Stick | 4060 DP |
| Expensive Gloves | 2360 DP |
| Good Shoes | 3520 DP |
| Heavy Charm | 1820 DP |
| Kite Bandana | 1840 DP |
| Scorpio Bracelet | 2800 DP |

## MOVIE SHOP

| | |
|---|---|
| Fake Bat | 20000 DP |
| Fake Frying Pan | 18000 DP |
| Red Hat | 2000 DP |
| Angel Ribbon | 1500 DP |
| Bag of Pork Chips | 20 DP |
| Pork Noodles | 80 DP |
| Big City Burger | 60 DP |
| Bag of Big City Fries | 40 DP |
| | |
| Hot Dog Sushi | 200 DP |
| | |
| Big City Cola | 50 DP |

# PORKY'S QUEST!

**PREMIERE TONIGHT!**

## FREE ADMISSION

## STUNNING! — THE WEEKLY LARDNA
## A TRIUMPH! — ALOYSIUS REVIEW

## SOURCE OF THE STENCH

Inside the theater some punk is babbling about a sewer leader, the nosy lady won't let you run, and everyone else is complaining about the awful stench. Sniff around until you've uncovered the source.

## SUBCULTURE

You can't just let Boney run off, but there's no way you can follow him either. A man at the arcade was complaining about the air quality, so perhaps you can check with him about getting into the underground scene.

## NEW PORK SEWERS

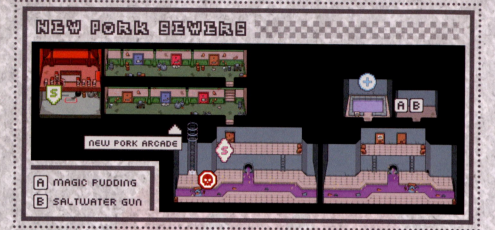

NEW PORK ARCADE

A MAGIC PUDDING

B SALTWATER GUN

## EENIE MEANIE

There's a trashy room in the sewer with a few surprises, but be careful: the can on the right isn't quite so pleasant.

## CRICKET SHOP

| | |
|---|---|
| Double Jerky | 240 DP |
| Antidote | 8 DP |
| Fresh Mint | 16 DP |
| Secret Herb | 600 DP |
| Cup of Lifenoodles | 1780 DP |

## MT APARTMENTS

As predicted by that guy in the theater, you'll discover the MT Apartments after a short trek through the sewer. This depressing slum doesn't seem like it was abandoned that long ago. What happened to the old tenants, and just how new is New Pork City?

## TAKE ME TO YOUR LEDER

In the west wing of the complex is a familiar-looking pair of legs, except that they're tied up! On the second floor, Boney will rejoin your party before you reunite with the mysterious "leader" you've been hearing about.

# LEDER'S STORY

Leder, the bell-ringer from Tazmily Village, is not only alive: he's speaking! He has remained voluntarily silent for all these years, waiting for this moment to tell you the truth. His tale is so staggering that you'll have a hard time taking it all in, so Mr. Stinkbug is recruited to write it down for safekeeping.

- Long ago, the world extended far beyond the Nowhere Islands and was filled with innumerable people. The world was eventually destroyed by mankind.

- The Nowhere Islands were specially protected from the destruction thanks to the dragon sleeping under the island, sealed there by the seven Needles of the ancient Magypsies. The people of the Nowhere Islands were the sole survivors of the end of the old world. They arrived at the Nowhere Islands on a "White Ship."

- To prevent a recurrence of the mindsets and circumstances which eventually destroyed the world, the survivors chose to erase their memories and replace them with an ideal "story" of their lives as the humble villagers of Tazmily.

- As a fail-safe measure, the original memories of the villagers were stored in the Hummingbird Egg. Wess and Duster were tasked with retrieving the Egg and restoring the memories of the townspeople in the event of a disaster.

- It was important that someone's memory remained intact to help "keep watch" over things. Due to his abnormal height, Leder was chosen. The bell he rang served to keep people's memories intact.

- Things went well for the villagers until a person named Porky arrived on the island in a "Time Distorter" which allowed him to travel through time and space. Using this machine, he began building an army with people he had brainwashed and brought from other eras.

- Treating the islands as his personal playpen, Porky began experimenting with Chimeras. Using them in conjunction with the Thunder Tower and his army, he began to seize control of the islands.

- At some point Porky met Locria, who betrayed her fellow Magypsies by telling him about the Needles and the Dragon. Realizing that the ultimate power could be his if he were to pull the needles, Porky started toward that goal.

- With three of the six Needles pulled by Porky's lifeless servant, it all comes down to the seventh Needle. It seems that Porky has brought everyone to New Pork City for some kind of twisted apocalypse party, and it is up to Lucas and his friends to stop it.

The Stinkbug. Don't hold your nose: a big whiff of this little guy will bring back important memories. He's small enough to fit in your key items, but big-hearted enough to remember the deepest secrets of the Nowhere Islands. If you want to listen to Leder's story again, the Stinkbug will recall it for you at any time. Take him with you as you approach Porky's skyscraper.

## NOT SO FAST

You're not out of the water yet! Just as you're about to escape the dank sewer, something explodes out of the water. A brassy, familiar song fills the air: Fassad! His interpreter takes a moment to describe Fassad's intense, loathing hatred in very precise terms. Fassad went to all the trouble of lurking in sewer water, so the least you can do is give him a fight!

# >> BOSS <<

## It came from the SEWERS

Fassad is nearly as unrecognizable as the Chimeras his army produced. He's got some amazing PSI attacks, but he won't use them until you really make him mad.

### FIRST HALF

▶ Miracle Fassad starts off with a shield, so you'll want Boney to use the Shield Snatcher immediately. Everyone else should stick with the standard routine: decrease the enemy's Offense/Defense and increase your own.

▶ You probably won't want to mess with shields, as Fassad's attacks aren't too threatening. Conserve your PP for the second half of the battle by attacking with combos.

### SECOND HALF

▶ Partway through the battle you'll knock off Fassad's gratuitous hornage, sending him into a PSI-powered rage. First he'll set up a PSI shield, so you should immediately use the Shield Snatcher. You'll also need Lucas to set up PSI Shield $\Omega$ immediately.

▶ At this point you should unleash everything you've got, meaning you finally get to use those two uber-attacks you just picked up: Starstorm and PK special $\Omega$!

▶ When he starts reinforcing his shields and scarfing bananas, you've got him on the ropes!

## BITTER DEFEAT

After you've beaten him, Fassad drops into the slimy waters as his interpreter makes an unceremonious exit. Next stop, Porky's Tower!

## GATHERING STORM

The streets are busier than ever! More and more people have arrived while you were listening to Leder's long story. If your way is blocked, you'll have to find another way around, but you can still get everywhere you need to go.

### BOMB SALESMAN

| | |
|---|---|
| PENCIL ROCKET | 500 DP |
| BOMB | 1000 DP |
| SUPER BOMB | 2000 DP |
| NEW YEAR'S EVE BOMB | 3000 DP |
| SALTWATER GUN | 400 DP |

**NEW YEAR'S EVE BOMB:** Potentially the most powerful weapon in the game: if it works, it reduces all enemies to 1 HP! Unfortunately it's not too reliable...

# SAVAGE STATUE

## 10 NP

Check out the eerie King Statue on the northeast side of the city a few times and you'll get a weird feeling. Return the favor and you'll find yourself in a battle for your life! There are only two ways to win: either use a New Year's Eve Bomb or have everyone guard while Lucas attempts PK Flash, which on rare occasion will instantly defeat your enemies.

# TRIVIA CARDS

If you somehow survive the King Statue's assault, speak to the man nearby and you'll be rewarded with the fourth and final Trivia Card. These trivia cards aren't useful, but they're fun to use in battle with members of the Pork Army. While you can get some entertaining wrong answers from any solider, below are the specific porkers which provide the right answers:

**1** Card answer: "This Game Stinks"
▶ Pigmask Major ▶ Pigmask Colonel

**2** Card answer: "Croquette Rolls"
▶ Pigmask ▶ Navy SQUEAL
▶ Pigmask Colonel

**3** Card answer: "Ape"
▶ Pigmask ▶ Pigmask Captain
▶ Pigmask Colonel

**4** Card answer: "The Civil War"
▶ Pigmask Major

# ENEMIES

## MIRACLE FASSAD

He's not too dangerous until you make him mad, at which point he busts out some wicked PSI. A PSI Shield will save you, as will the high-PP PSI attacks gained at the temple!

| HP: 5489 | OFF:164 DEF:140 | EXP:28636 DP:1540 |

## METAL ATTACK ROACH

This robo-roach is packing metallic mandibles! Beat on his exoskeleton or zap him with PK Thunder before he can hit you with a combo attack.

SECRET HERB (15%)

| HP: 475 | OFF:125 DEF:121 | EXP:3266 DP:340 |

## PUTRID MOLDYMAN

These malodorous mischief-makers hide in trash cans, waiting for unsuspecting adventurers in search of hamburgers. Their poisonous spores can leave a bad taste in your mouth.

ATTACK ATTRACTOR (5%)

| 389 | OFF:130 DEF:85 | EXP:3226 DP:154 |

## KING STATUE

The "divine protector" of the city can take you down in a single turn if you let it. It will flail its arms around and slam its feet into the ground to deal mortal damage to your entire party. The only way to last more than a few rounds is to Guard!

| HP: 100M | OFF:228 DEF:255 | EXP:17586 DP:2400 |

# CHAPTER NO 8

## PART TWO

### SCALING THE SCRAPER

## LEGEND OF THE DOORKNOB

The chances of a Doorknob being hired to a mining outfit were slim enough, even with his outstanding enforcement credentials, but he somehow landed the job. He was happy there, working amongst the massive clay beasts, but deep in his brass heart he knew his luck wouldn't hold. Sure enough, within a few months the suits showed up with pink slips. The jobs were moving to a massive metropolis, and the Pork Army troopers had seniority. Rolling back to his post to gather his personal effects, he happened across an argument. "What do you mean, passed over? Who worked overtime while the other Captains partied at that club?!" The peace-loving doorknob was about to step in when the irate Pigmask, furiously flailing his stubby arms, accidentally sent him flying. "Forget it, I've got an elevator security gig waiting for me..." Those were the last words Doorknob heard as he began his long descent into the depths of a seemingly endless mineshaft.

## LOBBY & THEATER

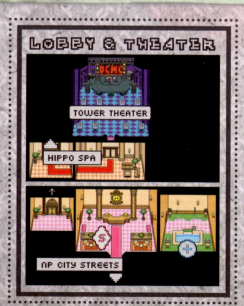

TOWER THEATER

HIPPO SPA

NP CITY STREETS

## GOING UP

The elevators in the Empire Porky Building are finally fixed, so you can begin your ascent to the vaunted 100th floor as soon as you're ready. Don't be surprised if Duster gets recognized en route, though...

## CRICKET SHOP

| | |
|---|---|
| GRILLED CHICKEN | 300 DP |
| SECRET HERB | 600 DP |
| CUP OF LIFENOODLES | 1780 DP |
| OFFENSE SPRAY | 1000 DP |
| DEFENSE SPRAY | 1000 DP |

## PRODIGAL PLAYER

OJ and the rest of the band heard that Lucky was coming, so they brought a special surprise with them to help sway him back onto the stage. The band members, smart enough to see through Porky's devious plan, are ready to make their final show one for the ages.

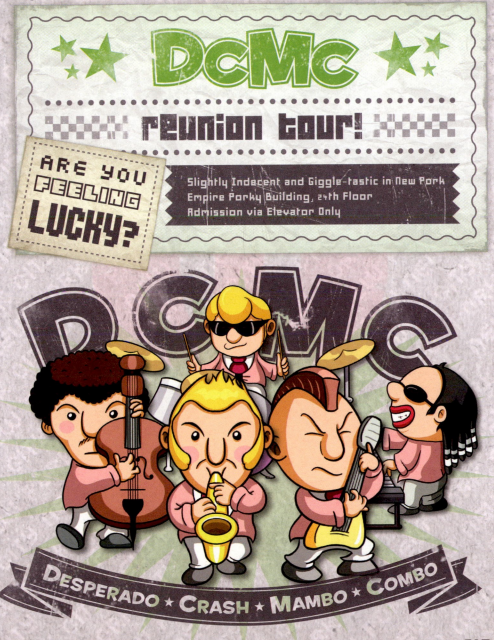

# ★★ DcMc ★★
## reunion tour!

### ARE YOU FEELING LUCKY?

Slightly Indecent and Giggle-tastic in New Pork
Empire Porky Building, 24th Floor
Admission via Elevator Only

DESPERADO ★ CRASH ★ MAMBO ★ COMBO

## BUZZKILL

As unexpectedly as it started, the concert ends. It seems the king pulled the plug. He wants you on the 100th floor, so don't keep him waiting. If you need to head back to the first floor for anything, the elevator will get you there. It might not be a bad idea to stock up before tackling the ominous 100th floor!

HIPPO SPA

HAREM SUITE

P-KORP

TOWER THEATER

| A | SUPER BOMB |
| B | ULTIMATE SHOES |
| C | GRILLED CHICKEN |
| D | CUP OF LIFENOODLES |

## HIPSTER VIBE

The hippos won't attack you unless you confront them first, so don't be scared to get in the water. Even if you get in a fight, there's an Instant Revitalizing Device to keep you in shape. Once you hop out of the pool, one of the more insecure researchers will consider you a threat.

## HAREM UPSTAIRS

The 'real' 100th floor seems to be occupied by King Porky's fans. You've got work to do, so don't be taken in by the lush surroundings, calorie-rich foods, or free oxygen.

## FLUSHING MEADOWS

Thinking back, many of the houses in Tazmily were sorely lacking in bathrooms. It's no wonder: King Porky was hoarding them for the 100th floor! Take care as you explore, there are plenty of surprises in store—some more pleasant than others.

# BATHROOMS

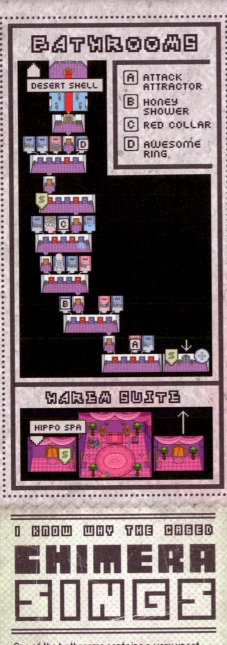

DESERT SHELL

| | |
|---|---|
| **A** | ATTACK ATTRACTOR |
| **B** | HONEY SHOWER |
| **C** | RED COLLAR |
| **D** | AWESOME RING |

## HAREM SUITE

HIPPO SPA

# ENEMIES

## HIPPO LAUNCHER

This isn't your average household hippopotamus. One blast from its mouth—missile and you're mincemeat! The ones in the water are more dangerous, so fight the ones on land if you're scared of sinking.

**THUD CHARM (3%)**

| HP: 1623 | OFF:182 | DEF:108 | EXP:Y566 | DP:254 |
|---|---|---|---|---|
| HP: 998 | OFF:182 | DEF:108 | EXP:Y566 | DP:238 |

## PIGMASK MAJOR

This oversized opponent isn't happy about the interruption. Take him out and then take yourself out of there before you realize what just happened.

**HOT DOG SUSHI (10%)**

| HP: 721 | OFF:147 | DEF:75 | EXP:2788 | DP:300 |
|---|---|---|---|---|

## MEN'S ROOM SIGN

You won't see it coming when this iconic irritation blows you to kingdom come with PK Starstorm. It's got tons of HP, so if you're not good with combos, setting up a PSI Shield might be a good idea.

**MAGIC PUDDING (10%)**

| HP: 1222 | OFF:99 | DEF:82 | EXP:3014 | DP:200 |
|---|---|---|---|---|

# I KNOW WHY THE CAGED CHIMERA SINGS

One of the bathrooms contains a very upset occupant. After two eerily familiar—sounding knocks, you'll be able to enter, but be ready to retreat! Once you've left the hall, you'll hear the Chimera bust out. If you return and dash through the Chimera—shaped hole you can snatch the coveted Awesome Ring, but don't get bitten or it's game over!

## I CRIED

You'll eventually stumble upon the throne, but the king is nowhere to be seen. Most of him, at least. Porky comes back on the horn to taunt you once again: did you really think this was the 100th floor? This is the Empire Porky Building, not some trifling tower.

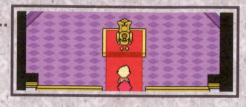

## LOCRIA, THE MYSTERY MAGYPSY

The sounds and smells on the 100th floor should serve to confirm any suspicions you might have had about the missing Magypsy. Locria has not only left bananas (and peels) all over the place, but he left his memento as well. Drop any old equipment you're carrying and stock up on presents. Be sure to comfort that poor mouse on your way to the 100th floor.

### DESERT SHELL

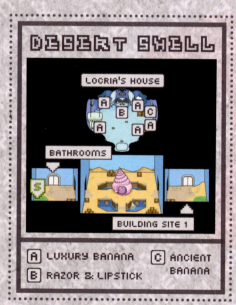

[A] LUXURY BANANA [C] ANCIENT BANANA
[B] RAZOR & LIPSTICK

### BUILDING SITE 1

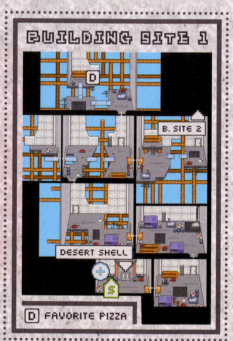

[D] FAVORITE PIZZA

### BUILDING SITE 2

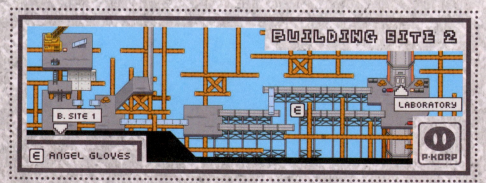

[E] ANGEL GLOVES

# RECONSTRUCTION SITE

Huh? This floor doesn't quite seem to be finished. Perhaps you're having difficulty reaching the top because they haven't even built the 100th floor yet? There are construction workers in your way and treacherous gaps in the unfinished floor, but you can solve both problems at once with a swift tackle!

# CRANE GAME

Building a giant swimming bath on the 100th floor of a skyscraper out of concrete and lumber is a labor-intensive process. Surely the construction workers would appreciate a hand—perhaps you could operate the crane?

# AL CABO DE LABO

Finally, the 100th floor! This futuristic laboratory is even more advanced than the Chimera lab, and twice as dangerous too. If you're willing to take a beating, you'll be able to pick up some great items on this floor. Make good use of that Instant Revitalizing Device!

# ENEMIES

## BOA TRANSISTOR

This annoyingly observant snake will try to trip you up, but its predictable weakness to lightning makes it pretty easy to shake.

**SALTWATER GUN (10%)**

| HP: 678 | OFF:131 DEF:87 | EXP:2623 DP:182 |

## K9000

This recursive pooch may irritate your metallurgies. Give it an obedience lesson before it blinds you with its dazzling light.

**NEW YEAR'S EVE BOMB (5%)**

| HP: 1086 | OFF:138 DEF:126 | EXP:3529 DP:230 |

## RHINOCEROCKET MARK II

The Rhinocerocket's moves haven't really changed, but it's still as dangerous as ever. A shot of PK Freeze should go a long way toward decommissioning it.

**PENCIL ROCKET (10%)**

| HP: 832 | OFF:159 DEF:89 | EXP:3628 DP:178 |

## LOVE WALKER

Don't get burned by these flaming lips. Its kisses are twice as disgusting as grandma's, but the difference is that you're free to use PK Fire on this thing.

**GODDESS RIBBON (3%)**

| HP: 847 | OFF:132 DEF:77 | EXP:3316 DP:121 |

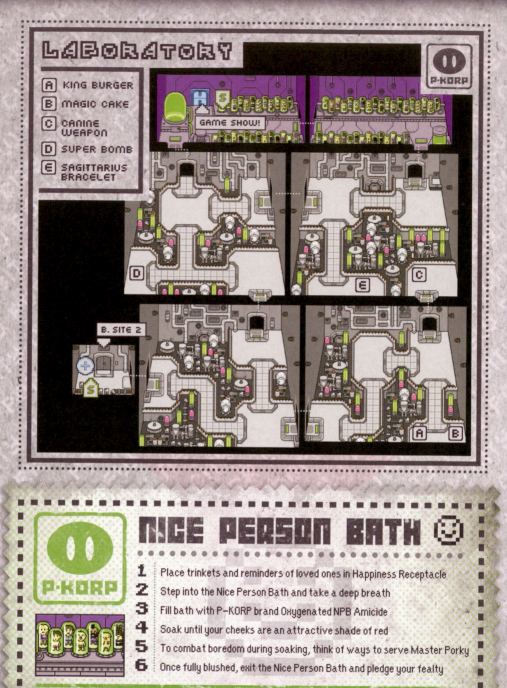

# LABORATORY

- **A** KING BURGER
- **B** MAGIC CAKE
- **C** CANINE WEAPON
- **D** SUPER BOMB
- **E** SAGITTARIUS BRACELET

P-KORP

GAME SHOW!

D

E

C

B. SITE 2

A   B

---

# NICE PERSON BATH ☺

P-KORP

1   Place trinkets and reminders of loved ones in Happiness Receptacle

2   Step into the Nice Person Bath and take a deep breath

3   Fill bath with P-KORP brand Oxygenated NPB Amicide

4   Soak until your cheeks are an attractive shade of red

5   To combat boredom during soaking, think of ways to serve Master Porky

6   Once fully blushed, exit the Nice Person Bath and pledge your fealty

SIDE EFFECTS MAY INCLUDE INCREASED APPETITE AND DESIRE TO HUMILIATE ONE'S ENEMIES. FALSE MEMORIES OF LIFE BEFORE PORKY ARE MERELY DELUSIONS AND SHOULD BE IGNORED.

## COME ON UP!

It seems that he's revisited the haberdashery, but just as he predicted, the limo driver greets you once again. His job is to ensure that you're "worthy" of meeting with Master Porky, and as such, he takes you to face the first of three fearsome tasks.

## GAME SHOW!

GAME SHOW #2

LABORATORY

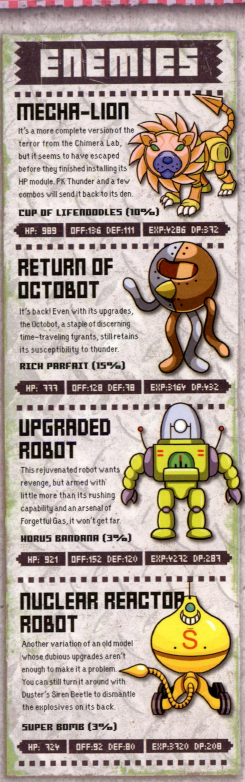

# ENEMIES

## MECHA-LION

It's a more complete version of the terror from the Chimera Lab, but it seems to have escaped before they finished installing its HP module. PK Thunder and a few combos will send it back to its den.

**CUP OF LIFENOODLES (10%)**

| HP: 989 | OFF:136 | DEF:111 | EXP:4286 | DP:372 |

## RETURN OF OCTOBOT

It's back! Even with its upgrades, the Octobot, a staple of discerning time-traveling tyrants, still retains its susceptibility to thunder.

**RICH PARFAIT (15%)**

| HP: 777 | OFF:128 | DEF:78 | EXP:3164 | DP:432 |

## UPGRADED ROBOT

This rejuvenated robot wants revenge, but armed with little more than its rushing capability and an arsenal of Forgetful Gas, it won't get far.

**HORUS BANDANA (3%)**

| HP: 921 | OFF:152 | DEF:120 | EXP:4272 | DP:287 |

## NUCLEAR REACTOR ROBOT

Another variation of an old model whose dubious upgrades aren't enough to make it a problem. You can still turn it around with Duster's Siren Beetle to dismantle the explosives on its back.

**SUPER BOMB (3%)**

| HP: 724 | OFF:92 | DEF:80 | EXP:3920 | DP:208 |

### SMILE OF VICTORY

As his many indentured servants make painfully clear, Master Porky loves to win, but he's got two unusual quirks:

#### HE MUST WIN BY A RAZOR-THIN MARGIN

▶ Winning is great, but nothing is as important as having a worthy adversary to destroy. What better way to humiliate your enemy than by snatching a narrow victory from their grasp?

#### HE DOES NOT ACTUALLY HAVE TO BE PRESENT

▶ As long as victory has his name attached, that's good enough. Porky is content to triumph vicariously through his robotic slave, Master Mini-Porky.

## ★ TRIUMVIRATE TEST OF TACT ★

### SUPER WHACK-A-MOLE

This is your first major test! You must whack the moles without hitting the hapless old construction workers. The idea is to make a good impression, so put in a serious effort, but... don't strain yourself too hard. If you're hopelessly confused, check the cue-card in the corner during your turn.

### PURPLE BRIDGE RACE

A perilous plank race across infested waters! You should try to make it interesting, but it wouldn't be a good idea to work up a sweat. Once again, if you find yourself unable to continue, reading the cue-card during the race might be advisable.

### TO WHOM GOES THE BOOM?

This cleverly-titled game is more than a test of agility; the psychological underpinnings of the game are designed to sniff out the proud and cold-hearted. If at first you don't under-succeed, try again... or read the cue-card.

# RESPITE ON THE LANDING

After a long series of trials you'll finally be invited into Master Porky's inner sanctum on the 100th floor. Before you go in, prepare yourself:

▶ Rest up on the stairwell couch.
▶ Make sure you've equipped the gear you picked up.
▶ Spread out your Magypsy mementos to your vital members.
▶ Give explosives and HP/PP restoring items to Boney (and Duster).
▶ Speak with the Save Frog before proceeding.

## >>> BOSS <<<

### GOT PORK ON THE BRAIN?

Talk about bad hospitality! Porky changes his mind at the last moment and decides he doesn't want to meet you after all, leaving you to grapple with his "toy".

**LUCAS** Use Counter Ω right away. NKC can't use PSI, and Counter will reflect its strongest attack, the "End Of The Century" beam. Next, use Defense Up Ω to protect the party, and Offense Up Ω to powerup Duster and Boney's attacks. If you've learned it, Refresh is useful for keeping everyone's HP up and preserving mementos.

**KUMATORA** Offense Down α yields huge benefits with up to three uses. PK Ground is incredibly efficient, if you've learned it. Starstorm and Thunder also work well, but don't bother with Freeze or Fire.

**DUSTER** The NKC's steady beat makes it easy to rack up big combos. The Tickle Stick can help, but the Scary Mask isn't needed if Kumatora is using Offense Down.

**BONEY** Bombs aren't very effective, so save them for later. You can take down NKC's Counter with the Shield Snatcher. Otherwise, it's combos all the way.

## PORKY'S SANCTUM

LOOOONG HALL

GAME SHOW #3

## ENEMIES

### NATURAL KILLER CYBORG

The N.K. Cyborg is a towering porcine tank with a wide arsenal of physical attacks, plus the occasional electric shock. Take down its Counter and set up your own to deflect its insane End of the Century beam. The time to use your most powerful PSI attacks is now!

| HP: 7548 | OFF: 232 | DEF: 189 | EXP: 34381 | DP: 1600 |

# CHAPTER NO. 8

## PART THREE
## REVELATIONS & REUNIONS

# NOSTALGIA ★ TRIP ★

Emerging from the tiring battle, you find yourself slowly pacing down an immensely long hallway as classical music plays overhead. In the next room is an unexpected sight: an indoor waterway. Board the houseboat and enjoy a tour of Porky's detached nostalgia.

LOOOONG HALL

PORKY'S HALL

100TH FLOOR - MUSEUM RIDE

# THE PENCIL ERASER

If only you'd had this at the beginning of your journey, and if only there were any other pencils to erase in the first place. Alas, the tool may be better suited for a different journey in a different time, but you can still erase the pencil statue in this room just for fun.

## 100TH FLOOR PORKY'S HALL

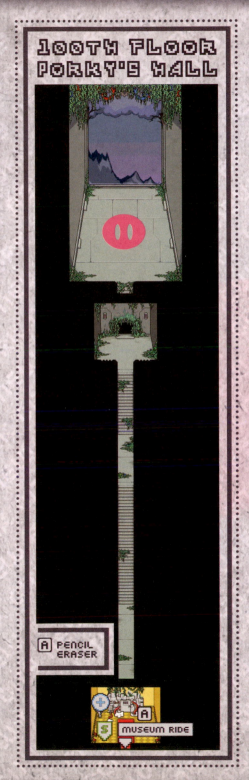

Ⓐ PENCIL ERASER

Ⓐ
Ⓢ MUSEUM RIDE

# PREP FOR THE UNKNOWN

Before you cross the vine-covered threshold to Porky's Inner Sanctum, you should make your final preparations. As usual, explosives and PP-restoring items are great for Boney, and your most vital characters should carry mementos.

## BEGINNING OF THE END

Within his inner sanctum, Porky finally appears... as a "meek" young boy! Could a child have possibly commissioned so many evil deeds? During your conversation the deception becomes clear: this is only the beginning of the end.

# >> BOSS <<

# MANGLING THE MECHA PORKIES

Individually the PORKY bots aren't much of a threat, but you're dealing with an entire pack. After you've demolished the first five, PORKY 06 will drop in with some Chimera reinforcements, and then PORKY 07. How many more can you handle?

## LUCAS

▶ Refresh is a good choice for a first-round cast, since this battle is destined to take a while.

▶ Counter $\Omega$ is another excellent choice for the beginning of the battle. Unfortunately, none of your defensive PSI will lessen the impact of the explosions.

▶ Avoid Lucas's offensive PSI. Flash is ineffective and his special attack will be reflected by the PORKY bot's PSI Counters!

## KUMATORA

▶ PK Thunder is great because it bypasses the bots' shields. It also attacks individually, rather than doling out excessive punishment to the entire group.

▶ The remainder of Kumatora's PK attacks will be reflected, and PK Ground is surprisingly inefficient, so stick with Thunder $\Omega$.

## DUSTER

▶ As usual, combos are Duster's best bet. No sense in wasting time with his Thief Tools when there are so many enemies to tackle.

## BONEY

▶ Explosives, especially Super Bombs and Pencil Rockets, work pretty well against the Mecha-Porkies.

▶ The Shield Snatcher works, but it's not a very good idea. Similarly, the New Year's Eve Bomb will prove to be a dud, so stick with combos when you run out of bombs.

## OFFSLAUGHT

After you've defeated the seventh Mecha-PORKY, another batch of three drops from the ceiling. Luckily they're not the only reinforcements arriving—out of nowhere, the DCMC busts into the room to back you up!

With the threat neutralized, former residents of Tazmily begin to stream into the room one by one. Wess wonders aloud whether they or Porky are the ones actually cornered, and on cue, Master Porky reveals himself at last.

## PORKY'S EXPOSITION

Lowered from the ceiling in a creepy casket-cradle, a withered Master Porky coughs and wheezes taunts. Without remorse he explains the source of his inspiration (an unnamed, selfish "hero"...?) and the motive behind his all-encompassing powerlust: boredom. The only remedy for his tedium is to toy with the last remnant of humanity before snuffing it out.

# ENEMIES

## MECHA PORKY

This mechanical menace may have a baby-face, but it possesses the mind of... a bomb! Not only will it explode when defeated, but you've got to grapple with more than half a dozen of them, so make sure you've got a good healing strategy.

| HP: 865 | OFF:135 | DEF:148 | EXP:1580 | DP:21 |

## THE SEVENTH NEEDLE

Almost on cue, an alarm echoes through the sanctuary: the final Needle has been located. Porky, always willing to prolong an entertaining spectacle, provides your party (plus Flint) a one-way trip to the caverns below the tower.

## MASTER PORKY MINCH

"I'm the most clever, most charming, and most trouble-making boy ever..." King of the Pigmask Army and wreaker of havoc on the Nowhere Islands. The power which enabled him to tear through space and time has aged his body, but his mind retains its twisted, childlike cruelty.

## FLINT AHEAD

Flint insists that you let him go ahead of you, offering no further explanation. Once he's gone, start your descent through the cavernous mining project. Eventually you'll come across a present with a helpful surprise inside! Check your distribution of healing items and then step into the cave.

## THE ADVENTURES OF DOORKNOB

Weeks passed, and Doorknob grew weaker. It seemed forever since he had first landed there on bedrock, unable to nurse the dents and scratches he suffered during his plunge through the factory mine. Every day Pigmasks and chubby construction workers ambled by, oblivious to his plight. Today was different, though; the footfalls were hard and fast as workers and captains rushed to and from the pit below. A new flurry of activity sprang up; a siren, a crash, and then a familiar figure scrambling down the rocks. Doorknob dragged himself to the precipice in hopes of catching a glimpse of the stranger's face. Right as he peered over the edge an unseen assailant grabbed him and then fumbled, sending him tumbling down. The last thing he saw as he fell from the face of the cliff was a smallish, calloused hand.

## DESCENDING SHAFT

PORKY'S HALL

A

THE CAVE OF THE FUTURE

B

[A] DOORKNOB
[B] HOT SPRING

## CAVE OF THE FUTURE

THE FINAL NEEDLE

A

DESCENDING SHAFT

[A] REAL BAT

## END SEARCH

Partway into the cave, you'll see a chilling sight. Kneeling on the ground ahead is Flint, battered but alive. He confirms what you may have already suspected about the identity of the Masked Man. Flint seems to have barely survived his encounter, so things certainly won't be any easier for you.

## FEAR OF A RECESSION

If you're feeling a little vindictive about being left alone for the past three years, take some time to pester Flint. Eventually he'll give you some insight on his, err, reluctant hairline. No wonder you've never seen him without his hat before!

# >> BOSS <<

## PORCINE PUNK

During the battle with Porky, he'll take a few moments to explain his immense battle superiority. He doesn't even know how old he is, but he is sure of one thing: he will never die.

### LUCAS

▶ Offense/Defense Up will be useful for boosting your stats, as well as recovering from Porky's devastating 'cough' attack.

▶ Refresh is, as always, a good choice once you've got everyone's stats boosted.

▶ Healing will be Lucas's most important role once the battle is underway.

▶ Combos are preferable to offensive PSI, since Porky maintains a PSI Counter.

### KUMATORA

▶ PK Ground is very powerful against Porky. If you don't have it, it will be worth your time to level up until you do (Level 60).

▶ PK Thunder is less efficient than Ground, but still effective.

▶ Thanks to Porky's constant reinforcement of his PSI Counter, none of the rest of your PK attacks will be useful.

### DUSTER

▶ Tickle Stick and Scary Mask are useful for a few turns.

▶ Combos, boosted by Lucas's Offense Up casts, should be Duster's main focus.

### BONEY

▶ Explosives work on Porky, but you might be better off with combos.

▶ Shield Snatcher works, but isn't very effective since Porky is constantly reinforcing his PSI Counter.

## NERVES IN THE BULLPEN

Not far from Flint you'll find the Real Bat, brimming with strength and courage. Equip it, heal your party, and get your healing items wisely distributed. As soon as you climb the ladder you'll be stopped by Porky, whose bizarre cradle has transformed into a nightmarish weapon. His nerves seem to be fraying ever so slightly, but that uncertainty won't keep him from flaunting his casual disregard for the history— or fate—of his masked servant.

# ENEMIES

## MINERALI

This enemy's appearance is surprisingly consistent, in spite of its erratic movements. If your levels are low, shock it with PK Thunder before it has a chance to rock you.

**CUP OF LIFENOODLES (10%)**

| HP: 924 | OFF:158 DEF:142 | EXP:¥546 DP:28 |
|---|---|---|

## FENOMENO

You don't have time to get zapped, so do your best to avoid these volatile volts. PK Freeze will help you give them the slip.

**MAGIC PUDDING (20%)**

| HP: 712 | OFF:152 DEF:92 | EXP:¥113 DP:0 |
|---|---|---|

## PORKY

Porky's incomprehensible attacks and well-maintained PSI Counter make him a formidable foe. In addition to physical attacks, he calmly doles out stat damage, status effects, and shield-bypassing explosions. Even after you've shut down his cradle-mech, he retreats into the ultimate defense. He was right when he said he was unbeatable.

| HP: 6569 | OFF:170 DEF:182 | EXP:0 DP:0 |
|---|---|---|

# ABSOLUTE

Even after his machine runs out of juice, Porky refuses to admit defeat. He'll flee into his Absolutely Safe Capsule, a machine he "tricked" Mr. Saturn and Dr. Andonuts into creating. What he doesn't realize is that it's a double-edged sword: while Porky cannot be harmed inside the Capsule, neither can he do any harm to everything on the outside. In the pursuit of absolute safety, Porky, the interdimensional menace, seems to have been contained for good.

# PREPARATIONS

Just behind you, the Item Guy finally catches up. Stock up and then forge ahead to the final hot spring. If you have any Magypsy mementos left, give them to Lucas, along with any PP-restoring items you can spare.

# FINALITY

Your party reaches the Masked Man as he prepares to pull the final Needle. With a flash of recognition, he whirls around and strikes down your party with lightning. Lucas's Franklin Badge deflects the attack, and he enters the battle alone.

# FUTILITY

With your party members wiped out, you have the option of using Healing $\Omega$ to quickly revive them. However, your efforts will be in vain as the Masked Man will immediately wipe them out with a powerful bolt of lightning, leaving Lucas to fend for himself.

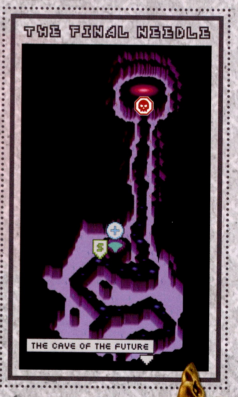

THE FINAL NEEDLE

THE CAVE OF THE FUTURE

# THE MASKED MAN

## PACIFIST

Lucas can't bring himself to attack, either with PSI or with his bat. Your only choice is to stand your ground. Guard as much as you can, and use Lifeup γ when your health meter falls below 100. Even if you mistime your recovery, a Memento can revive you.

## SACRIFICE

As the fight wears on, you'll hear a voice trying to reach Claus. After each attempt the air becomes more charged and the Masked Man becomes more frantic. He'll eventually resort to the most powerful attack at his disposal. Flint, who has caught up despite his injuries, intervenes with disastrous results.

## SPARKS

Following Flint's sacrifice, Lucas's anger is enough to overcome his uncertainty. With his conscience suppressed he is free to attack, but the voice will return with a motherly correction. As the increasingly unstable Masked Man doles out more and more violent punishment, a vision fills their minds.

## MEMORIES

Snapping from the dream, Lucas and the Masked Man face each other. Lucas is able to attack, but only with stinging remorse, sometimes missing purposely. Likewise, the Masked Man's attacks are dazed, without force or intention. The voice continues to call out to the Masked Man, who finally responds. Removing his helmet, Claus summons one final bolt.

## REQUIEM

Claus falters into the arms of his family, speaking softly to Lucas and Flint before joining his mother. Flint instructs you to pull the final Needle and bring the Dragon out from the darkness. Regardless of your choice, Lucas will pull the Needle.

## ROLLING

When you use Guard, your rolling HP meter slows to a crawl. With this advantage, you can withstand repeated mortal wounds from the Masked Man and save your Lifeup γ until the last second. After you've healed, wait for your health meter to tick back up before resuming the battle.

The final needle pulled, the dark
Dragon awakens from its ancient
slumber. Earthquakes and violent
cyclones celebrate the rise of the
pitch-black horror as destruction
rains down upon the Nowhere
Islands, wiping every last trace of the
twisted Pork Army from the earth.

In the inky black aftermath you'll
find yourself miraculously able to walk.
Stumbling through the darkness,
you'll be greeted by characters you
met along your journey, trying to
comprehend the miracle of their
survival. Confusion gives way to
joy as the former inhabitants of
Tazmily realize what has happened
in the wake of destruction.

The wishes of Lucas's heart have
been fulfilled. All things have
passed, giving rise to a new world
where evil has been washed away
and life once again shines brightly.

# MOTHER3
## HANDBOOK

# INDEX

# ENEMY INDEX

| MINIBOSS | BIG BOSS | RARE FOE | UNIQUE | EXPLOSIVE! | POISONOUS | CAUTION! | MYSTERY |
|----------|----------|----------|--------|------------|-----------|----------|---------|
| 💀 | 💀 | RARE | ① | ✷! | ☠ | ⚠ | ? |

| NORM | HIGH | SUSCEPTIBILTY | EXPLOIT FOE USING |
|------|------|---------------|-------------------|
| 🔥 | 🔥 | FIRE | PK Fire |
| ❄ | ❄ | FREEZE | PK Freeze |
| ⚡ | ⚡ | THUNDER | PK Thunder, Thunder Bomb |
| 💣 | 💣 | BOMB | Bomb, Running Bomb, Sprinting Bomb, Super Bomb, Pencil Rocket |
| DCMC | DCMC | DCMC SWAG | DCMC Pamphlet, DCMC Hat, DCMC Boxers, DCMC Shirt, DCMC Ring |
| ⚡⚡ | ⚡⚡ | NUMBNESS | PSI Paralyisis, PK Thunder |
| zZ | zZ | SLEEP | PSI Hypnosis, Duster's Pendulum |
| ◎ | ◎ | STRANGENESS | PSI Brainshock |
| 👁 | 👁 | CRYING | PK Flash, Duster's Smoke Bomb |
| « | « | WALL STAPLES | Duster's Wall Staples |
| ☮ | ☮ | APOLOGIZING | Salsa's Apologize |
| 😄 | 😄 | LAUGHTER | Duster's Tickle Stick Salsa's Make Laugh |

## AGITATED BOAR
**LVL 14**

*front*  *back*

| HP | 133 | EXP | 62 |
|----|-----|-----|-----|
| PP | 0 | DP | 0 |

Beef Jerky (70%)
DROPS

| | FRONT | BACK |
|-----|-------|------|
| Off. | 58 | 1 |
| Def. | 25 | 11 |
| IQ | 6 | 6 |
| Spd. | 20 | 1 |
| Chp | 1 | |

What a pig! These aggressive animals charge at anything they see, so try to maneuver around them while they make a beeline for where you were standing.

**WEAKNESS** 🔥 ❄ ⚡ 💣 ⚡⚡ ◎ 👁 « ☮ 😄

## ALMOST MECHA-LION
**LVL 35**

💀

| HP | 1684 | EXP | 4560 |
|----|------|-----|------|
| PP | 0 | DP | 848 |

DROPS

| | FRONT | BACK |
|-----|-------|------|
| Off. | 126 | 1 |
| Def. | 60 | 42 |
| IQ | 155 | 36 |
| Spd. | 155 | 1 |
| Chp | 7 | |

This almost beast is extremely powerful, and its only exploitable weakness is a vulnerability to crying. Have Lucas use these attacks while Boney keeps your party healed: PK Flash, PSI Counter, Defense/Offense Up, Thunder Bombs.

**WEAKNESS** 🔥 ❄ ⚡ 💣 ⚡⚡ ◎ 👁 « ☮ 😄

MOTHER 3

## ANCIENT DRAGONFLY
LVL 45

front · back

| HP | 402 | EXP | 612 |
|----|-----|-----|-----|
| PP | 0 | DP | 98 |

Beef Jerky (15%)

| | FRONT | BACK |
|----|----|----|
| Off. | 118 | 1 |
| Def. | 55 | 54 |
| IQ | 30 | 30 |
| Spd. | 84 | 1 |
| Chp | 7 | |

As the name and appearance imply, this insect can breathe fire at you. Luckily its HP and Defense are so low that a couple decent combos can knock it out of the canopy.

WEAKNESS

## ARACHNID!
LVL 12

front · back

| HP | 60 | EXP | 20 |
|----|-----|-----|-----|
| PP | 0 | DP | 0 |

Fresh Mint (20%)

| | FRONT | BACK |
|----|----|----|
| Off. | 43 | 1 |
| Def. | 5 | 1 |
| IQ | 12 | 12 |
| Spd. | 24 | 1 |
| Chp | 2,7 | |

They'll try to trap you in their webs and may call for backup, but their defense is so low that they don't pose a real threat.

WEAKNESS

## ARACHNID!!!
LVL 20

front · back

| HP | 178 | EXP | 41 |
|----|-----|-----|-----|
| PP | 0 | DP | 18 |

Antidote (10%)

| | FRONT | BACK |
|----|----|----|
| Off. | 58 | 1 |
| Def. | 10 | 5 |
| IQ | 12 | 14 |
| Spd. | 18 | 1 |
| Chp | 4 | |

The extra emphasis really doesn't make these spiders much more intimidating, but they can still poison you. Always use your Antidotes first—Lucas needs to conserve his PP!

WEAKNESS

## ARTSY GHOST
LVL 15

front · back

| HP | 187 | EXP | 46 |
|----|-----|-----|-----|
| PP | 10 | DP | 0 |

Peculiar Cheese (15%)

| | FRONT | BACK |
|----|----|----|
| Off. | 55 | 1 |
| Def. | 18 | 13 |
| IQ | 20 | 20 |
| Spd. | 21 | 1 |
| Chp | 2 | |

He may divide opinion, but his PSI Freeze leaves most critics cold. Tack him to the wall with some staples if you want to live!

WEAKNESS

## ATOMIC POWER ROBOT
LVL 27

front · back

| HP | 350 | EXP | 105 |
|----|-----|-----|-----|
| PP | 0 | DP | 68 |

Bomb (3%)

| | FRONT | BACK |
|----|----|----|
| Off. | 64 | 1 |
| Def. | 26 | 20 |
| IQ | 23 | 23 |
| Spd. | 27 | 1 |
| Chp | 5,7 | |

This refueling bot has deadly beams and an annoying capacity for recharging itself. Upon defeat, the machine will self-destruct! End the battle quickly to lessen the damage.

WEAKNESS

## BAKED YAMMONSTER
LVL 12

front · back

| HP | 154 | EXP | 42 |
|----|-----|-----|-----|
| PP | 0 | DP | 0 |

Baked Yam (50%)

| | FRONT | BACK |
|----|----|----|
| Off. | 48 | 1 |
| Def. | 8 | 3 |
| IQ | 13 | 13 |
| Spd. | 15 | 1 |
| Chp | 1 | |

This bitter sweet potato-like foe may look sinister, but it's not much of a fighter. A few attacks ought to put it one step closer to the dinner table.

WEAKNESS

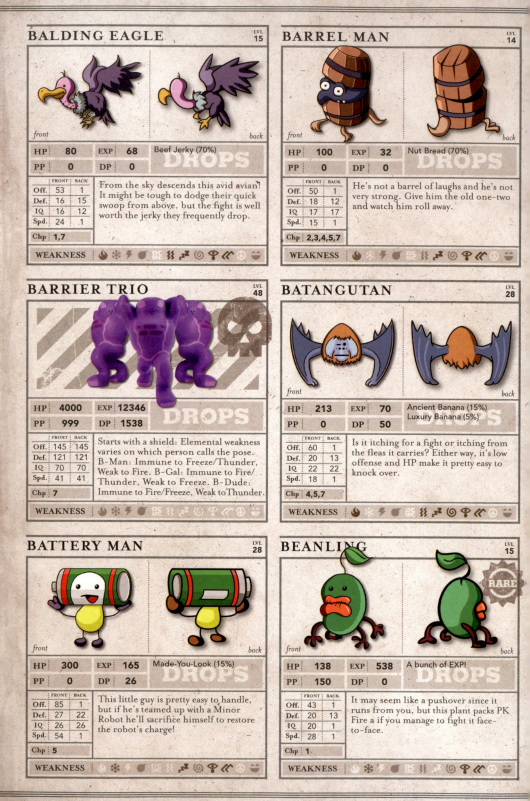

# BALDING EAGLE

LVL 15

| | FRONT | BACK |
|---|---|---|
| HP | 80 | EXP 68 | Beef Jerky (70%) |
| PP | 0 | DP 0 |

| | FRONT | BACK |
|---|---|---|
| Off. | 53 | 1 |
| Def. | 16 | 15 |
| IQ | 16 | 12 |
| Spd. | 24 | 1 |
| Chp | 1,7 | |

From the sky descends this avid avian! It might be tough to dodge their quick swoop from above, but the fight is well worth the jerky they frequently drop.

WEAKNESS

# BARREL MAN

LVL 14

| HP | 100 | EXP 32 | Nut Bread (70%) |
| PP | 0 | DP 0 |

| | FRONT | BACK |
|---|---|---|
| Off. | 50 | 1 |
| Def. | 18 | 12 |
| IQ | 17 | 17 |
| Spd. | 15 | 1 |
| Chp | 2,3,4,5,7 | |

He's not a barrel of laughs and he's not very strong. Give him the old one-two and watch him roll away.

WEAKNESS

# BARRIER TRIO

LVL 48

| HP | 4000 | EXP 12346 |
| PP | 999 | DP 1538 |

| | FRONT | BACK |
|---|---|---|
| Off. | 145 | 145 |
| Def. | 121 | 121 |
| IQ | 70 | 70 |
| Spd. | 41 | 41 |
| Chp | 7 | |

Starts with a shield: Elemental weakness varies on which person calls the pose. B-Man: Immune to Freeze/Thunder, Weak to Fire. B-Gal: Immune to Fire/Thunder, Weak to Freeze. B-Dude: Immune to Fire/Freeze, Weak to Thunder.

WEAKNESS

# BATANGUTAN

LVL 28

| HP | 213 | EXP 70 | Ancient Banana (15%) |
| PP | 0 | DP 50 | Luxury Banana (5%) |

| | FRONT | BACK |
|---|---|---|
| Off. | 60 | 1 |
| Def. | 20 | 13 |
| IQ | 22 | 22 |
| Spd. | 18 | 1 |
| Chp | 4,5,7 | |

Is it itching for a fight or itching from the fleas it carries? Either way, it's low offense and HP make it pretty easy to knock over.

WEAKNESS

# BATTERY MAN

LVL 28

| HP | 300 | EXP 165 | Made-You-Look (15%) |
| PP | 0 | DP 26 |

| | FRONT | BACK |
|---|---|---|
| Off. | 85 | 1 |
| Def. | 27 | 22 |
| IQ | 26 | 26 |
| Spd. | 54 | 1 |
| Chp | 5 | |

This little guy is pretty easy to handle, but if he's teamed up with a Minor Robot he'll sacrifice himself to restore the robot's charge!

WEAKNESS

# BEANLING

LVL 15

RARE

| HP | 138 | EXP 538 | A bunch of EXP! |
| PP | 150 | DP 0 |

| | FRONT | BACK |
|---|---|---|
| Off. | 43 | 1 |
| Def. | 20 | 13 |
| IQ | 20 | 1 |
| Spd. | 28 | 1 |
| Chp | 1 | |

It may seem like a pushover since it runs from you, but this plant packs PK Fire a if you manage to fight it face-to-face.

WEAKNESS

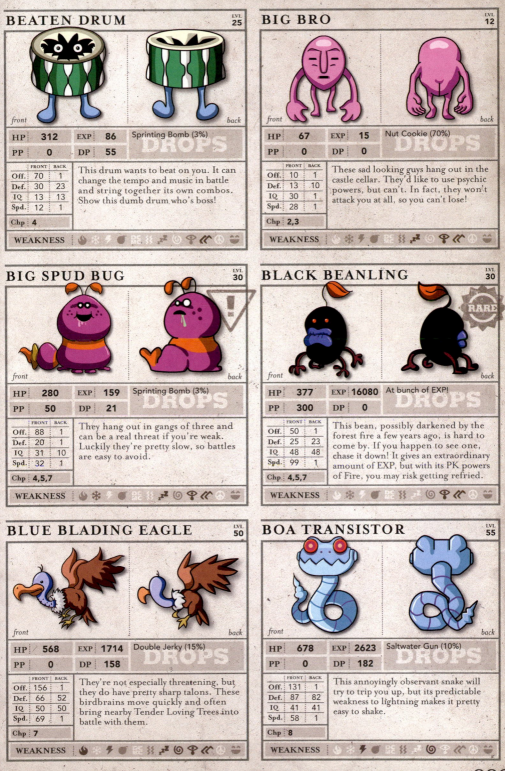

## BEATEN DRUM

LVL 25

front · back

| HP | 312 | EXP | 86 |
|---|---|---|---|
| PP | 0 | DP | 55 |

Sprinting Bomb (3%)

| | FRONT | BACK |
|---|---|---|
| Off. | 70 | 1 |
| Def. | 30 | 23 |
| IQ | 13 | 13 |
| Spd. | 12 | 1 |
| Chp | 4 | |

This drum wants to beat on you. It can change the tempo and music in battle and string together its own combos. Show this dumb drum who's boss!

WEAKNESS

## BIG BRO

LVL 12

front · back

| HP | 67 | EXP | 15 |
|---|---|---|---|
| PP | 0 | DP | 0 |

Nut Cookie (70%)

| | FRONT | BACK |
|---|---|---|
| Off. | 10 | 1 |
| Def. | 13 | 10 |
| IQ | 30 | 1 |
| Spd. | 28 | 1 |
| Chp | 2,3 | |

These sad looking guys hang out in the castle cellar. They'd like to use psychic powers, but can't. In fact, they won't attack you at all, so you can't lose!

WEAKNESS

## BIG SPUD BUG

LVL 30

front · back

| HP | 280 | EXP | 159 |
|---|---|---|---|
| PP | 50 | DP | 21 |

Sprinting Bomb (3%)

| | FRONT | BACK |
|---|---|---|
| Off. | 88 | 1 |
| Def. | 20 | 1 |
| IQ | 31 | 10 |
| Spd. | 32 | 1 |
| Chp | 4,5,7 | |

They hang out in gangs of three and can be a real threat if you're weak. Luckily they're pretty slow, so battles are easy to avoid.

WEAKNESS

## BLACK BEANLING

LVL 30

RARE

front · back

| HP | 377 | EXP | 16080 |
|---|---|---|---|
| PP | 300 | DP | 0 |

At bunch of EXP!

| | FRONT | BACK |
|---|---|---|
| Off. | 50 | 1 |
| Def. | 25 | 23 |
| IQ | 48 | 48 |
| Spd. | 99 | 1 |
| Chp | 4,5,7 | |

This bean, possibly darkened by the forest fire a few years ago, is hard to come by. If you happen to see one, chase it down! It gives an extraordinary amount of EXP, but with its PK powers of Fire, you may risk getting refried.

WEAKNESS

## BLUE BLADING EAGLE

LVL 50

front · back

| HP | 568 | EXP | 1714 |
|---|---|---|---|
| PP | 0 | DP | 158 |

Double Jerky (15%)

| | FRONT | BACK |
|---|---|---|
| Off. | 156 | 1 |
| Def. | 66 | 52 |
| IQ | 50 | 50 |
| Spd. | 69 | 1 |
| Chp | 7 | |

They're not especially threatening, but they do have pretty sharp talons. These birdbrains move quickly and often bring nearby Tender Loving Trees into battle with them.

WEAKNESS

## BOA TRANSISTOR

LVL 55

front · back

| HP | 678 | EXP | 2623 |
|---|---|---|---|
| PP | 0 | DP | 182 |

Saltwater Gun (10%)

| | FRONT | BACK |
|---|---|---|
| Off. | 131 | 1 |
| Def. | 87 | 82 |
| IQ | 41 | 41 |
| Spd. | 58 | 1 |
| Chp | 8 | |

This annoyingly observant snake will try to trip you up, but its predictable weakness to lightning makes it pretty easy to shake.

WEAKNESS

## BRIGHT SMILE

LVL 30

RARE

front | back

| HP | 278 | EXP | 90 |
| PP | 128 | DP | 2000 |

DROPS

A bunch of DP!

| | FRONT | BACK |
| Off. | 67 | 1 |
| Def. | 30 | 8 |
| IQ | 35 | 68 |
| Spd. | 65 | 1 |
| Chp | 5,7 | |

This dazzling foe's appearances are as short as they are rare, so make the most of your time by using super-powerful attacks. Wipe the smile off its face and you'll get a huge cash reward.

WEAKNESS

## BRO TEAM

LVL 35

front | back

| HP | 380 | EXP | 447 |
| PP | 182 | DP | 70 |

DROPS

Nut Cookie (50%)
Beef Jerky (30%)

| | FRONT | BACK |
| Off. | 104 | 1 |
| Def. | 45 | 30 |
| IQ | 38 | 38 |
| Spd. | 32 | 1 |
| Chp | 7 | |

These guys are much tougher when they work together, serving as a valuable lesson to siblings everywhere. Use Flash to make them cry or just avoid them altogether.

WEAKNESS

## CACTUS WOLF

LVL 10

| HP | 468 | EXP | 143 |
| PP | 0 | DP | 0 |

DROPS

Beef Jerky (100%)

| | FRONT | BACK |
| Off. | 43 | 1 |
| Def. | 20 | 11 |
| IQ | 10 | 12 |
| Spd. | 11 | 1 |
| Chp | 3 | |

Use Running Bombs, if you have them. This foe has no status affecting skills, but it does use some tough attacks. Apologize is useless and Make Laugh has a low chance of success, so use Monkey Mimic when out of bombs.

WEAKNESS

## CAREFREE JELLYFISH

LVL 45

front | back

| HP | 485 | EXP | 579 |
| PP | 0 | DP | 86 |

DROPS

Anti-Paralysis (20%)

| | FRONT | BACK |
| Off. | 111 | 1 |
| Def. | 50 | 31 |
| IQ | 30 | 50 |
| Spd. | 56 | 1 |
| Chp | 7 | |

They're so carefree you can easily walk up behind them and get in a sneak attack. Watch out for their stinging tentacles, though, as you may end up paralyzed.

WEAKNESS

## CARPET MONSTER

LVL 14

front | back

| HP | 132 | EXP | 67 |
| PP | 24 | DP | 0 |

DROPS

Beef Jerky (15%)

| | FRONT | BACK |
| Off. | 50 | 1 |
| Def. | 21 | 3 |
| IQ | 19 | 19 |
| Spd. | 28 | 1 |
| Chp | 2,5,7 | |

Never smile at this crocodile. With thief tools it's easy to send him scurrying back to the safety of his carpet.

WEAKNESS

## CATTLESNAKE

LVL 40

front | back

| HP | 536 | EXP | 536 |
| PP | 162 | DP | 162 |

DROPS

Fresh Milk (50%)

| | FRONT | BACK |
| Off. | 90 | 1 |
| Def. | 50 | 43 |
| IQ | 27 | 27 |
| Spd. | 22 | 1 |
| Chp | 4,5,7 | |

These chimeras might seem like easy targets, but defeating one requires serious physical and mental strength. Their HP is astronomical! Watch out, they can take you out easily if your level is too low.

WEAKNESS

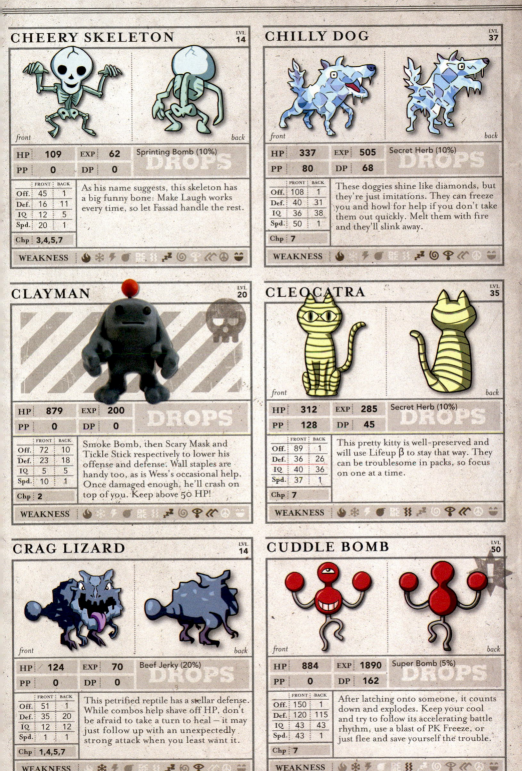

## CHEERY SKELETON — LVL 14

*front* *back*

| HP | 109 | EXP | 62 | Sprinting Bomb (10%) |
|----|-----|-----|----|------|
| PP | 0 | DP | 0 | |

| | FRONT | BACK |
|----|-------|------|
| Off. | 45 | 1 |
| Def. | 16 | 11 |
| IQ | 12 | 5 |
| Spd. | 20 | 1 |
| Chp | 3,4,5,7 | |

As his name suggests, this skeleton has a big funny bone: Make Laugh works every time, so let Fassad handle the rest.

WEAKNESS

## CHILLY DOG — LVL 37

*front* *back*

| HP | 337 | EXP | 505 | Secret Herb (10%) |
|----|-----|-----|-----|------|
| PP | 80 | DP | 68 | |

| | FRONT | BACK |
|----|-------|------|
| Off. | 108 | 1 |
| Def. | 40 | 31 |
| IQ | 36 | 38 |
| Spd. | 50 | 1 |
| Chp | 7 | |

These doggies shine like diamonds, but they're just imitations. They can freeze you and howl for help if you don't take them out quickly. Melt them with fire and they'll slink away.

WEAKNESS

## CLAYMAN — LVL 20

| HP | 879 | EXP | 200 | |
|----|-----|-----|-----|------|
| PP | 0 | DP | 0 | |

| | FRONT | BACK |
|----|-------|------|
| Off. | 72 | 10 |
| Def. | 23 | 18 |
| IQ | 5 | 5 |
| Spd. | 10 | 1 |
| Chp | 2 | |

Smoke Bomb, then Scary Mask and Tickle Stick respectively to lower his offense and defense. Wall staples are handy too, as is Wess's occasional help. Once damaged enough, he'll crash on top of you. Keep above 50 HP!

WEAKNESS

## CLEOCATRA — LVL 35

*front* *back*

| HP | 312 | EXP | 285 | Secret Herb (10%) |
|----|-----|-----|-----|------|
| PP | 128 | DP | 45 | |

| | FRONT | BACK |
|----|-------|------|
| Off. | 89 | 1 |
| Def. | 36 | 26 |
| IQ | 40 | 36 |
| Spd. | 37 | 1 |
| Chp | 7 | |

This pretty kitty is well-preserved and will use Lifeup β to stay that way. They can be troublesome in packs, so focus on one at a time.

WEAKNESS

## CRAG LIZARD — LVL 14

*front* *back*

| HP | 124 | EXP | 70 | Beef Jerky (20%) |
|----|-----|-----|----|------|
| PP | 0 | DP | 0 | |

| | FRONT | BACK |
|----|-------|------|
| Off. | 51 | 1 |
| Def. | 35 | 20 |
| IQ | 12 | 12 |
| Spd. | 1 | 1 |
| Chp | 1,4,5,7 | |

This petrified reptile has a stellar defense. While combos help shave off HP, don't be afraid to take a turn to heal — it may just follow up with an unexpectedly strong attack when you least want it.

WEAKNESS

## CUDDLE BOMB — LVL 50

*front* *back*

| HP | 884 | EXP | 1890 | Super Bomb (5%) |
|----|-----|-----|------|------|
| PP | 0 | DP | 162 | |

| | FRONT | BACK |
|----|-------|------|
| Off. | 150 | 1 |
| Def. | 120 | 115 |
| IQ | 43 | 43 |
| Spd. | 43 | 1 |
| Chp | 7 | |

After latching onto someone, it counts down and explodes. Keep your cool and try to follow its accelerating battle rhythm, use a blast of PK Freeze, or just flee and save yourself the trouble.

WEAKNESS

## DETACHED LEECH

LVL 13

front        back

| HP | 61 | EXP | 21 | Edible Mushroom (70%) |
|----|----|-----|----|----|
| PP | 0 | DP | 0 | **DROPS** |

| | FRONT | BACK |
|----|----|----|
| Off. | 33 | 1 |
| Def. | 5 | 1 |
| IQ | 11 | 11 |
| Spd. | 26 | 1 |
| Chp | 2 | |

Great leaping leeches! This sucker is fairly easy to overpower, but beware of large groups – there's safety in numbers, but not for you.

**WEAKNESS**

## DOGFISH

LVL 35

| HP | 368 | EXP | 322 | Doggy Biscuit (15%) |
|----|----|-----|----|----|
| PP | 38 | DP | 45 | Doggy Jerky (10%) |

| | FRONT | BACK |
|----|----|----|
| Off. | 102 | 1 |
| Def. | 42 | 33 |
| IQ | 24 | 24 |
| Spd. | 35 | 1 |
| Chp | 4,5,7 | |

Chimera experiments have turned this dog into man's worst friend. Watch out for its deadly PK Freeze attack! If you double back to where it leaps from its pond, you may be able to score an easy surprise attack.

**WEAKNESS**

## DUNG BEETLE

LVL 4

front        back

| HP | 43 | EXP | 2 | Dung (60%) |
|----|----|-----|----|----|
| PP | 0 | DP | 0 | **DROPS** |

| | FRONT | BACK |
|----|----|----|
| Off. | 15 | 1 |
| Def. | 2 | 1 |
| IQ | 6 | 5 |
| Spd. | 2 | 1 |
| Chp | 3 | |

It's easy to sneak up on a Dung Beetle because it will be too preoccupied with diligently rolling its dung around. You won't gain much experience, but if you're "lucky" you'll get to keep the dung…

**WEAKNESS**

## EERIE SMILE

LVL ~45

| HP | ??? | EXP | ??? | ??????????? |
|----|----|-----|----|----|
| PP | ??? | DP | ??? | **DROPS** |

| | FRONT | BACK |
|----|----|----|
| Off. | ??? | ??? |
| Def. | ??? | ??? |
| IQ | ??? | ??? |
| Spd. | ??? | ??? |
| Chp | 7 | |

This foe won't show it's true face until its HP is low. You can usually figure out which enemy it really is from its battle actions, though, or by relying on Boney's nose.

**WEAKNESS**

## EINSWINE

LVL 37

front        back

| HP | 387 | EXP | 422 | Magic Tart (10%) |
|----|----|-----|----|----|
| PP | 255 | DP | 83 | **DROPS** |

| | FRONT | BACK |
|----|----|----|
| Off. | 94 | 1 |
| Def. | 43 | 35 |
| IQ | 45 | 45 |
| Spd. | 35 | 1 |
| Chp | 7 | |

Einswine won't pick a fight, but don't underestimate them: their PSI attacks are powerful and can easily overwhelm you. Take them out quickly or deplete their PP.

**WEAKNESS**

## ELDER BATTY

LVL 20

front        back

| HP | 288 | EXP | 50 | Bug Spray (15%) |
|----|----|-----|----|----|
| PP | 0 | DP | 31 | **DROPS** |

| | FRONT | BACK |
|----|----|----|
| Off. | 66 | 1 |
| Def. | 16 | 10 |
| IQ | 17 | 16 |
| Spd. | 20 | 1 |
| Chp | 4,7 | |

Your mom told you to obey your elders, but she'd probably make an exception for these old bats. Watch your HP, as they can suck it away to heal themselves!

**WEAKNESS**

## FENOMENO

**LVL 65**

*front*      *back*

| HP | 712 | EXP | 4113 | Magic Pudding (20%) |
|---|---|---|---|---|
| PP | 0 | DP | 0 | |

| | FRONT | BACK |
|---|---|---|
| Off. | 152 | 0 |
| Def. | 92 | 80 |
| IQ | 70 | 70 |
| Spd. | 60 | 1 |
| Chp | 7 | |

You don't have time to get zapped, so do your best to avoid these volatile volts. PK Freeze will help you give them the slip.

**WEAKNESS**

---

## FIERCE PORK TROOPER

**LVL 28**

| HP | 1758 | EXP | 1548 | Pickled Veggie Plate (100%) |
|---|---|---|---|---|
| PP | 0 | DP | 620 | |

| | FRONT | BACK |
|---|---|---|
| Off. | 125 | 1 |
| Def. | 46 | 42 |
| IQ | 15 | 15 |
| Spd. | 25 | 1 |
| Chp | 5 | |

He's the toughest Pigmask around, but this big guy has a not-so-secret soft spot for DCMC merchandise. Keep him distracted while you knock his offense/ defense down.

**WEAKNESS**

---

## FIERCE PORK TROOPER II

**LVL 30**

| HP | 2064 | EXP | 3286 | |
|---|---|---|---|---|
| PP | 0 | DP | 650 | |

| | FRONT | BACK |
|---|---|---|
| Off. | 159 | 1 |
| Def. | 59 | 44 |
| IQ | 18 | 18 |
| Spd. | 28 | 1 |
| Chp | 5 | |

This is the same guy, just tougher thanks to his combat suit. If you don't keep him distracted with merch, get ready to deal with his fists and powerful bum rush. Swag is more than just a good idea—its a necessity.

**WEAKNESS**

---

## FILTHY ATTACK ROACH

**LVL 39**

*front*      *back*

| HP | 335 | EXP | 450 | Paper Fan (10%) |
|---|---|---|---|---|
| PP | 0 | DP | 92 | |

| | FRONT | BACK |
|---|---|---|
| Off. | 118 | 1 |
| Def. | 40 | 22 |
| IQ | 30 | 30 |
| Spd. | 54 | 1 |
| Chp | 7 | |

These roaches are not only more resilient than mole crickets, but they're also the undisputed champions of the inter-species insectoid martial arts tournaments.

**WEAKNESS**

---

## FIREFLY

**LVL 10**

| HP | 53 | EXP | 17 | Nut Bread (100%) |
|---|---|---|---|---|
| PP | 0 | DP | 0 | |

| | FRONT | BACK |
|---|---|---|
| Off. | 35 | 1 |
| Def. | 10 | 6 |
| IQ | 8 | 8 |
| Spd. | 17 | 1 |
| Chp | 1 | |

These bugs attack in groups of three, with powerful charges in addition to their weaker fire attacks. Use Flint's special 'Swing' ability twice to extinguish them in two turns

**WEAKNESS**

---

## FISH ROE MAN

**LVL 45**

*front*      *back*

| HP | 1856 | EXP | 943 | Awesome Crown 100% In giftbox after battle. |
|---|---|---|---|---|
| PP | 0 | DP | 200 | |

| | FRONT | BACK |
|---|---|---|
| Off. | 168 | 0 |
| Def. | 65 | 57 |
| IQ | 34 | 34 |
| Spd. | 57 | 1 |
| Chp | 7 | |

For a pile of unfertilized eggs, this thing is well-developed fighter. It can launch attacks to hit 3 party members for pretty huge damage. Give it a little freezer burn with PK Freeze.

**WEAKNESS**

# FLYING MOUSE

LVL 14

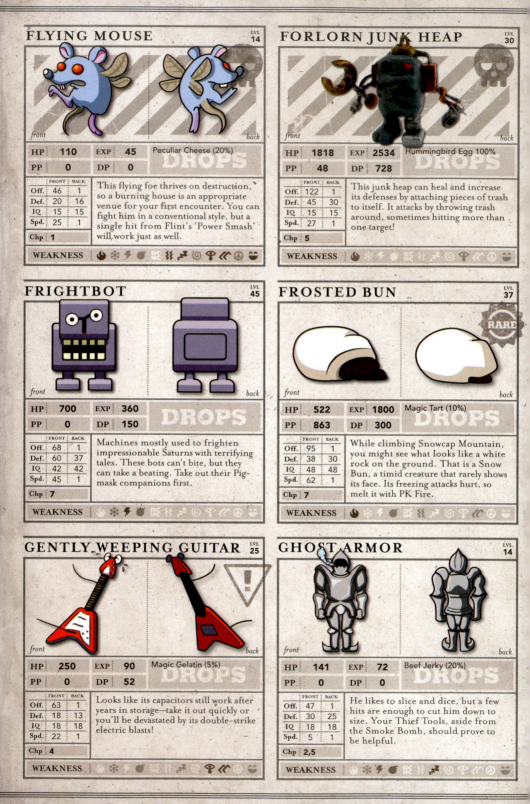

| HP | 110 | EXP | 45 | Peculiar Cheese (20%) |
|----|-----|-----|-----|----|
| PP | 0 | DP | 0 | DROPS |

|  | FRONT | BACK |
|----|----|----|
| Off. | 46 | 1 |
| Def. | 20 | 16 |
| IQ | 15 | 15 |
| Spd. | 25 | 1 |
| Chp | 1 | |

This flying foe thrives on destruction, so a burning house is an appropriate venue for your first encounter. You can fight him in a conventional style, but a single hit from Flint's 'Power Smash' will work just as well.

**WEAKNESS**

# FORLORN JUNK HEAP

LVL 30

| HP | 1818 | EXP | 2534 | Hummingbird Egg 100% |
|----|------|-----|------|----|
| PP | 48 | DP | 728 | DROPS |

|  | FRONT | BACK |
|----|----|----|
| Off. | 122 | 1 |
| Def. | 45 | 30 |
| IQ | 15 | 15 |
| Spd. | 27 | 1 |
| Chp | 5 | |

This junk heap can heal and increase its defenses by attaching pieces of trash to itself. It attacks by throwing trash around, sometimes hitting more than one target!

**WEAKNESS**

# FRIGHTBOT

LVL 45

| HP | 700 | EXP | 360 | |
|----|-----|-----|-----|----|
| PP | 0 | DP | 150 | DROPS |

|  | FRONT | BACK |
|----|----|----|
| Off. | 68 | 1 |
| Def. | 60 | 37 |
| IQ | 42 | 42 |
| Spd. | 45 | 1 |
| Chp | 7 | |

Machines mostly used to frighten impressionable Saturns with terrifying tales. These bots can't bite, but they can take a beating. Take out their Pig-mask companions first.

**WEAKNESS**

# FROSTED BUN

LVL 37

RARE

| HP | 522 | EXP | 1800 | Magic Tart (10%) |
|----|-----|-----|------|----|
| PP | 863 | DP | 300 | DROPS |

|  | FRONT | BACK |
|----|----|----|
| Off. | 95 | 1 |
| Def. | 38 | 30 |
| IQ | 48 | 48 |
| Spd. | 62 | 1 |
| Chp | 7 | |

While climbing Snowcap Mountain, you might see what looks like a white rock on the ground. That is a Snow Bun, a timid creature that rarely shows its face. Its freezing attacks hurt, so melt it with PK Fire.

**WEAKNESS**

# GENTLY WEEPING GUITAR

LVL 25

| HP | 250 | EXP | 90 | Magic Gelatin (5%) |
|----|-----|-----|-----|----|
| PP | 0 | DP | 52 | DROPS |

|  | FRONT | BACK |
|----|----|----|
| Off. | 63 | 1 |
| Def. | 18 | 13 |
| IQ | 18 | 18 |
| Spd. | 22 | 1 |
| Chp | 4 | |

Looks like its capacitors still work after years in storage—take it out quickly or you'll be devastated by its double-strike electric blasts!

**WEAKNESS**

# GHOST ARMOR

LVL 14

| HP | 141 | EXP | 72 | Beef Jerky (20%) |
|----|-----|-----|-----|----|
| PP | 0 | DP | 0 | DROPS |

|  | FRONT | BACK |
|----|----|----|
| Off. | 47 | 1 |
| Def. | 30 | 24 |
| IQ | 18 | 18 |
| Spd. | 5 | 1 |
| Chp | 2,5 | |

He likes to slice and dice, but a few hits are enough to cut him down to size. Your Thief Tools, aside from the Smoke Bomb, should prove to be helpful.

**WEAKNESS**

## GHOST KNIGHT
LVL 20

| | FRONT | BACK |
|---|---|---|
| Off. | 68 | 1 |
| Def. | 36 | 31 |
| IQ | 22 | 22 |
| Spd. | 5 | 1 |
| Chp | 2 | |

HP **200** EXP **180** PP **20** DP **0**

Yogurt (70%)

Hardheaded ghost disliked by all the other ghosts in the castle. Keep your health up and lower his offense and defense frequently! Your thief tools (except for the smoke bomb) will come in handy.

## GHOST SHIELD
LVL 14

| | FRONT | BACK |
|---|---|---|
| Off. | 45 | 1 |
| Def. | 33 | 27 |
| IQ | 17 | 17 |
| Spd. | 10 | 1 |
| Chp | 2,5 | |

HP **124** EXP **37** PP **14** DP **0**

Rotten Milk (10%)

Don't be taken in by his toothy grin—although this chap isn't too aggressive, he has good defense. Send him looking for an orthodontist.

## GHOST SWORD
LVL 14

| | FRONT | BACK |
|---|---|---|
| Off. | 57 | 1 |
| Def. | 24 | 11 |
| IQ | 15 | 15 |
| Spd. | 26 | 1 |
| Chp | 2,5 | |

HP **108** EXP **48** PP **12** DP **0**

Peculiar Cheese (10%)

He likes to slice and dice, but a few hits are enough to cut him down to size.

## GOOEY GOO
LVL 12

| | FRONT | BACK |
|---|---|---|
| Off. | 35 | 1 |
| Def. | 12 | 4 |
| IQ | 1 | 1 |
| Spd. | 1 | 1 |
| Chp | 3 | |

HP **92** EXP **82** PP **0** DP **0**

Mosquito Charm (100%)

You'll face three at once — a perfect time for a Running Bomb. You'll find one in the nearby gift box. Use Make Laugh and let Fassad take care of the fighting. If you kill all but one and allow it to duplicate, you can rack EXP!

## GRATED YAMMONSTER
LVL 35

| | FRONT | BACK |
|---|---|---|
| Off. | 92 | 1 |
| Def. | 42 | 1 |
| IQ | 28 | 14 |
| Spd. | 38 | 1 |
| Chp | 4,5,7 | |

HP **387** EXP **344** PP **60** DP **100**

Magic Tart (5%)

These starch-nemeses can use PK Freeze attacks, easily doing 150 damage in one round. Thankfully they like to stay in one place! It might be best to return when you're stronger.

## GREAT ANTLION
LVL 6

| | FRONT | BACK |
|---|---|---|
| Off. | 41 | 1 |
| Def. | 15 | 5 |
| IQ | 13 | 1 |
| Spd. | 5 | 1 |
| Chp | 3 | |

HP **121** EXP **27** PP **0** DP **0**

Flea Charm (100%) Miniboss
Beef Jerky (10%) Regular

There is a miniboss version and a regular type. When the sand whirls, an antlion is lurking. They can make you cry uncontrollably or lose a turn, so use Monkey Mimic to inflict the most damage, or defend and let Fassad fight.

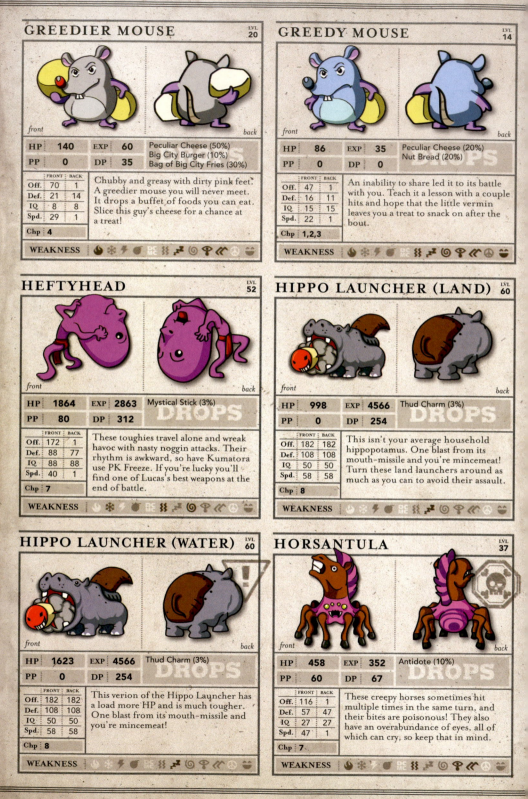

## GREEDIER MOUSE

LVL **20**

*front*          *back*

| HP | 140 | EXP | 60 | Peculiar Cheese (50%) |
|----|-----|-----|----|-----|
| PP | 0 | DP | 35 | Big City Burger (10%) |
| | | | | Bag of Big City Fries (30%) |

| | FRONT | BACK | |
|----|----|----|----|
| Off. | 70 | 1 | Chubby and greasy with dirty pink feet. |
| Def. | 21 | 14 | A greedier mouse you will never meet. |
| IQ | 8 | 8 | It drops a buffet of foods you can eat. |
| Spd. | 29 | 1 | Slice this guy's cheese for a chance at |
| Chp | 4 | | a treat! |

WEAKNESS

## GREEDY MOUSE

LVL **14**

*front*          *back*

| HP | 86 | EXP | 35 | Peculiar Cheese (20%) |
|----|-----|-----|----|-----|
| PP | 0 | DP | 0 | Nut Bread (20%) |

| | FRONT | BACK | |
|----|----|----|----|
| Off. | 47 | 1 | An inability to share led it to its battle |
| Def. | 16 | 11 | with you. Teach it a lesson with a couple |
| IQ | 15 | 15 | hits and hope that the little vermin |
| Spd. | 22 | 1 | leaves you a treat to snack on after the |
| Chp | 1,2,3 | | bout. |

WEAKNESS

## HEFTYHEAD

LVL **52**

*front*          *back*

| HP | 1864 | EXP | 2863 | Mystical Stick (3%) |
|----|-----|-----|----|-----|
| PP | 80 | DP | 312 | |

| | FRONT | BACK | |
|----|----|----|----|
| Off. | 172 | 1 | These toughies travel alone and wreak |
| Def. | 88 | 77 | havoc with nasty noggin attacks. Their |
| IQ | 88 | 88 | rhythm is awkward, so have Kumatora |
| Spd. | 40 | 1 | use PK Freeze. If you're lucky you'll |
| Chp | 7 | | find one of Lucas's best weapons at the |
| | | | end of battle. |

WEAKNESS

## HIPPO LAUNCHER (LAND)

LVL **60**

*front*          *back*

| HP | 998 | EXP | 4566 | Thud Charm (3%) |
|----|-----|-----|----|-----|
| PP | 0 | DP | 254 | |

| | FRONT | BACK | |
|----|----|----|----|
| Off. | 182 | 182 | This isn't your average household |
| Def. | 108 | 108 | hippopotamus. One blast from its |
| IQ | 50 | 50 | mouth-missile and you're mincemeat! |
| Spd. | 58 | 58 | Turn these land launchers around as |
| Chp | 8 | | much as you can to avoid their assault. |

WEAKNESS

## HIPPO LAUNCHER (WATER)

LVL **60**

*front*          *back*

| HP | 1623 | EXP | 4566 | Thud Charm (3%) |
|----|-----|-----|----|-----|
| PP | 0 | DP | 254 | |

| | FRONT | BACK | |
|----|----|----|----|
| Off. | 182 | 182 | This verion of the Hippo Launcher has |
| Def. | 108 | 108 | a load more HP and is much tougher. |
| IQ | 50 | 50 | One blast from its mouth-missile and |
| Spd. | 58 | 58 | you're mincemeat! |
| Chp | 8 | | |

WEAKNESS

## HORSANTULA

LVL **37**

*front*          *back*

| HP | 458 | EXP | 352 | Antidote (10%) |
|----|-----|-----|----|-----|
| PP | 60 | DP | 67 | |

| | FRONT | BACK | |
|----|----|----|----|
| Off. | 116 | 1 | These creepy horses sometimes hit |
| Def. | 57 | 47 | multiple times in the same turn, and |
| IQ | 27 | 27 | their bites are poisonous! They also |
| Spd. | 47 | 1 | have an overabundance of eyes, all of |
| Chp | 7 | | which can cry, so keep that in mind. |

WEAKNESS

## HUGE PILLBUG
**LVL 10**

*front* ... *back*

| HP | 60 | EXP | 30 | Nut Bread (30%) |
|---|---|---|---|---|
| PP | 0 | DP | 0 | **DROPS** |

| | FRONT | BACK |
|---|---|---|
| Off. | 35 | 1 |
| Def. | 20 | 12 |
| IQ | 10 | 10 |
| Spd. | 1 | 1 |
| Chp | 3 | |

Avoid this guy altogether by running it over with the Pork Bean. If you approach one, it will roll up into a ball. Just press A next to it to initiate battle. HUGE Pillbugs are very easy to take out and give a nice amount of EXP.

**WEAKNESS**

---

## JEALOUS BASS
**LVL 25**

| HP | 978 | EXP | 1176 | |
|---|---|---|---|---|
| PP | 32 | DP | 624 | **DROPS** |

| | FRONT | BACK |
|---|---|---|
| Off. | 58 | 1 |
| Def. | 25 | 20 |
| IQ | 20 | 20 |
| Spd. | 26 | 1 |
| Chp | 4 | |

It has powerful attacks on its own, it can team up with its cohorts to make groovy group attacks that put the hurt on you. Stop the music by using a PK LOVE blast and a bomb in the first round, then focus on covering your basses.

**WEAKNESS**

---

## K9000
**LVL 57**

*front* ... *back*

| HP | 1086 | EXP | 3529 | New Year's Eve Bomb (5%) |
|---|---|---|---|---|
| PP | 0 | DP | 230 | **DROPS** |

| | FRONT | BACK |
|---|---|---|
| Off. | 138 | 1 |
| Def. | 126 | 112 |
| IQ | 57 | 57 |
| Spd. | 38 | 1 |
| Chp | 8 | |

This recursive pooch may irritate your metallurgies. Give it an obedience lesson before it blinds you with its dazzling light.

**WEAKNESS**

---

## KING STATUE
**LVL 99**

| HP | 1 Million | EXP | 17586 | A bunch of DP! |
|---|---|---|---|---|
| PP | 0 | DP | 2400 | **DROPS** |

| | FRONT | BACK |
|---|---|---|
| Off. | 228 | 228 |
| Def. | 255 | 255 |
| IQ | 200 | 200 |
| Spd. | 78 | 1 |
| Chp | 8 | |

The "divine protector" of the city can take you down in a single turn if you let it. It will flail its arms around and slam its feet to deal mortal damage to your entire party. Guard and use the New Year's Eve Bomb, it's your only hope!

**WEAKNESS**

---

## LI'L BIG BRO
**LVL 14**

*front* ... *back*

| HP | 138 | EXP | 85 | Beef Jerky (70%) |
|---|---|---|---|---|
| PP | 0 | DP | 0 | **DROPS** |

| | FRONT | BACK |
|---|---|---|
| Off. | 47 | 1 |
| Def. | 20 | 1 |
| IQ | 15 | 11 |
| Spd. | 12 | 1 |
| Chp | 3 | |

That confused look on his face makes you wonder if he really wants to battle. Lighten the mood by making him laugh.

**WEAKNESS**

---

## LI'L MISS MARSHMALLOW
**LVL 30**

| HP | 2300 | EXP | 2864 | Friend's Yo-Yo 100% |
|---|---|---|---|---|
| PP | 0 | DP | 824 | **DROPS** |

| | FRONT | BACK |
|---|---|---|
| Off. | 110 | 132 |
| Def. | 46 | 55 |
| IQ | 23 | 30 |
| Spd. | 35 | 40 |
| Chp | 5 | |

This metal maniacal maid's insane HP and Offense stats belie her kindly steel exterior. Stick to the Offense/Defense Down strategy. Marshmallow's stats, PK Thunder is her best attack. Feel free to make use of a Saltwater gun.

**WEAKNESS**

## LINGERING SPIRIT

LVL 18

| | FRONT | BACK |
|---|---|---|
| HP | 65 | |
| PP | 18 | |
| EXP | 59 | |
| DP | 0 | |

Magic Gelatin (20%)

| | FRONT | BACK |
|---|---|---|
| Off. | 44 | 1 |
| Def. | 50 | 46 |
| IQ | 21 | 21 |
| Spd. | 17 | 1 |
| Chp | 2,5 | |

There's no use crying over past sorrows, especially if they're not yours. Put a stop to the flow of tears with a round of PSI Freeze!

WEAKNESS

## LORD PASSION

LVL 24

| | | |
|---|---|---|
| HP | 2897 | |
| PP | 0 | |
| EXP | 1086 | |
| DP | 280 | |

Mystical Shoes 100%

| | FRONT | BACK |
|---|---|---|
| Off. | 82 | 0 |
| Def. | 43 | 43 |
| IQ | 45 | 1 |
| Spd. | 34 | 1 |
| Chp | 5 | |

Take down this passionate poltergeist with a mix of PSI and combos. Kumatora's PK Fire works well, while Duster's Scary Mask and Smoke Bomb will make the battle easier.

WEAKNESS

## LOVE WALKER

LVL 56

LOVE

| | | |
|---|---|---|
| HP | 847 | |
| PP | 300 | |
| EXP | 3316 | |
| DP | 121 | |

Goddess Ribbon (3%)

| | FRONT | BACK |
|---|---|---|
| Off. | 132 | 1 |
| Def. | 77 | 64 |
| IQ | 68 | 68 |
| Spd. | 53 | 1 |
| Chp | 7 | |

Don't get burnt by these flaming lips. Its kisses are twice as disgusting as grandma's, but the difference is that you're free to use PK Fire on this thing.

WEAKNESS

## MAGMAN

LVL 40

| | | |
|---|---|---|
| HP | 594 | |
| PP | 150 | |
| EXP | 1194 | |
| DP | 278 | |

Double Jerky (20%)

| | FRONT | BACK |
|---|---|---|
| Off. | 135 | 1 |
| Def. | 72 | 60 |
| IQ | 39 | 39 |
| Spd. | 40 | 0 |
| Chp | 7 | |

The Magman is the toughest creature in the volcano. He has high HP and defense, can hurt everyone at once with fiery blasts, and can produce Pyreflies at will. Freeze him first — and fast!

WEAKNESS

## MASKED MAN

LVL 65

| | | |
|---|---|---|
| HP | 5000 | |
| PP | 999 | |
| EXP | 15474 | |
| DP | 1321 | |

| | FRONT | BACK |
|---|---|---|
| Off. | 165 | 1 |
| Def. | 120 | 110 |
| IQ | 64 | 64 |
| Spd. | 43 | 1 |
| Chp | 7 | |

His elemental defenses are tight, so raising your offense and going all-out physically may be your best bet. You're definitely going to need Lifeup Ω, and if Kumatora has learned it, PK Ground will make your life much easier.

WEAKNESS

## MASTER EDDY

LVL 47

| | | |
|---|---|---|
| HP | 2568 | |
| PP | 500 | |
| EXP | 0 | |
| DP | 721 | |

| | FRONT | BACK |
|---|---|---|
| Off. | 127 | 1 |
| Def. | 81 | 81 |
| IQ | 58 | 52 |
| Spd. | 52 | 1 |
| Chp | 7 | |

Master Eddy musters malicious maelstroms! His whirlpools will ebb away your HP, but you can strike back with PK Thunder and explosives. You might not last long without a shield, though...

WEAKNESS

## MECHA-DRAGO

LVL 20

| | FRONT | BACK |
|---|---|---|
| Off. | 60 | 1 |
| Def. | 34 | 23 |
| IQ | 8 | 8 |
| Spd. | 8 | 1 |
| Chp | 1 | |

| HP | 724 | EXP | 486 |
|---|---|---|---|
| PP | 0 | DP | 0 |

**DROPS**

Use the Drago Fang to pierce its hide. Without it, it's only one HP damage. Drago's War Cry reduces Flint's offense one level while Flint's 'Strengthen Up' increases it one level. Always keep your HP above 60, over 40 on the last blow.

WEAKNESS

## MECHA-LION

LVL 58

*front* *back*

| HP | 989 | EXP | 4286 | Cup of Lifenoodles (10%) |
|---|---|---|---|---|
| PP | 0 | DP | 372 | |

| | FRONT | BACK |
|---|---|---|
| Off. | 136 | 1 |
| Def. | 111 | 92 |
| IQ | 65 | 65 |
| Spd. | 68 | 1 |
| Chp | 8 | |

**DROPS**

It's a more complete version of the terror from the Chimera Lab, but it seems to have escaped before they finished installing its HP module. PK Thunder and a few combos will send it back to its den.

WEAKNESS

## MECHA-MOLE!

LVL 48

*front* *back*

| HP | 564 | EXP | 1590 | Bomb (3%) |
|---|---|---|---|---|
| PP | 0 | DP | 115 | |

| | FRONT | BACK |
|---|---|---|
| Off. | 142 | 1 |
| Def. | 72 | 61 |
| IQ | 56 | 56 |
| Spd. | 51 | 1 |
| Chp | 7 | |

**DROPS**

The bright red light atop their heads can signal other moles to aid in battle, so take them out before you're facing a squadron!

WEAKNESS

## MECHA-PORKY

LVL 60

| HP | 865 | EXP | 1580 |
|---|---|---|---|
| PP | 0 | DP | 21 |

| | FRONT | BACK |
|---|---|---|
| Off. | 135 | 1 |
| Def. | 148 | 1 |
| IQ | 45 | 1 |
| Spd. | 49 | 1 |
| Chp | 8 | |

**DROPS**

Not only will it explode when defeated, but you've got more than half a dozen of them, so make sure you've got a good healing strategy. PK Thunder passes by their PSI Shields. Stick with combos and bombs (no theif tools).

WEAKNESS

## MECHA-TURTLE

LVL 27

*front* *back*

| HP | 400 | EXP | 100 | Saltwater Gun (3%) |
|---|---|---|---|---|
| PP | 0 | DP | 69 | |

| | FRONT | BACK |
|---|---|---|
| Off. | 80 | 80 |
| Def. | 40 | 32 |
| IQ | 31 | 32 |
| Spd. | 10 | 27 |
| Chp | 5,7 | |

**DROPS**

Sneaking up on this turtle is not such a good idea—strapped to the back of its shell is an array of weapons! Fight this reptile head on.

WEAKNESS

## MEN'S ROOM SIGN

LVL 57

*front* *back*

| HP | 1222 | EXP | 3014 | Magic Pudding (10%) |
|---|---|---|---|---|
| PP | 0 | DP | 200 | |

| | FRONT | BACK |
|---|---|---|
| Off. | 99 | 1 |
| Def. | 82 | 72 |
| IQ | 64 | 64 |
| Spd. | 42 | 1 |
| Chp | 8 | |

**DROPS**

You won't see it coming when this iconic irritation blows you to kingdom come with PK Starstorm. It's got tons of HP, so if you're not good with combos, setting up a PSI Shield might be a good idea.

WEAKNESS

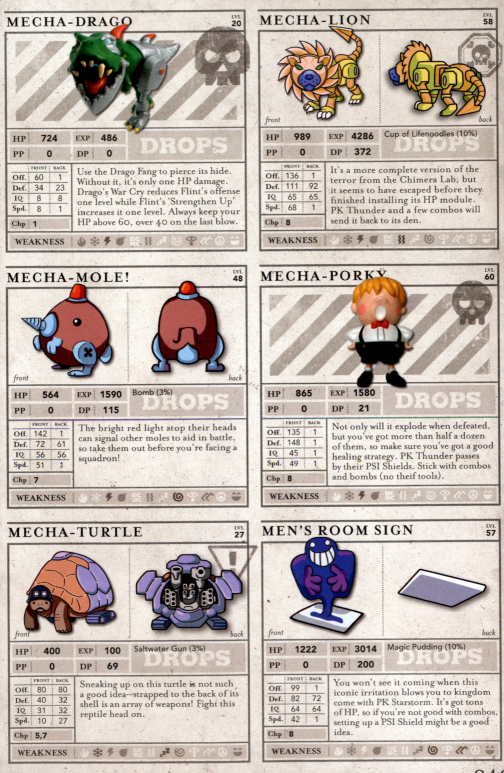

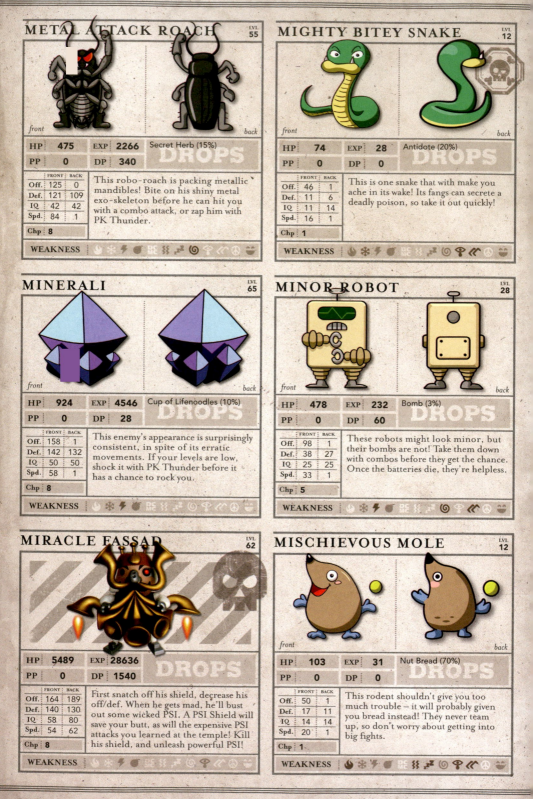

## METAL ATTACK ROACH
LVL 55

*front*    *back*

| | | | | |
|---|---|---|---|---|
| HP | 475 | EXP | 2266 | Secret Herb (15%) |
| PP | 0 | DP | 340 | DROPS |

| | FRONT | BACK |
|---|---|---|
| Off. | 125 | 0 |
| Def. | 121 | 109 |
| IQ | 42 | 42 |
| Spd. | 84 | 1 |
| Chp | 8 | |

This robo-roach is packing metallic mandibles! Bite on his shiny metal exo-skeleton before he can hit you with a combo attack, or zap him with PK Thunder.

WEAKNESS

## MIGHTY BITEY SNAKE
LVL 12

*front*    *back*

| | | | | |
|---|---|---|---|---|
| HP | 74 | EXP | 28 | Antidote (20%) |
| PP | 0 | DP | 0 | DROPS |

| | FRONT | BACK |
|---|---|---|
| Off. | 46 | 1 |
| Def. | 11 | 6 |
| IQ | 11 | 14 |
| Spd. | 16 | 1 |
| Chp | 1 | |

This is one snake that with make you ache in its wake! Its fangs can secrete a deadly poison, so take it out quickly!

WEAKNESS

## MINERALI
LVL 65

*front*    *back*

| | | | | |
|---|---|---|---|---|
| HP | 924 | EXP | 4546 | Cup of Lifenoodles (10%) |
| PP | 0 | DP | 28 | DROPS |

| | FRONT | BACK |
|---|---|---|
| Off. | 158 | 1 |
| Def. | 142 | 132 |
| IQ | 50 | 50 |
| Spd. | 58 | 1 |
| Chp | 8 | |

This enemy's appearance is surprisingly consistent, in spite of its erratic movements. If your levels are low, shock it with PK Thunder before it has a chance to rock you.

WEAKNESS

## MINOR ROBOT
LVL 28

*front*    *back*

| | | | | |
|---|---|---|---|---|
| HP | 478 | EXP | 232 | Bomb (3%) |
| PP | 0 | DP | 60 | DROPS |

| | FRONT | BACK |
|---|---|---|
| Off. | 98 | 1 |
| Def. | 38 | 27 |
| IQ | 25 | 25 |
| Spd. | 33 | 1 |
| Chp | 5 | |

These robots might look minor, but their bombs are not! Take them down with combos before they get the chance. Once the batteries die, they're helpless.

WEAKNESS

## MIRACLE FASSAD
LVL 62

| | | | | |
|---|---|---|---|---|
| HP | 5489 | EXP | 28636 | DROPS |
| PP | 0 | DP | 1540 | |

| | FRONT | BACK |
|---|---|---|
| Off. | 164 | 189 |
| Def. | 140 | 130 |
| IQ | 58 | 80 |
| Spd. | 54 | 62 |
| Chp | 8 | |

First snatch off his shield, decrease his off/def. When he gets mad, he'll bust out some wicked PSI. A PSI Shield will save your butt, as will the expensive PSI attacks you learned at the temple! Kill his shield, and unleash powerful PSI!

WEAKNESS

## MISCHIEVOUS MOLE
LVL 12

*front*    *back*

| | | | | |
|---|---|---|---|---|
| HP | 103 | EXP | 31 | Nut Bread (70%) |
| PP | 0 | DP | 0 | DROPS |

| | FRONT | BACK |
|---|---|---|
| Off. | 50 | 1 |
| Def. | 17 | 11 |
| IQ | 14 | 14 |
| Spd. | 20 | 1 |
| Chp | 1 | |

This rodent shouldn't give you too much trouble – it will probably given you bread instead! They never team up, so don't worry about getting into big fights.

WEAKNESS

## MOBILE GRAVE
LVL 15

| HP | 158 | EXP | 60 |
|----|-----|-----|----|
| PP | 0 | DP | 0 |

**DROPS** Running Bomb (10%)

| | FRONT | BACK |
|----|----|----|
| Off. | 63 | 1 |
| Def. | 26 | 23 |
| IQ | 10 | 1 |
| Spd. | 4 | 1 |
| Chp | 2,3 | |

At night it's not just the dead that go walking. Stoneface here can be a tough customer, but a Thunder Bomb will help bring him down.

WEAKNESS

## MOLE CRICKET
LVL 5

| HP | 45 | EXP | 2 |
|----|-----|-----|----|
| PP | 0 | DP | 0 |

**DROPS**

| | FRONT | BACK |
|----|----|----|
| Off. | 10 | 1 |
| Def. | 3 | 1 |
| IQ | 2 | 1 |
| Spd. | 1 | 1 |
| Chp | Prologue | |

He may talk tough, but even against a couple of kids this insect doesn't stand much of a chance. It's your first battle, so take it slow and keep it simple! In the second battle with the Mole Cricket, his speed rose to 255, but it doesn't help.

WEAKNESS

## MONKALRUS
LVL 47

| HP | 668 | EXP | 1071 |
|----|-----|-----|----|
| PP | 0 | DP | 273 |

Luxury Banana (15%)
Mystical Gloves (3%)

| | FRONT | BACK |
|----|----|----|
| Off. | 168 | 1 |
| Def. | 80 | 70 |
| IQ | 32 | 32 |
| Spd. | 43 | 1 |
| Chp | 7 | |

You must stay on tusk if you want to triumph over this ape. He hits hard and can spread fleas, so try to take him out fast. Perhaps you'll get lucky and find the powerful gloves he drops!

WEAKNESS

## MR. BATTY
LVL 10

| HP | 56 | EXP | 20 |
|----|-----|-----|----|
| PP | 0 | DP | 0 |

Nut Cookie (2%)
Nut Bread (20%)

| | FRONT | BACK |
|----|----|----|
| Off. | 41 | 1 |
| Def. | 14 | 9 |
| IQ | 10 | 10 |
| Spd. | 15 | 1 |
| Chp | 1,2,7 | |

It's nothing more than an average bat, man. A few simple swats at this nocturnal nuisance will send it flying back to its cave.

WEAKNESS

## MR. GENETOR
LVL 35

| HP | 3333 | EXP | 4389 |
|----|-----|-----|----|
| PP | 0 | DP | 840 |

**DROPS**

| | FRONT | BACK |
|----|----|----|
| Off. | 120 | 1 |
| Def. | 55 | 42 |
| IQ | 35 | 35 |
| Spd. | 38 | 1 |
| Chp | 5 | |

Don't hit him directly while he's charged up. Use PK Special, Freeze, Off/Def down tools, and explosives. When the discharge zap occurs, heal up and start attacking him with physical attacks when he is down.

WEAKNESS

## MR. PASSION
LVL 20

| HP | 630 | EXP | 340 |
|----|-----|-----|----|
| PP | 0 | DP | 0 |

**DROPS**

| | FRONT | BACK |
|----|----|----|
| Off. | 60 | 1 |
| Def. | 25 | 1 |
| IQ | 18 | 1 |
| Spd. | 20 | 1 |
| Chp | 2 | |

Use your Smoke Bomb to reduce him to tears and decrease his accuracy. With that out of the way, lower his offense and defense a few times, and then start attacking him with any bombs you've picked up along the way.

WEAKNESS

## MRS. LAVA

LVL 40

*front* *back*

| | | | | |
|---|---|---|---|---|
| HP | 461 | EXP | 837 | Meteotite (5%) |
| PP | 120 | DP | 484 | |

| | FRONT | BACK |
|---|---|---|
| Off. | 108 | 1 |
| Def. | 58 | 48 |
| IQ | 43 | 43 |
| Spd. | 45 | 0 |
| Chp | 7 | |

Ice this old flame as soon as possible. Otherwise, her PK Fire γ will quickly sap your party's HP. Of course, if you brought along some Flame Pendants you won't have too much trouble.

WEAKNESS

## MUTTSHROOM

LVL 18

*front* *back*

| | | | | |
|---|---|---|---|---|
| HP | 248 | EXP | 62 | Doggy Biscuit (10%) |
| PP | 0 | DP | 40 | |

| | FRONT | BACK |
|---|---|---|
| Off. | 58 | 1 |
| Def. | 25 | 10 |
| IQ | 17 | 17 |
| Spd. | 27 | 1 |
| Chp | 4,5,7 | |

Mush, boy! As the name implies, this pooch can spread its spores and make you feel funky. These dangerous dogs are slow enough to outrun, so conserve your healing supplies unless you're looking to level up.

WEAKNESS

## MYSTERY METAL MONKEY

LVL 50

RARE

*front* *back*

| | | | | |
|---|---|---|---|---|
| HP | 12 | EXP | Good Time | Made-You-Look (20%) |
| PP | 125 | DP | 120 | |

| | FRONT | BACK |
|---|---|---|
| Off. | 120 | 1 |
| Def. | 255 | 255 |
| IQ | 50 | 50 |
| Spd. | 255 | 1 |
| Chp | 7 | |

You can usually get a free round of attacks on these shy simians. Speed and defense are top-notch, so string together a good combo. If they get an attack in, they pack PK Fire, so use PK Thunder to short-circuit them.

WEAKNESS

## N.K. CYBORG

LVL 64

*front* *back*

| | | | | |
|---|---|---|---|---|
| HP | 7548 | EXP | 34381 | |
| PP | 0 | DP | 1600 | |

| | FRONT | BACK |
|---|---|---|
| Off. | 232 | 232 |
| Def. | 189 | 189 |
| IQ | 52 | 52 |
| Spd. | 43 | 43 |
| Chp | 7 | |

A tank with a wide arsenal of physical attacks, plus the occasional electric shock. Take down its Counter and set up your own to deflect its insane "End of the Century" beam. The time to use your most powerful PSI attacks is now!

WEAKNESS

## NAUGHTY MUSHROOM

LVL 39

*front* *back*

| | | | | |
|---|---|---|---|---|
| HP | 361 | EXP | 486 | Bread Roll (15%) |
| PP | 0 | DP | 102 | |

| | FRONT | BACK |
|---|---|---|
| Off. | 98 | 1 |
| Def. | 48 | 43 |
| IQ | 32 | 32 |
| Spd. | 40 | 1 |
| Chp | 7 | |

These seemingly arrogant tunnel fungi can't be trusted. If you're cornered by a gang of them, burn them up with PK Fire before they start spreading their spores.

WEAKNESS

## NAVY SQUEAL

LVL 45

*front* *back*

| | | | | |
|---|---|---|---|---|
| HP | 563 | EXP | 774 | Pork Stew (10%) |
| PP | 0 | DP | 118 | |

| | FRONT | BACK |
|---|---|---|
| Off. | 115 | 1 |
| Def. | 70 | 58 |
| IQ | 37 | 45 |
| Spd. | 45 | 1 |
| Chp | 7 | |

These underwater Pigmasks show no new battle tactics and usually travel solo. They're also so severely underpaid that they might just vacate the battle on a whim.

WEAKNESS

## NEGATIVE MAN

LVL 50

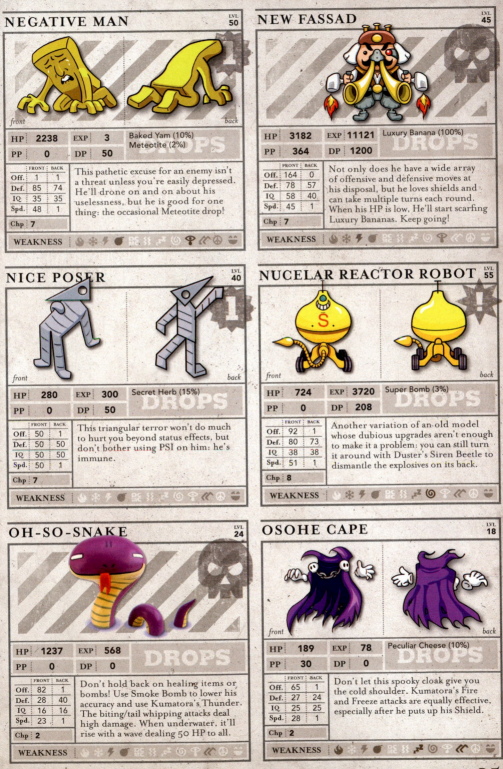

*front* *back*

| HP | 2238 | EXP | 3 | Baked Yam (10%) |
|----|------|-----|---|-----------------|
| PP | 0 | DP | 50 | Meteotite (2%) |

| | FRONT | BACK |
|-----|-------|------|
| Off. | 1 | 1 |
| Def. | 85 | 74 |
| IQ | 35 | 35 |
| Spd. | 48 | 1 |
| Chp | 7 | |

This pathetic excuse for an enemy isn't a threat unless you're easily depressed. He'll drone on and on about his uselessness, but he is good for one thing: the occasional Meteotite drop!

WEAKNESS

## NEW FASSAD

LVL 45

| HP | 3182 | EXP | 11121 | Luxury Banana (100%) |
|----|------|-----|-------|----------------------|
| PP | 364 | DP | 1200 | |

| | FRONT | BACK |
|-----|-------|------|
| Off. | 164 | 0 |
| Def. | 78 | 57 |
| IQ | 58 | 40 |
| Spd. | 45 | 1 |
| Chp | 7 | |

Not only does he have a wide array of offensive and defensive moves at his disposal, but he loves shields and can take multiple turns each round. When his HP is low, He'll start scarfing Luxury Bananas. Keep going!

WEAKNESS

## NICE POSER

LVL 40

*front* *back*

| HP | 280 | EXP | 300 | Secret Herb (15%) |
|----|-----|-----|-----|-------------------|
| PP | 0 | DP | 50 | |

| | FRONT | BACK |
|-----|-------|------|
| Off. | 50 | 1 |
| Def. | 50 | 50 |
| IQ | 50 | 50 |
| Spd. | 50 | 1 |
| Chp | 7 | |

This triangular terror won't do much to hurt you beyond status effects, but don't bother using PSI on him: he's immune.

WEAKNESS

## NUCELAR REACTOR ROBOT

LVL 55

*front* *back*

| HP | 724 | EXP | 3720 | Super Bomb (3%) |
|----|-----|-----|------|-----------------|
| PP | 0 | DP | 208 | |

| | FRONT | BACK |
|-----|-------|------|
| Off. | 92 | 1 |
| Def. | 80 | 73 |
| IQ | 38 | 38 |
| Spd. | 51 | 1 |
| Chp | 8 | |

Another variation of an old model whose dubious upgrades aren't enough to make it a problem: you can still turn it around with Duster's Siren Beetle to dismantle the explosives on its back.

WEAKNESS

## OH-SO-SNAKE

LVL 24

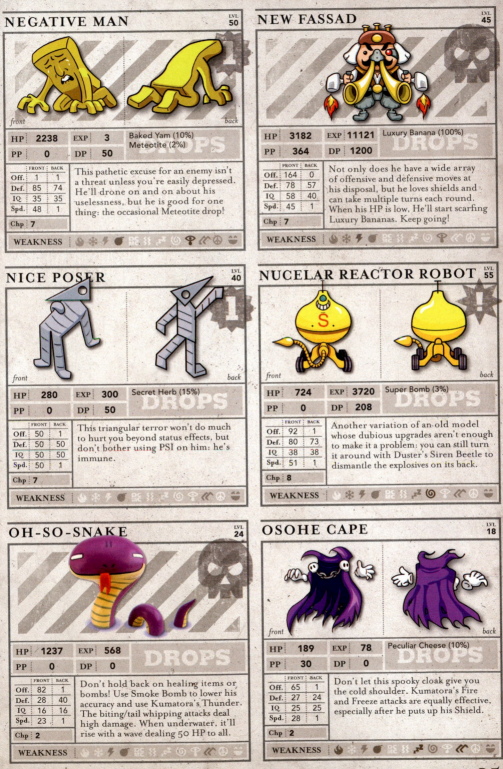

| HP | 1237 | EXP | 568 | |
|----|------|-----|-----|---|
| PP | 0 | DP | 0 | |

| | FRONT | BACK |
|-----|-------|------|
| Off. | 82 | 1 |
| Def. | 28 | 40 |
| IQ | 16 | 16 |
| Spd. | 23 | 1 |
| Chp | 2 | |

Don't hold back on healing items or bombs! Use Smoke Bomb to lower his accuracy and use Kumatora's Thunder. The biting/tail whipping attacks deal high damage. When underwater, it'll rise with a wave dealing 50 HP to all.

WEAKNESS

## OSOHE CAPE

LVL 18

*front* *back*

| HP | 189 | EXP | 78 | Peculiar Cheese (10%) |
|----|-----|-----|----|----------------------|
| PP | 30 | DP | 0 | |

| | FRONT | BACK |
|-----|-------|------|
| Off. | 65 | 1 |
| Def. | 27 | 24 |
| IQ | 25 | 25 |
| Spd. | 28 | 1 |
| Chp | 2 | |

Don't let this spooky cloak give you the cold shoulder. Kumatora's Fire and Freeze attacks are equally effective, especially after he puts up his Shield.

WEAKNESS

## OSTRELEPHANT

LVL 37

*front* *back*

| HP | 400 | EXP | 374 | Beef Jerky (5%) |
|----|-----|-----|-----|-----|
| PP | 0 | DP | 75 | DROPS |

| | FRONT | BACK |
|----|----|----|
| Off. | 105 | 1 |
| Def. | 50 | 42 |
| IQ | 25 | 25 |
| Spd. | 48 | 1 |
| Chp | 4,5,7 | |

The odd roar/squawk they emit as they dash toward you is truly gut-wrenching. They may look silly, but their physical strength is something you'll always remember! Steer clear unless you've got plenty of PP and healing items.

WEAKNESS

## PARENTAL KANGASHARK

LVL 25

*front* *back*

| HP | 289 | EXP | 93 | Beef Jerky (10%) |
|----|-----|-----|-----|-----|
| PP | 0 | DP | 50 | DROPS |

| | FRONT | BACK |
|----|----|----|
| Off. | 82 | 1 |
| Def. | 24 | 14 |
| IQ | 17 | 18 |
| Spd. | 28 | 1 |
| Chp | 5,7 | |

This overprotective mother is a formidable foe who child can provide more than just moral support! Use PK Freeze to stop it cold.

WEAKNESS

## PIGMASK

LVL 18

*front* *back*

| HP | 160 | EXP | 61 | Bag of Pork Chips (50%) |
|----|-----|-----|-----|-----|
| PP | 0 | DP | 0 | DROPS |

| | FRONT | BACK |
|----|----|----|
| Off. | 55 | 1 |
| Def. | 20 | 15 |
| IQ | 10 | 22 |
| Spd. | 23 | 1 |
| Chp | 2,3,7 | |

They may be tough on the eye and the ear, but they're not too tough in battle. Look out for their defense-lowering beams and cowardly kicks.

WEAKNESS

## PIGMASK CAPTAIN

LVL 42

*front* *back*

| HP | 453 | EXP | 854 | Cup of Pork Noodles (10%) |
|----|-----|-----|-----|-----|
| PP | 0 | DP | 150 | DROPS |

| | FRONT | BACK |
|----|----|----|
| Off. | 121 | 1 |
| Def. | 52 | 47 |
| IQ | 28 | 28 |
| Spd. | 43 | 0 |
| Chp | 7 | |

You might want to take this Pigmask seriously. His gun is pretty strong and he can take quite a few hits. DCMC goods might distract him, but you should focus on taking him out quick.

WEAKNESS

## PIGMASK COLONEL

LVL 64

*front* *back*

| HP | 895 | EXP | 3910 | King Burger (15%) |
|----|-----|-----|-----|-----|
| PP | 0 | DP | 500 | Awesome Cloak (5%) |

| | FRONT | BACK |
|----|----|----|
| Off. | 168 | 1 |
| Def. | 100 | 88 |
| IQ | 45 | 45 |
| Spd. | 59 | 1 |
| Chp | 7,8 | |

You'll need a Shield Snatcher in the first round, and maybe later if he uses his shield device. PK Freeze and Bombs are effective against him, and while he can really put up a fight, don't waste your PP; there's a bigger battle coming!

WEAKNESS

## PIGMASK MAJOR

LVL 60

*front* *back*

| HP | 721 | EXP | 2788 | Hot Dog Sushi (10%) |
|----|-----|-----|-----|-----|
| PP | 0 | DP | 300 | DROPS |

| | FRONT | BACK |
|----|----|----|
| Off. | 147 | 1 |
| Def. | 75 | 64 |
| IQ | 38 | 38 |
| Spd. | 62 | 1 |
| Chp | 7,8 | |

These higher-ranking Pigmasks are rather tough, as far as Pigmasks go. Their guns pack a punch, and sometimes they'll try to stick a time bomb on you. Use PK Fire and PK Love to take groups out quickly.

WEAKNESS

## PIGTUNIA
**LVL 35**

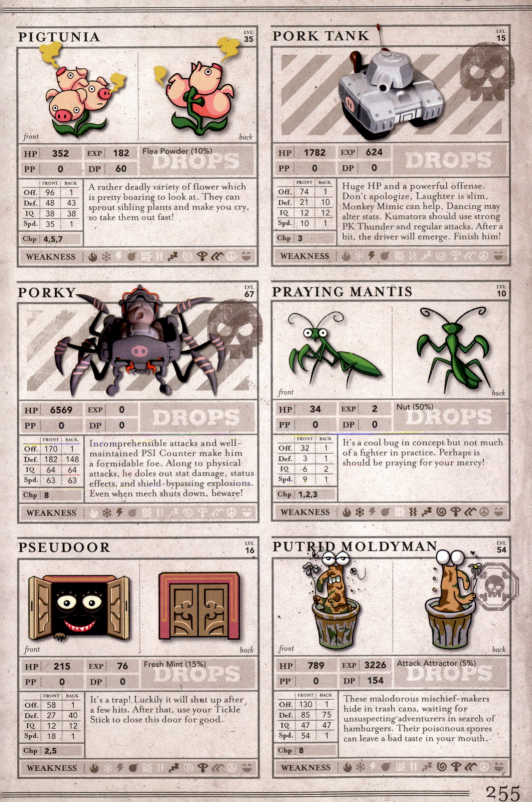

*front*     *back*

| HP | 352 | EXP | 182 | Flea Powder (10%) |
|---|---|---|---|---|
| PP | 0 | DP | 60 | **DROPS** |

| | FRONT | BACK |
|---|---|---|
| Off. | 96 | 1 |
| Def. | 48 | 43 |
| IQ | 38 | 38 |
| Spd. | 35 | 1 |
| Chp | 4,5,7 | |

A rather deadly variety of flower which is pretty boaring to look at. They can sprout sibling plants and make you cry, so take them out fast!

**WEAKNESS**

## PORK TANK
**LVL 15**

| HP | 1782 | EXP | 624 | |
|---|---|---|---|---|
| PP | 0 | DP | 0 | **DROPS** |

| | FRONT | BACK |
|---|---|---|
| Off. | 74 | 1 |
| Def. | 21 | 10 |
| IQ | 12 | 12 |
| Spd. | 10 | 1 |
| Chp | 3 | |

Huge HP and a powerful offense. Don't apologize, Laughter is slim, Monkey Mimic can help, Dancing may alter stats. Kumatora should use strong PK Thunder and regular attacks. After a bit, the driver will emerge. Finish him!

**WEAKNESS**

## PORKY
**LVL 67**

| HP | 6569 | EXP | 0 | |
|---|---|---|---|---|
| PP | 0 | DP | 0 | **DROPS** |

| | FRONT | BACK |
|---|---|---|
| Off. | 170 | 1 |
| Def. | 182 | 148 |
| IQ | 64 | 64 |
| Spd. | 63 | 63 |
| Chp | 8 | |

Incomprehensible attacks and well-maintained PSI Counter make him a formidable foe. Along to physical attacks, he doles out stat damage, status effects, and shield-bypassing explosions. Even when mech shuts down, beware!

**WEAKNESS**

## PRAYING MANTIS
**LVL 10**

*front*     *back*

| HP | 34 | EXP | 2 | Nut (50%) |
|---|---|---|---|---|
| PP | 0 | DP | 0 | **DROPS** |

| | FRONT | BACK |
|---|---|---|
| Off. | 32 | 1 |
| Def. | 3 | 1 |
| IQ | 6 | 2 |
| Spd. | 9 | 1 |
| Chp | 1,2,3 | |

It's a cool bug in concept but not much of a fighter in practice. Perhaps is should be praying for your mercy!

**WEAKNESS**

## PSEUDOOR
**LVL 16**

*front*     *back*

| HP | 215 | EXP | 76 | Fresh Mint (15%) |
|---|---|---|---|---|
| PP | 0 | DP | 0 | **DROPS** |

| | FRONT | BACK |
|---|---|---|
| Off. | 58 | 1 |
| Def. | 27 | 40 |
| IQ | 12 | 12 |
| Spd. | 18 | 1 |
| Chp | 2,5 | |

It's a trap! Luckily it will shut up after a few hits. After that, use your Tickle Stick to close this door for good.

**WEAKNESS**

## PUTRID MOLDYMAN
**LVL 54**

*front*     *back*

| HP | 789 | EXP | 3226 | Attack Attractor (5%) |
|---|---|---|---|---|
| PP | 0 | DP | 154 | **DROPS** |

| | FRONT | BACK |
|---|---|---|
| Off. | 130 | 1 |
| Def. | 85 | 75 |
| IQ | 47 | 47 |
| Spd. | 54 | 1 |
| Chp | 8 | |

These malodorous mischief-makers hide in trash cans, waiting for unsuspecting adventurers in search of hamburgers. Their poisonous spores can leave a bad taste in your mouth.

**WEAKNESS**

## PYREFLY
LVL 37

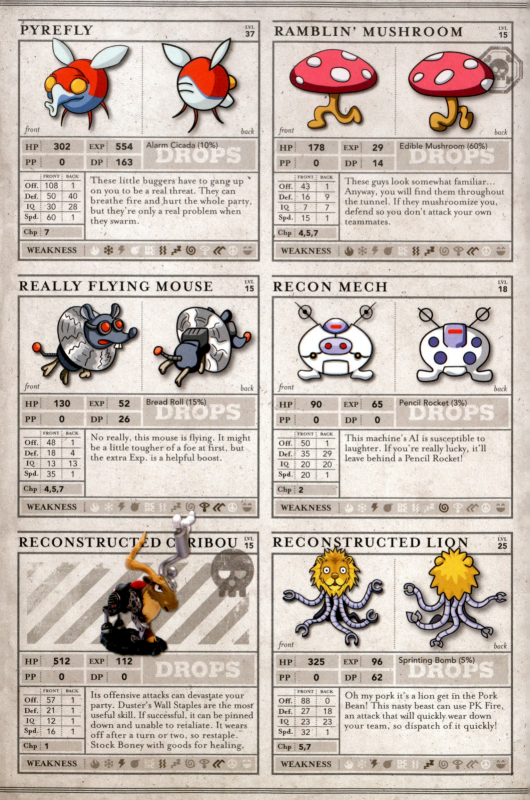

*front*    *back*

| HP | 302 | EXP | 554 | DROPS |
|---|---|---|---|---|
| PP | 0 | DP | 163 | Alarm Cicada (10%) |

| | FRONT | BACK |
|---|---|---|
| Off. | 108 | 1 |
| Def. | 50 | 40 |
| IQ | 30 | 28 |
| Spd. | 60 | 1 |
| Chp | 7 | |

These little buggers have to gang up on you to be a real threat. They can breathe fire and hurt the whole party, but they're only a real problem when they swarm.

WEAKNESS

## RAMBLIN' MUSHROOM
LVL 15

*front*    *back*

| HP | 178 | EXP | 29 | DROPS |
|---|---|---|---|---|
| PP | 0 | DP | 14 | Edible Mushroom (60%) |

| | FRONT | BACK |
|---|---|---|
| Off. | 43 | 1 |
| Def. | 16 | 9 |
| IQ | 7 | 7 |
| Spd. | 15 | 1 |
| Chp | 4,5,7 | |

These guys look somewhat familiar... Anyway, you will find them throughout the tunnel. If they mushroomize you, defend so you don't attack your own teammates.

WEAKNESS

## REALLY FLYING MOUSE
LVL 15

*front*    *back*

| HP | 130 | EXP | 52 | DROPS |
|---|---|---|---|---|
| PP | 0 | DP | 26 | Bread Roll (15%) |

| | FRONT | BACK |
|---|---|---|
| Off. | 48 | 1 |
| Def. | 18 | 4 |
| IQ | 13 | 13 |
| Spd. | 35 | 1 |
| Chp | 4,5,7 | |

No really, this mouse is flying. It might be a little tougher of a foe at first, but the extra Exp. is a helpful boost.

WEAKNESS

## RECON MECH
LVL 18

*front*    *back*

| HP | 90 | EXP | 65 | DROPS |
|---|---|---|---|---|
| PP | 0 | DP | 0 | Pencil Rocket (3%) |

| | FRONT | BACK |
|---|---|---|
| Off. | 50 | 1 |
| Def. | 35 | 29 |
| IQ | 20 | 20 |
| Spd. | 20 | 1 |
| Chp | 2 | |

This machine's AI is susceptible to laughter. If you're really lucky, it'll leave behind a Pencil Rocket!

WEAKNESS

## RECONSTRUCTED CARIBOU
LVL 15

| HP | 512 | EXP | 112 | DROPS |
|---|---|---|---|---|
| PP | 0 | DP | 0 | |

| | FRONT | BACK |
|---|---|---|
| Off. | 57 | 1 |
| Def. | 21 | 1 |
| IQ | 12 | 1 |
| Spd. | 16 | 1 |
| Chp | 1 | |

Its offensive attacks can devastate your party. Duster's Wall Staples are the most useful skill. If successful, it can be pinned down and unable to retaliate. It wears off after a turn or two, so restaple. Stock Boney with goods for healing.

WEAKNESS

## RECONSTRUCTED LION
LVL 25

*front*    *back*

| HP | 325 | EXP | 96 | DROPS |
|---|---|---|---|---|
| PP | 0 | DP | 62 | Sprinting Bomb (5%) |

| | FRONT | BACK |
|---|---|---|
| Off. | 88 | 0 |
| Def. | 27 | 18 |
| IQ | 23 | 23 |
| Spd. | 32 | 1 |
| Chp | 5,7 | |

Oh my pork it's a lion get in the Pork Bean! This nasty beast can use PK Fire, an attack that will quickly wear down your team, so dispatch of it quickly!

WEAKNESS

## RECONSTRUCTED MOLE
**LVL 16**

*front* *back*

| HP | 165 | EXP | 42 | **DROPS** Bread Roll (10%) |
| PP | 0 | DP | 33 | |

| | FRONT | BACK |
| Off. | 64 | 1 |
| Def. | 18 | 8 |
| IQ | 14 | 14 |
| Spd. | 18 | 1 |
| Chp | 4,5,7 | |

As if a mole needed a more effective way to tear up a lawn. Don't let them gang up on you because those drills are powerful!

**WEAKNESS**

---

## RETURN OF OCTOBOT
**LVL 57**

*front* *back*

| HP | 777 | EXP | 3164 | **DROPS** Rich Parfait (15%) |
| PP | 0 | DP | 432 | |

| | FRONT | BACK |
| Off. | 128 | 1 |
| Def. | 78 | 68 |
| IQ | 35 | 35 |
| Spd. | 58 | 1 |
| Chp | 8 | |

It's back! Even with its upgrades, the Octobot, a staple of discerning time-traveling tyrants, still retains its susceptibility to thunder.

**WEAKNESS**

---

## RHINOCEROCKET
**LVL 27**

*front* *back*

| HP | 400 | EXP | 171 | **DROPS** Pencil Rocket (10%) |
| PP | 0 | DP | 178 | |

| | FRONT | BACK |
| Off. | 80 | 1 |
| Def. | 27 | 30 |
| IQ | 19 | 19 |
| Spd. | 34 | 1 |
| Chp | 5,7 | |

This speedy foe flies through the air with the greatest of ease and malice. When he attacks, he hits everyone in the party—twice! Take him down fast with your strongest attacks.

**WEAKNESS**

---

## RHINOCEROCKET MARK II
**LVL 56**

*front* *back*

| HP | 832 | EXP | 3628 | **DROPS** Pencil Rocket (10%) |
| PP | 0 | DP | 178 | |

| | FRONT | BACK |
| Off. | 159 | 1 |
| Def. | 89 | 76 |
| IQ | 47 | 83 |
| Spd. | 59 | 1 |
| Chp | 8 | |

The Rhinocerocket's moves haven't really changed, but it's still as dangerous as ever. A shot of PK Freeze should go a long way towards decommissioning it.

**WEAKNESS**

---

## ROAD BLOCK
**LVL 28**

*front* *back*

| HP | 333 | EXP | 108 | **DROPS** Fresh Mint (20%) |
| PP | 68 | DP | 75 | |

| | FRONT | BACK |
| Off. | 90 | 1 |
| Def. | 39 | 32 |
| IQ | 23 | 23 |
| Spd. | 40 | 1 |
| Chp | 5,7 | |

These traffic enforcers will try Hypnosis α on you, and if that doesn't work they'll call in reinforcements!

**WEAKNESS**

---

## ROCK LOBSTER
**LVL 45**

*front* *back*

| HP | 589 | EXP | 865 | **DROPS** Giant Abalone Steak (10%) |
| PP | 48 | DP | 148 | |

| | FRONT | BACK |
| Off. | 172 | 1 |
| Def. | 100 | 85 |
| IQ | 28 | 28 |
| Spd. | 40 | 1 |
| Chp | 7 | |

You may find yourself in a pinch with these guys. Their defenses are rock-solid, so hit them hard with PK Thunder or Freeze. With any luck you'll fry 'em or freeze 'em solid!

**WEAKNESS**

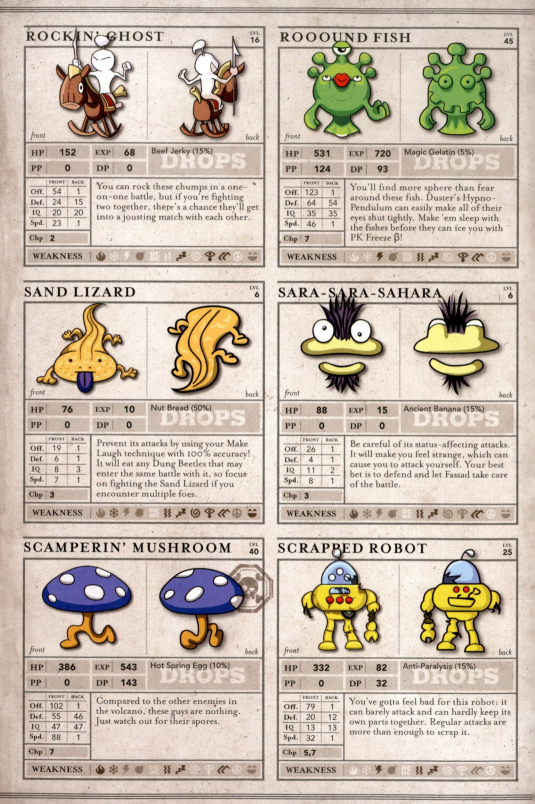

## ROCKIN' GHOST

**LVL 16**

| | | | |
|---|---|---|---|
| HP | 152 | EXP | 68 |
| PP | 0 | DP | 0 |

| | FRONT | BACK |
|---|---|---|
| Off. | 54 | 1 |
| Def. | 24 | 15 |
| IQ | 20 | 20 |
| Spd. | 23 | 1 |
| Chp | 2 | |

Beef Jerky (15%)

**DROPS**

You can rock these chumps in a one-on-one battle, but if you're fighting two together, there's a chance they'll get into a jousting match with each other.

**WEAKNESS**

## ROOOUND FISH

**LVL 45**

| | | | |
|---|---|---|---|
| HP | 531 | EXP | 720 |
| PP | 124 | DP | 93 |

| | FRONT | BACK |
|---|---|---|
| Off. | 123 | 1 |
| Def. | 64 | 54 |
| IQ | 35 | 35 |
| Spd. | 46 | 1 |
| Chp | 7 | |

Magic Gelatin (5%)

**DROPS**

You'll find more sphere than fear around these fish. Duster's Hypno-Pendulum can easily make all of their eyes shut tightly. Make 'em sleep with the fishes before they can ice you with PK Freeze β!

**WEAKNESS**

## SAND LIZARD

**LVL 6**

| | | | |
|---|---|---|---|
| HP | 76 | EXP | 10 |
| PP | 0 | DP | 0 |

| | FRONT | BACK |
|---|---|---|
| Off. | 19 | 1 |
| Def. | 6 | 1 |
| IQ | 8 | 3 |
| Spd. | 7 | 1 |
| Chp | 3 | |

Nut Bread (50%)

**DROPS**

Prevent its attacks by using your Make Laugh technique with 100% accuracy! It will eat any Dung Beetles that may enter the same battle with it, so focus on fighting the Sand Lizard if you encounter multiple foes.

**WEAKNESS**

## SARA-SARA-SAHARA

**LVL 6**

| | | | |
|---|---|---|---|
| HP | 88 | EXP | 15 |
| PP | 0 | DP | 0 |

| | FRONT | BACK |
|---|---|---|
| Off. | 26 | 1 |
| Def. | 4 | 1 |
| IQ | 11 | 2 |
| Spd. | 8 | 1 |
| Chp | 3 | |

Ancient Banana (15%)

**DROPS**

Be careful of its status-affecting attacks. It will make you feel strange, which can cause you to attack yourself. Your best bet is to defend and let Fassad take care of the battle.

**WEAKNESS**

## SCAMPERIN' MUSHROOM

**LVL 40**

| | | | |
|---|---|---|---|
| HP | 386 | EXP | 543 |
| PP | 0 | DP | 143 |

| | FRONT | BACK |
|---|---|---|
| Off. | 102 | 1 |
| Def. | 55 | 46 |
| IQ | 47 | 47 |
| Spd. | 88 | 1 |
| Chp | 7 | |

Hot Spring Egg (10%)

**DROPS**

Compared to the other enemies in the volcano, these guys are nothing. Just watch out for their spores.

**WEAKNESS**

## SCRAPPED ROBOT

**LVL 25**

| | | | |
|---|---|---|---|
| HP | 332 | EXP | 82 |
| PP | 0 | DP | 32 |

| | FRONT | BACK |
|---|---|---|
| Off. | 79 | 1 |
| Def. | 20 | 12 |
| IQ | 13 | 13 |
| Spd. | 32 | 1 |
| Chp | 5,7 | |

Anti-Paralysis (15%)

**DROPS**

You've gotta feel bad for this robot; it can barely attack and can hardly keep its own parts together. Regular attacks are more than enough to scrap it.

**WEAKNESS**

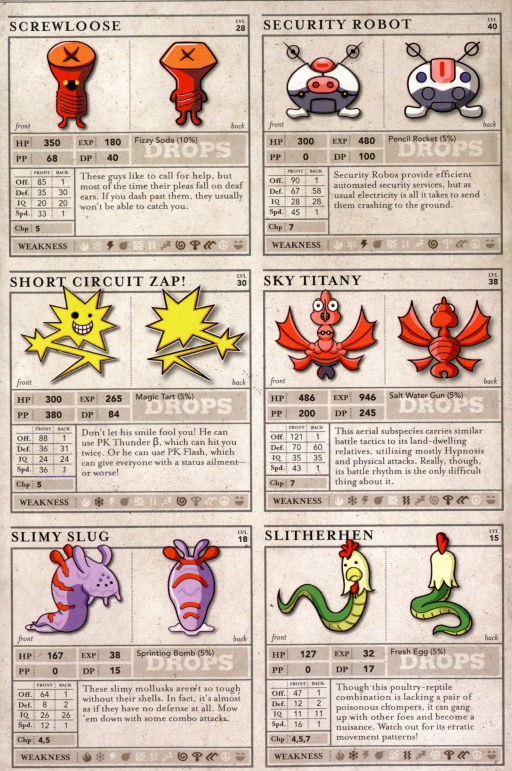

## SCREWLOOSE

LVL 28

*front* — *back*

| HP | 350 | EXP | 180 |
|---|---|---|---|
| PP | 68 | DP | 40 |

Fizzy Soda (10%)

**DROPS**

| | FRONT | BACK |
|---|---|---|
| Off. | 85 | 1 |
| Def. | 35 | 30 |
| IQ | 20 | 20 |
| Spd. | 33 | 1 |
| Chp | 5 | |

These guys like to call for help, but most of the time their pleas fall on deaf ears. If you dash past them, they usually won't be able to catch you.

**WEAKNESS**

## SECURITY ROBOT

LVL 40

*front* — *back*

| HP | 300 | EXP | 480 |
|---|---|---|---|
| PP | 0 | DP | 100 |

Pencil Rocket (5%)

**DROPS**

| | FRONT | BACK |
|---|---|---|
| Off. | 90 | 1 |
| Def. | 67 | 58 |
| IQ | 28 | 28 |
| Spd. | 45 | 1 |
| Chp | 7 | |

Security Robos provide efficient automated security services, but as usual electricity is all it takes to send them crashing to the ground.

**WEAKNESS**

## SHORT CIRCUIT ZAP!

LVL 30

*front* — *back*

| HP | 300 | EXP | 265 |
|---|---|---|---|
| PP | 380 | DP | 84 |

Magic Tart (5%)

**DROPS**

| | FRONT | BACK |
|---|---|---|
| Off. | 88 | 1 |
| Def. | 36 | 31 |
| IQ | 24 | 24 |
| Spd. | 36 | 1 |
| Chp | 5 | |

Don't let his smile fool you! He can use PK Thunder β, which can hit you twice. Or he can use PK Flash, which can give everyone with a status ailment—or worse!

**WEAKNESS**

## SKY TITANY

LVL 38

*front* — *back*

| HP | 486 | EXP | 946 |
|---|---|---|---|
| PP | 200 | DP | 245 |

Salt Water Gun (5%)

**DROPS**

| | FRONT | BACK |
|---|---|---|
| Off. | 121 | 1 |
| Def. | 70 | 60 |
| IQ | 35 | 35 |
| Spd. | 43 | 1 |
| Chp | 7 | |

This aerial subspecies carries similar battle tactics to its land-dwelling relatives, utilizing mostly Hypnosis and physical attacks. Really, though, its battle rhythm is the only difficult thing about it.

**WEAKNESS**

## SLIMY SLUG

LVL 18

*front* — *back*

| HP | 167 | EXP | 38 |
|---|---|---|---|
| PP | 0 | DP | 15 |

Sprinting Bomb (5%)

**DROPS**

| | FRONT | BACK |
|---|---|---|
| Off. | 64 | 1 |
| Def. | 8 | 2 |
| IQ | 26 | 26 |
| Spd. | 12 | 1 |
| Chp | 4,5 | |

These slimy mollusks aren't so tough without their shells. In fact, it's almost as if they have no defense at all. Mow 'em down with some combo attacks.

**WEAKNESS**

## SLITHERHEN

LVL 15

*front* — *back*

| HP | 127 | EXP | 32 |
|---|---|---|---|
| PP | 0 | DP | 17 |

Fresh Egg (5%)

**DROPS**

| | FRONT | BACK |
|---|---|---|
| Off. | 47 | 1 |
| Def. | 12 | 2 |
| IQ | 11 | 11 |
| Spd. | 16 | 1 |
| Chp | 4,5,7 | |

Though this poultry-reptile combination is lacking a pair of poisonous chompers, it can gang up with other foes and become a nuisance. Watch out for its erratic movement patterns!

**WEAKNESS**

## SOOT DUMPLING

LVL 15

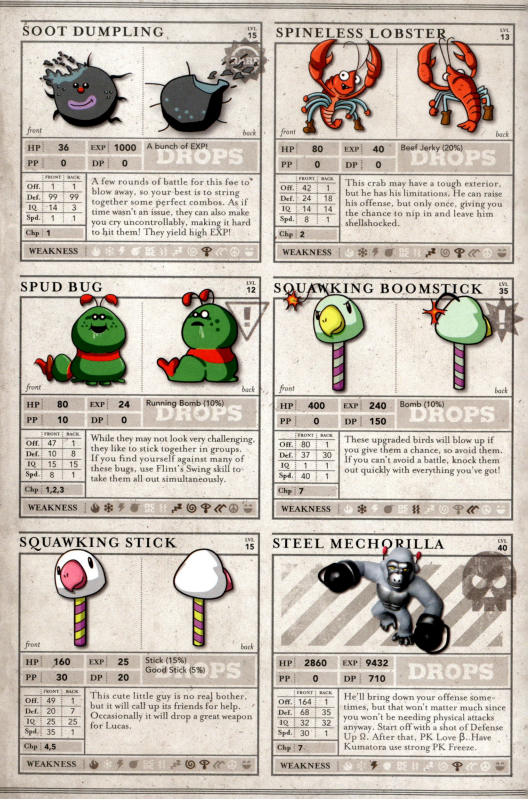

*front* — *back*

| HP | 36 | EXP | 1000 | A bunch of EXP! |
|---|---|---|---|---|
| PP | 0 | DP | 0 | DROPS |

| | FRONT | BACK |
|---|---|---|
| Off. | 1 | 1 |
| Def. | 99 | 99 |
| IQ | 14 | 3 |
| Spd. | 1 | 1 |
| Chp | 1 | |

A few rounds of battle for this foe to blow away, so your best is to string together some perfect combos. As if time wasn't an issue, they can also make you cry uncontrollably, making it hard to hit them! They yield high EXP!

WEAKNESS

## SPINELESS LOBSTER

LVL 13

*front* — *back*

| HP | 80 | EXP | 40 | Beef Jerky (20%) |
|---|---|---|---|---|
| PP | 0 | DP | 0 | DROPS |

| | FRONT | BACK |
|---|---|---|
| Off. | 42 | 1 |
| Def. | 24 | 18 |
| IQ | 14 | 14 |
| Spd. | 8 | 1 |
| Chp | 2 | |

This crab may have a tough exterior, but he has his limitations. He can raise his offense, but only once, giving you the chance to nip in and leave him shellshocked.

WEAKNESS

## SPUD BUG

LVL 12

*front* — *back*

| HP | 80 | EXP | 24 | Running Bomb (10%) |
|---|---|---|---|---|
| PP | 10 | DP | 0 | DROPS |

| | FRONT | BACK |
|---|---|---|
| Off. | 47 | 1 |
| Def. | 10 | 8 |
| IQ | 15 | 15 |
| Spd. | 8 | 1 |
| Chp | 1,2,3 | |

While they may not look very challenging, they like to stick together in groups. If you find yourself against many of these bugs, use Flint's Swing skill to take them all out simultaneously.

WEAKNESS

## SQUAWKING BOOMSTICK

LVL 35

*front* — *back*

| HP | 400 | EXP | 240 | Bomb (10%) |
|---|---|---|---|---|
| PP | 0 | DP | 150 | DROPS |

| | FRONT | BACK |
|---|---|---|
| Off. | 80 | 1 |
| Def. | 37 | 30 |
| IQ | 1 | 1 |
| Spd. | 40 | 1 |
| Chp | 7 | |

These upgraded birds will blow up if you give them a chance, so avoid them. If you can't avoid a battle, knock them out quickly with everything you've got!

WEAKNESS

## SQUAWKING STICK

LVL 15

*front* — *back*

| HP | 160 | EXP | 25 | Stick (15%) |
|---|---|---|---|---|
| PP | 30 | DP | 20 | Good Stick (5%) DROPS |

| | FRONT | BACK |
|---|---|---|
| Off. | 49 | 1 |
| Def. | 20 | 7 |
| IQ | 25 | 25 |
| Spd. | 35 | 1 |
| Chp | 4,5 | |

This cute little guy is no real bother, but it will call up its friends for help. Occasionally it will drop a great weapon for Lucas.

WEAKNESS

## STEEL MECHORILLA

LVL 40

| HP | 2860 | EXP | 9432 | |
|---|---|---|---|---|
| PP | 0 | DP | 710 | DROPS |

| | FRONT | BACK |
|---|---|---|
| Off. | 164 | 1 |
| Def. | 68 | 35 |
| IQ | 32 | 32 |
| Spd. | 30 | 1 |
| Chp | 7 | |

He'll bring down your offense sometimes, but that won't matter much since you won't be needing physical attacks anyway. Start off with a shot of Defense Up Ω. After that, PK Love β. Have Kumatora use strong PK Freeze.

WEAKNESS

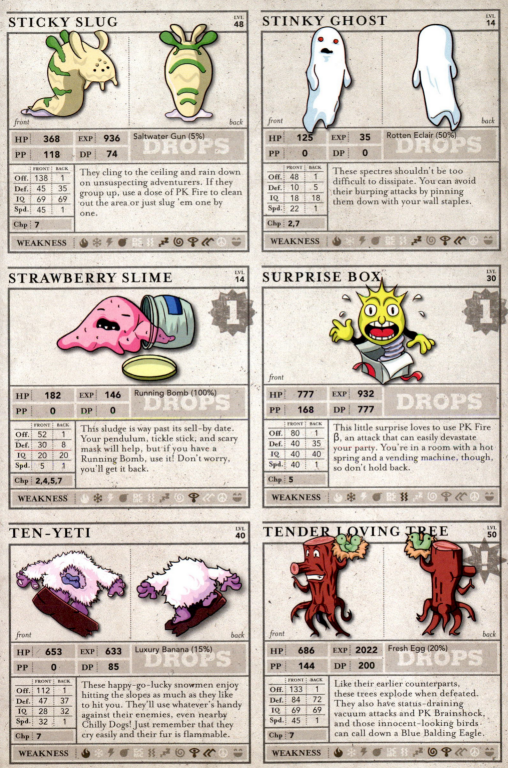

## STICKY SLUG

LVL 48

| HP | 368 | EXP | 936 |
|----|-----|-----|-----|
| PP | 118 | DP | 74 |

Saltwater Gun (5%)

**DROPS**

| | FRONT | BACK |
|------|-------|------|
| Off. | 138 | 1 |
| Def. | 45 | 35 |
| IQ | 69 | 69 |
| Spd. | 45 | 1 |
| Chp | 7 | |

They cling to the ceiling and rain down on unsuspecting adventurers. If they group up, use a dose of PK Fire to clean out the area or just slug 'em one by one.

**WEAKNESS**

## STINKY GHOST

LVL 14

| HP | 125 | EXP | 35 |
|----|-----|-----|-----|
| PP | 0 | DP | 0 |

Rotten Eclair (50%)

**DROPS**

| | FRONT | BACK |
|------|-------|------|
| Off. | 48 | 1 |
| Def. | 10 | 5 |
| IQ | 18 | 18 |
| Spd. | 22 | 1 |
| Chp | 2,7 | |

These spectres shouldn't be too difficult to dissipate. You can avoid their burping attacks by pinning them down with your wall staples.

**WEAKNESS**

## STRAWBERRY SLIME

LVL 14

| HP | 182 | EXP | 146 |
|----|-----|-----|-----|
| PP | 0 | DP | 0 |

Running Bomb (100%)

**DROPS**

| | FRONT | BACK |
|------|-------|------|
| Off. | 52 | 1 |
| Def. | 30 | 8 |
| IQ | 20 | 20 |
| Spd. | 5 | 1 |
| Chp | 2,4,5,7 | |

This sludge is way past its sell-by date. Your pendulum, tickle stick, and scary mask will help, but if you have a Running Bomb, use it! Don't worry, you'll get it back.

**WEAKNESS**

## SURPRISE BOX

LVL 30

| HP | 777 | EXP | 932 |
|----|-----|-----|-----|
| PP | 168 | DP | 777 |

**DROPS**

| | FRONT | BACK |
|------|-------|------|
| Off. | 80 | 1 |
| Def. | 40 | 35 |
| IQ | 40 | 40 |
| Spd. | 40 | 1 |
| Chp | 5 | |

This little surprise loves to use PK Fire β, an attack that can easily devastate your party. You're in a room with a hot spring and a vending machine, though, so don't hold back.

**WEAKNESS**

## TEN-YETI

LVL 40

| HP | 653 | EXP | 633 |
|----|-----|-----|-----|
| PP | 0 | DP | 85 |

Luxury Banana (15%)

**DROPS**

| | FRONT | BACK |
|------|-------|------|
| Off. | 112 | 1 |
| Def. | 47 | 37 |
| IQ | 28 | 32 |
| Spd. | 32 | 1 |
| Chp | 7 | |

These happy-go-lucky snowmen enjoy hitting the slopes as much as they like to hit you. They'll use whatever's handy against their enemies, even nearby Chilly Dogs! Just remember that they cry easily and their fur is flammable.

**WEAKNESS**

## TENDER LOVING TREE

LVL 50

| HP | 686 | EXP | 2022 |
|----|-----|-----|-----|
| PP | 144 | DP | 200 |

Fresh Egg (20%)

**DROPS**

| | FRONT | BACK |
|------|-------|------|
| Off. | 133 | 1 |
| Def. | 84 | 72 |
| IQ | 69 | 69 |
| Spd. | 45 | 1 |
| Chp | 7 | |

Like their earlier counterparts, these trees explode when defeated. They also have status-draining vacuum attacks and PK Brainshock, and those innocent-looking birds can call down a Blue Balding Eagle.

**WEAKNESS**

## THE SQUEEKZ

LVL 25

| | FRONT | BACK |
|---|---|---|
| Off. | 78 | 1 |
| Def. | 41 | 36 |
| IQ | 58 | 58 |
| Spd. | 52 | 1 |
| Chp | 7 | |

| HP | 320 | EXP | 157 |
|---|---|---|---|
| PP | 0 | DP | 23 |

DROPS

'Eyyyyy! He may act street-savvy, but a single round of combat is probably enough to send him back to the highway.

WEAKNESS

## TITANIAN

LVL 45

*front*  *back*

| HP | 450 | EXP | 1005 |
|---|---|---|---|
| PP | 38 | DP | 325 |

Secret Herb (10%)

DROPS

| | FRONT | BACK |
|---|---|---|
| Off. | 135 | 1 |
| Def. | 110 | 98 |
| IQ | 44 | 44 |
| Spd. | 46 | 1 |
| Chp | 7 | |

A rock-hard defense makes these bugs tough to squash. Watch out for its frequent use of Hypnosis and use PK Freeze or Bug Spray to kill it quickly.

WEAKNESS

## TITANY

LVL 15

*front*  *back*

| HP | 119 | EXP | 63 |
|---|---|---|---|
| PP | 12 | DP | 0 |

Running Bomb (10%)

DROPS

| | FRONT | BACK |
|---|---|---|
| Off. | 50 | 1 |
| Def. | 30 | 25 |
| IQ | 16 | 16 |
| Spd. | 13 | 1 |
| Chp | 1 | |

What exactly is this creature? You don't know, but what is clear is that it's unfriendly. You may want to Toughen Up to better penetrate its rough outer shells.

WEAKNESS

## TOP DOGFISH

LVL 48

RARE

*front*  *back*

| HP | 861 | EXP | 2032 |
|---|---|---|---|
| PP | 120 | DP | 869 |

Meteotite (100%)
A bunch of EXP!

| | FRONT | BACK |
|---|---|---|
| Off. | 132 | 1 |
| Def. | 58 | 44 |
| IQ | 38 | 38 |
| Spd. | 40 | 1 |
| Chp | 4,5,7 | |

WARNING! This rare chimera is ultra-powerful! As leader of the pack it doesn't make many public experiences. If you can take it down you'll be rewarded with a huge amount of Exp., DP, and a valuable Meteotite.

WEAKNESS

## TREE

LVL 15

*front*  *back*

| HP | 160 | EXP | 72 |
|---|---|---|---|
| PP | 12 | DP | 0 |

Nut Bread (20%)

DROPS

| | FRONT | BACK |
|---|---|---|
| Off. | 56 | 1 |
| Def. | 24 | 20 |
| IQ | 10 | 10 |
| Spd. | 14 | 1 |
| Chp | 1,7 | |

Fighting this lumbering foe is not recommended, as it contains a deadly mixture of chemicals that cause it to explode when defeated.

WEAKNESS

## UNWELCOME GUST

LVL 46

*front*  *back*

| HP | 598 | EXP | 1456 |
|---|---|---|---|
| PP | 0 | DP | 281 |

Magic Pudding (5%)

DROPS

| | FRONT | BACK |
|---|---|---|
| Off. | 145 | 1 |
| Def. | 64 | 54 |
| IQ | 46 | 46 |
| Spd. | 54 | 1 |
| Chp | 7 | |

These swirling goons love pelting unassuming travelers with rough winds. If you must fight them, use PK Thunder.

WEAKNESS

## UPGRADED ROBOT
**LVL 58**

*front* *back*

| | | | | |
|---|---|---|---|---|
| HP | 921 | EXP | 4272 | Horus Bandana (3%) |
| PP | 0 | DP | 287 | DROPS |

| | FRONT | BACK | |
|---|---|---|---|
| Off. | 152 | 1 | This rejuvenated robot wants revenge, but armed with little more than its rushing capability and an arsenal of Forgetful Gas, it won't get far. |
| Def. | 120 | 92 | |
| IQ | 52 | 52 | |
| Spd. | 44 | 1 | |
| Chp | 8 | | |

**WEAKNESS**

## VIOLENT ATTACK ROACH
**LVL 14**

*front* *back*

| | | | | |
|---|---|---|---|---|
| HP | 88 | EXP | 40 | Nut Bread (10%) |
| PP | 0 | DP | 0 | DROPS |

| | FRONT | BACK | |
|---|---|---|---|
| Off. | 55 | 1 | They may be small, but they pack quite a punch, which can take its toll on your health if you're not careful. |
| Def. | 11 | 6 | |
| IQ | 18 | 18 | |
| Spd. | 35 | 1 | |
| Chp | 2,3,7 | | |

**WEAKNESS**

## WALKING BUSHIE
**LVL 15**

*front* *back*

| | | | | |
|---|---|---|---|---|
| HP | 108 | EXP | 8 | Antidote (10%) |
| PP | 84 | DP | 0 | DROPS |

| | FRONT | BACK | |
|---|---|---|---|
| Off. | 45 | 1 | The experience you gain from defeating this helpful herb is far less useful than the healing it gives you if you don't hurt it in battle. |
| Def. | 22 | 15 | |
| IQ | 18 | 18 | |
| Spd. | 20 | 1 | |
| Chp | 1,4,5,7 | | |

**WEAKNESS**

## WHATEVER
**LVL 28**

*front* *back*

| | | | | |
|---|---|---|---|---|
| HP | 264 | EXP | 98 | Magic Gelatin (10%) |
| PP | 52 | DP | 12 | DROPS |

| | FRONT | BACK | |
|---|---|---|---|
| Off. | 80 | 1 | These little guys aren't much of a threat. They'd rather give you a hug than a bruise, and you can even walk up to them without getting into a fight. |
| Def. | 25 | 20 | |
| IQ | 36 | 36 | |
| Spd. | 39 | 1 | |
| Chp | 5 | | |

**WEAKNESS**

## WOBBLY ROBO
**LVL 27**

*front* *back*

| | | | | |
|---|---|---|---|---|
| HP | 412 | EXP | 126 | Secret Herb (5%) |
| PP | 0 | DP | 64 | DROPS |

| | FRONT | BACK | |
|---|---|---|---|
| Off. | 93 | 1 | This robot may look like a pushover, but he is not like his broken brethren. He can emit an electromagnetic pulse that will make you feel numb and leave you motionless! |
| Def. | 28 | 22 | |
| IQ | 13 | 13 | |
| Spd. | 33 | 1 | |
| Chp | 7 | | |

**WEAKNESS**

## WOUND-UP ROAD HOG
**LVL 27**

*front* *back*

| | | | | |
|---|---|---|---|---|
| HP | 420 | EXP | 150 | Secret Herb (10%) |
| PP | 0 | DP | 53 | DROPS |

| | FRONT | BACK | |
|---|---|---|---|
| Off. | 98 | 1 | This road hog will often break his wind-up spring during his charge attack. If you're lucky, it will drop a valuable Secret Herb! |
| Def. | 36 | 26 | |
| IQ | 10 | 10 | |
| Spd. | 34 | 1 | |
| Chp | 5,7 | | |

**WEAKNESS**

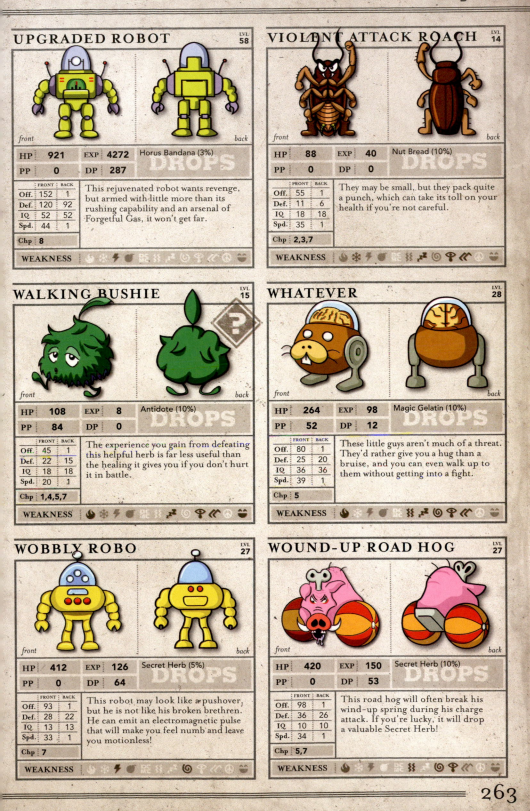

## YAMMONSTER

LVL 10

| HP | 33 | EXP | 26 |
|---|---|---|---|
| PP | 0 | DP | 0 |

Nut Bread (60%)

|  | FRONT | BACK |
|---|---|---|
| Off. | 35 | 1 |
| Def. | 22 | 20 |
| IQ | 12 | 1 |
| Spd. | 5 | 1 |
| Chp | 1 | |

This deranged tuber won't chase you, but it might get in the way. Take advantage of its poor depth perception by dashing up when it's not looking— you'll get plenty of Exp. and, often, a Nut Bread.

WEAKNESS

## ZOMBIDILLO

LVL 42

| HP | 372 | EXP | 522 |
|---|---|---|---|
| PP | 0 | DP | 47 |

Rotten Milk (5%)

|  | FRONT | BACK |
|---|---|---|
| Off. | 108 | 1 |
| Def. | 37 | 32 |
| IQ | 40 | 40 |
| Spd. | 43 | 1 |
| Chp | 7 | |

These sickly roller rats can be found in the depths of the Chimera Lab basement. They're too weak to really be a major issue.

WEAKNESS

## ZOMBIE DOG

LVL 12

| HP | 115 | EXP | 29 |
|---|---|---|---|
| PP | 0 | DP | 0 |

Nut Bread (70%)

|  | FRONT | BACK |
|---|---|---|
| Off. | 42 | 1 |
| Def. | 5 | 2 |
| IQ | 6 | 15 |
| Spd. | 25 | 1 |
| Chp | 2,3 | |

Don't let his winning smile fool you. He's not the toughest enemy around – his bark is worse than his bite. A few hits should be enough to tame him.

WEAKNESS

## ZOMBIE LADY

LVL 12

| HP | 87 | EXP | 25 |
|---|---|---|---|
| PP | 0 | DP | 0 |

Rotten Eclair (10%)

|  | FRONT | BACK |
|---|---|---|
| Off. | 44 | 1 |
| Def. | 7 | 3 |
| IQ | 5 | 1 |
| Spd. | 1 | 1 |
| Chp | 2,3 | |

She's back from the dead and fighting fit! She's not a lot different from the Zombie Man, so use the same attack techniques to send her back to the grave.

WEAKNESS

## ZOMBIE MAN

LVL 12

| HP | 95 | EXP | 25 |
|---|---|---|---|
| PP | 0 | DP | 0 |

Rotten Eclair (10%)

|  | FRONT | BACK |
|---|---|---|
| Off. | 44 | 1 |
| Def. | 7 | 3 |
| IQ | 5 | 1 |
| Spd. | 1 | 1 |
| Chp | 2,3 | |

The dead walk the earth — and they're hungry! And a little chatty. Zombies make up for being slow and weak by attacking in groups, so hit them with wall staples and focus your attacks on one at a time.

WEAKNESS

## ZOMBIESHROOM

LVL 45

| HP | 2489 | EXP | 6336 |
|---|---|---|---|
| PP | 0 | DP | 780 |

DROPS

|  | FRONT | BACK |
|---|---|---|
| Off. | 151 | 1 |
| Def. | 65 | 52 |
| IQ | 32 | 32 |
| Spd. | 150 | 1 |
| Chp | 7 | |

This towering toadstool is not a fun guy. Its spore attacks can poison you, but you can fight back with PK Fire and numbness-inducing attacks.

WEAKNESS

# BATTLE MEMORY

- Do battle with every enemy in the game and you'll get a **silver star** in your Battle Memory! With silver star in hand, the final save frog (the one you stumble across in the darkness at the end of the game) will tell you about a **secret Memo Menu**. To access it, press start and hover over the 'Status' icon, but don't select it. Instead, hold down L and R and then press 'A'. You'll be taken to the secret Memo Menu, which is filled with interesting information about the game.

- Once you've gotten the silver star, consider going for the **gold star**. This is considerably more difficult because you're required to record every pose/view of every enemy in the game. Most enemies have front and back views, but others (like the N.K. Cyborg) simply have different poses, and some don't have alternate views at all! Once you've earned your gold star, the frog at the end of the game will tell you about **Hard Mode**: simply enter your name as "HARD MODE" at the Forest Sanctuary to make the game more challenging. You can actually turn it off (or on!) later by changing your name again at the factory.

# TRICKSTER TIPS

### DUSTER'S SIREN BEETLE
This is the most efficient way to glimpse an enemy's back: by making them turn and cover their ears.

### MADE-YOU-LOOK
Stock up when Duster's not around. These cheap items are like a Siren Beetle that anyone can use.

### INVINCIBILITY APPROACH
After battle, your party members are temporarily 'invincible' even though enemies will still see you.

### SNARING
Some enemies simply home in on you, but others make direct approaches. Fake out a charging foe by circling around them mid-tackle!

### POWERLEVELING
An easy method of sneaking up on an enemy is to be really strong so you can approach a fleeing enemy at your leisure.

## BEANLING
Beanlings are not only tough to find, they're tough to catch! If it buries itself, wait around until a small hole emerges nearby.

## SOOT DUMPLING
These can be found rolling around Lighter's house after Flint escapes from jail. If you find one, approach it slowly. An Ancient Banana can help you beat it.

## BLACK BEANLING
These miniature melanistic legumes are just like their green Beanling cousins.

## BRIGHT SMILE
It occasionally shows up on the highway. It comes equipped with some truly deadly attacks and shields!

## TOP DOGFISH
These can be found on the west side of the pond next to the Chimera Lab. Careful! They know PK Freeze γ and have other powerful attacks.

## FROSTED BUN
This enemy appears only on a tiny cliffside in the Snowcap Mountains. It looks like a small white circle that only responds if you talk to it.

# ONE-SHOT WONDERS

Listed here are the foes that Duster can't battle against. Make sure to prioritize these enemies during their respective chapters!

CHAPTER 4 - You can buy Made-You-Looks from the mouse at the Attic's entrance, so stock up! The Elder Batties show up in Murki Cave in Chapter 7, so you can get them later.

CHAPTER 7 - Yes, you have to engage the Zombieshroom in a fight before eating shrooms, resulting in a game over. A small price to pay for a more thorough Memory!

## CHP 1
Yammonster
Mighty Bitey Snake
Baked Yammonster
Flying Mouse
Greedy Mouse
Beanling
Soot Dumpling
Spud Bug
Agitated Boar

## CHP 7
Cleocatra
Zombieshroom

## CHP 3
Dung Beetle
Sand Lizard
Sara-Sara-Sahara
Ant Lion
HUGE Pillbug
Li'l Big Bro

## CHP 4
Slimy Slug
Greedier Mouse
Arachnid!!!!
Gently Weeping Guitar
Beaten Drum

# KEY ITEMS
## ITEMS PIVOTAL TO COMPLETING THE STORY.

| |  |  |
|---|---|---|
| | Battle Memory | A list of all monsters encountered so far. Lets you relive memories of past battles. |
| | Bird | A bird that inhabits the Saturn Valley area. |
| | Carrier Pidgeon | A messenger pigeon noted for its skill and work ethic. |
| | Child's Shoe | A small, familiar-looking shoe. Its counterpart is still missing. |
| | Courage Badge | The rust and dirt conceals the design underneath. It's incredibly old. |
| | Drawbridge Key | Nippolyte's key for lowering Osohe Castle's drawbridge. |
| | Hummingbird Egg | This is said to have the power to create or destroy an entire world. |
| | Encouraging Words | No matter how down in the dumps you are, these choice words will lift your mood. |
| | Franklin Badge | A badge that reflects lightning. |
| | Hypno Pendulum | Sway it in front of an enemy to lull it into a deep sleep. |
| | Jar of Yummy Pickles | Delicious pickles inside an easy-to-drop, easy-to-roll jar. |
| | Mole Cricket Brother | Leads the way back to the start point if you get lost in the Mole Cricket Hole. |
| | Nail File | A metal file that's bound to break after one more usage. |
| | Noble Spittoon | A mysterious spittoon from Osohe Castle. |
| | Pencil Eraser | This machine will eradicate all iron, pencil-shaped figures in just one second. |
| | Pendant | A pendant dropped by a girl seen inside Osohe Castle. |
| | Phrygia's Notebook | A notebook containing important information written down by Phrygia. |
| | Pig Mark Notebook | A notebook with a pig-like symbol on it. The handwriting inside is terrible. |
| | Rope Snake | A snake that seems like a good replacement for a rope. |
| | Scary Mask | Scares an enemy, lowering its offense. |
| | Scrap of Cloth | A familiar scrap of red cloth. It was stuck in a tree on top of a cliff. |
| | Siren Beetle | A beetle that makes a shrill noise. Causes an enemy to stop and cover its ears. |
| | Smoke Bomb | Explodes into an acrid smoke, bringing an enemy to tears. |
| | Stinkbug's Memory | A record of Leder's long and important story, in case you need to hear it again. |
| | Ticket | Tickets to go to Club Titiboo, received after working in the factory. |
| | Tickle Stick | Tickles an enemy, lowering its defense. |
| | Transceiver | A high-powered transceiver left behind by a Pigmask. |
| | Wall Staple | Stick these in a wall for a quick ladder. Use in battle to briefly pin an enemy down. |
| | Waters of Time | Time is said to speed up for whatever this water is poured onto. |

# WEAPONS

**F: FLINT | L: LUCAS | B: BONEY | D: DUSTER | K: KUMATORA | S: SALSA**

| | Weapon | OFF | BUY/SELL | Char | Source |
|---|---|---|---|---|---|
| | Angel Gloves | OFF +67 | BUY: --- / SELL: 860 | K | box |
| | Better Stick | OFF +20 | BUY: 500 / SELL: --- | F, L | trade |
| | Barefoot Shoes | OFF +38 | BUY: 1,520 / SELL: 760 | D | shop |
| | Canine Weapon | OFF +15 | BUY: --- / SELL: 900 | B | box |
| | Chic Gloves | OFF +23 | BUY: --- / SELL: 300 | K | box |
| | Clever Stick | OFF +62 | BUY: 3,980 / SELL: 1,990 | L | shop |
| | DCMC Pamphlet | OFF +8 | BUY: 100 / SELL: 50 | F, L, D, K | box, shop, NPC |
| | Durable Gloves | OFF +16 | BUY: 300 / SELL: 150 | K | shop |
| | Durable Shoes | OFF +12 | BUY: --- / SELL: 85 | D | box |
| | Easy Grip Stick | OFF +15 | BUY: --- / SELL: 100 | F, L | pre-equip |
| | Expensive Gloves | OFF +58 | BUY: 2,360 / SELL: 1,180 | K | shop |
| | Fake Bat | OFF +30 | BUY: 20,000 / SELL: 10,000 | L | shop |
| | Fake Frying Pan | OFF +26 | BUY: 18,000 / SELL: 9,000 | K | box |
| | Fresh Lumber | OFF +16 SPD -4 | BUY: --- / SELL: 150 | F | box |
| | Friend's Yoyo | OFF +30 SPD +5 | BUY: --- / SELL: 1000 | L, D, K | in the open |
| | Funny Stick | OFF +40 | BUY: 2,400 / SELL: 1,200 | F, L | shop |
| | Gloves | OFF +9 | BUY: --- / SELL: 65 | K | pre-equip |
| | Good Shoes | OFF +70 | BUY: 3,520 / SELL: 1,760 | D | shop |
| | Good Stick | OFF +27 | BUY: 1,500 / SELL: 750 | F, L | foe, shop |
| | Handy Yoyo | OFF +20 | BUY: 650 / SELL: 325 | F, L, D, K | shop |
| | Lighter's Lumber | OFF +6 SPD -3 | BUY: --- / SELL: 50 | F | in the open |
| | Magic Gloves | OFF +30 PP +10 | BUY: --- / SELL: 400 | K | box |
| | Master Stick | OFF +75 | BUY: 4,860 / SELL: 2,430 | F, L | shop |
| | Mystical Gloves | OFF +55 | BUY: --- / SELL: 10 | K | foe |
| | Mystical Shoes | OFF +40 SPD +7 HP +15 IQ +5 | BUY: --- / SELL: 10 | D | foe |
| | Mystical Stick | OFF +90 SPD +5 HP&PP +10 IQ +5 | BUY: --- / SELL: 10 | F, L | foe |
| | Non-Slip Shoes | OFF +58 | BUY: 3,660 / SELL: 1,830 | D | shop |
| | Ordinary Shoes | OFF +6 | BUY: --- / SELL: 15 | D | pre-equip |
| | Real Bat | OFF +100 | BUY: --- / SELL: --- | L | box |
| | Rubber Boots | OFF +25 | BUY: 1,360 / SELL: 680 | D | shop |
| | Sevolg | OFF +35 | BUY: 1,200 / SELL: 600 | K | shop |
| | Sharp Shoes | OFF +17 | BUY: 480 / SELL: 240 | D | shop |
| | Spiky Weapon | OFF +47 | BUY: 3,240 / SELL: 1,620 | L, D, K | shop |
| | Stick | OFF +2 | BUY: --- / SELL: 10 | F, L | foe, NPC |
| | Strong Gloves | OFF +50 | BUY: 2,690 / SELL: 1,345 | K | shop |
| | Ultimate Shoes | OFF +82 | BUY: --- / SELL: 1,000 | D | box |
| | Very Good Stick | OFF +34 | BUY: 2,000 / SELL: 1,000 | F, L | shop |
| | Vigor Stick | OFF +50 | BUY: --- / SELL: 1,800 | F, L | box |

# HEAD GEAR

| | Item | Stats | Price | Equip | Source |
|---|---|---|---|---|---|
| | Alligator Hat | DEF +20 no fleas | BUY: --- SELL: 740 | L, B, S | box |
| | Angel Ribbon | DEF+27 | BUY: 1,500 SELL: 750 | B, K | shop |
| | Awesome Crown | DEF +20 PP +30 | BUY: --- SELL: 2,000 | L | box |
| | Azure Ribbon | DEF +8 | BUY: 180 SELL: 90 | B, K | shop |
| | Bear Hat | DEF +15 | BUY: 720 SELL: 360 | L, B, S | shop |
| | Boing Ribbon | DEF +14 no forget | BUY: 780 SELL: 390 | B, K | shop |
| | Chick Bandana | DEF +5 | BUY: --- SELL: 10 | D, S | box |
| | Cow Hat | DEF +10 | BUY: --- SELL: 250 | L, B, S | box |
| | Crow Bandana | DEF +25 | BUY:1,520 SELL: 760 | D, S | shop |
| | DCMC Hat | DEF +7 SPD +2 | BUY: 200 SELL: 100 | L, B, D | shop |
| | Fairy Ribbon | DEF +18 no sleep | BUY: --- SELL: 680 | B, K | box |
| | Goddess Ribbon | DEF +32 | BUY: --- SELL: 1,150 | B, K | foe |
| | Horus Bandana | DEF +35 no sleep | BUY: --- SELL: 880 | D, S | foe |
| | Kid's Hat | DEF + 3 | BUY: 50 SELL: 25 | L, B, S | shop |
| | Kite Bandana | DEF +30 | BUY: 1,840 SELL: 920 | D, S | shop |
| | Manly Bandana | DEF +1 OFF +2 | BUY: --- SELL: 15 | F, D, S | NPC |
| | Ordinary Hat | DEF +3 | BUY: --- SELL: 50 | F, L, B, S | pre-equip |
| | Otter Hat | DEF +25 | BUY: 1,640 SELL: 820 | L, B, S | shop |
| | Rail Bandana | DEF +15 | BUY: 940 SELL: 470 | D, S | shop |
| | Red Hat | DEF +30 | BUY: 2,000 SELL: 1,000 | L, B, S | shop |
| | Scarlet Ribbon | DEF +2 | BUY: --- SELL: 25 | B, K | pre-equip |
| | Sparrow Bandana | DEF +9 | BUY: 200 SELL: 100 | D, S | shop |
| | Swallow Bandana | DEF +20 | BUY: 1,396 SELL: 698 | D, S | box |
| | White Ribbon | DEF +12 | BUY: 520 SELL: 260 | B, K, S | shop |

# BODY GEAR

| | Item | Stats | Price | Equip | Source |
|---|---|---|---|---|---|
| | Aloha Coat | DEF +8 fire-strong | BUY: 1,600 SELL: 800 | F, L, D, K | shop |
| | Awesome Cloak | DEF +23 lightning, fire, & ice strong | BUY: --- SELL: 2,500 | L | foe |
| | Bantam Charm | DEF +15 | BUY: 540 SELL: 270 | ALL | shop |
| | Black Collar | DEF +30 OFF +30 | BUY: --- SELL: 1,080 | B | box |
| | Brown Collar | DEF +20 OFF +20 | BUY: 1,600 SELL: 800 | B | box, shop |
| | DCMC Boxers | DEF +7 | BUY: --- SELL: 150 | D | pre-equip |
| | DCMC Shirt | DEF +10 SPD +1 | BUY: 360 SELL: 180 | F, L, D, K | shop |
| | Feather Charm | DEF +18 | BUY: 1,280 SELL: 640 | ALL | shop |
| | Flame Pendant | DEF +15 fire-strong | BUY: 1,500 SELL: 750 | L, B, D, K | shop |
| | Flea Charm | DEF +5 | BUY: --- SELL: 35 | ALL | foe, box, trade |
| | Fly Charm | DEF +10 | BUY: 350 SELL: 175 | ALL | shop |
| | Goddess Bustier | DEF +20 fire & ice strong | BUY: --- SELL: 2,300 | K | box |
| | Good Kid's Shirt | DEF +17 IQ +10 | BUY: --- SELL: 1,000 | L | box |
| | Heavy Charm | DEF +26 | BUY: 1,820 SELL: 910 | ALL | shop, in the open |
| | Ice Pendant | DEF +15 ice-strong | BUY: 1,500 SELL: 720 | L, B, D, K | shop |
| | Kid's Shirt | DEF +7 | BUY: 100 SELL: 50 | F, L, D, K | shop |
| | Knit Sweater | DEF +8 some HP every turn | BUY: --- SELL: 30 | F, L, D, K | box |
| | Magic Pendant | DEF +3 PP +5 | BUY: --- SELL: 100 | K | pre-equip |
| | Mini-Mini Charm | DEF +2 | BUY: --- SELL: 15 | ALL | box, pre-equip |
| | Mosquito Charm | DEF +7 | BUY: --- SELL: 75 | ALL | foe, pre-equip |
| | Pumice Charm | DEF +23 | BUY: 1,540 SELL: 770 | ALL | shop, in the open |
| | Red Collar | DEF +50 OFF +50 | BUY: --- SELL: 2,300 | B | box |
| | Rubber Cape | DEF +8 lightning-strong | BUY: 1,200 SELL: 600 | F, L, D, K | shop |
| | Souvenir Dress | DEF + 13 | BUY: 1,400 SELL: 700 | K | shop |
| | Striped Collar | DEF +40 OFF +40 | BUY: --- SELL: 1,650 | B | box |
| | Thud Charm | DEF +30 protect from all ailments | BUY: --- SELL: 1,800 | ALL | foe, in the open |
| | Thunder Pendant | DEF +15 lightning-strong | BUY: 1,500 SELL: 750 | L, B, D, K | shop |
| | Warm Sweater | DEF +8 ice-strong | BUY: 1,000 SELL: 500 | F, L, D, K | shop |
| | White Collar | DEF +10 OFF +10 | BUY: --- SELL: 490 | B | pre-equip |

# BRACELETS

| | Item | Stats | Price | Equip | Source |
|---|---|---|---|---|---|
| | Aquarius Bracelet | DEF +5 | BUY: --- SELL: 50 | F, L, D, K, S | box, pre-equip |
| | Aries Bracelet | DEF +3 | BUY: --- SELL: 25 | F, L, D, K, S | box, pre-equip |
| | Awesome Ring | DEF +30 PP +30 | BUY: --- SELL: 2,400 | L | box |
| | Cancer Bracelet | DEF +20 | BUY: 1,400 SELL: 700 | F, L, D, K, S | box, shop |
| | Capricorn Bracelet | DEF +9 | BUY: 600 SELL: 300 | F, L, D, K, S | box, shop |
| | DCMC Ring | DEF +7 SPD +5 | BUY: 400 SELL: 200 | L, D, K | shop |
| | Gemini Bracelet | DEF +12 OFF +10 | BUY: --- SELL: 650 | L | box |
| | Leo Bracelet | DEF +25 | BUY: 1,600 SELL: 800 | F, L, D, K, S | shop |
| | Libra Bracelet | DEF +30 | BUY: 2,400 SELL: 1,200 | F, L, D, K, S | shop |
| | Pisces Bracelet | DEF +7 | BUY: 160 SELL: 80 | F, L, D, K, S | box, shop |
| | Sagittarius Bracelet | DEF +45 | BUY: --- SELL: 1,600 | F, L, D, K, S | box |
| | Scorpio Bracelet | DEF +35 | BUY: 2,800 SELL: 1,400 | F, L, D, K, S | box |
| | Taurus Bracelet | DEF +15 | BUY: 1,200 SELL: 600 | F, L, D, K, S | shop |
| | Virgo Bracelet | DEF +26 PP +10 | BUY: --- SELL: 900 | K | box |

## RECOVERY ITEMS (HP)

| Item | Effect | Buy/Sell | Source |
|---|---|---|---|
| Bag of Big City Fries | Restores 70 HP | BUY: 40 SELL: 20 | foe, box, shop |
| Bag of Pork Chips | Restores 50 HP | BUY: 28 SELL: 14 | foe, shop |
| Baked Yam | Restores 40 HP | BUY: --- SELL: 50 | foe, box |
| Beef Jerky | Restores 60 HP | BUY: 26 SELL: 13 | foe, box, shop, trade, NPC |
| Beefsteak | Restores 300 HP | BUY: 2,000 SELL: 1,000 | shop |
| Big City Burger | Restores 100 HP | BUY: 60 SELL: 30 | foe, shop |
| Big City Cola | Restores 30 HP | BUY: 10 SELL: 5 | shop |
| Big City Soda | Restores 20 HP | BUY: 8 SELL: 4 | shop |
| Bread Roll | Restores 60 HP | BUY: 30 SELL: 15 | foe, shop |
| Cup of Pork Noodles | Restores 80 HP | BUY: 80 SELL: 40 | foe, shop |
| Doggy Biscuit | Restores 60 HP | BUY: 16 SELL: 8 | foe, box, shop |
| Doggy Jerky | Restores 150 HP | BUY: 54 SELL: 27 | foe, shop |
| Double Jerky | Restores 160 HP | BUY: 240 SELL: 120 | foe, shop |
| Edible Mushroom | Restores 20 HP | BUY: --- SELL: 5 | foe, box, in the open, trade |
| Favorite Pizza | Restores 250 HP | BUY: 1,560 SELL: 780 | box, shop |
| Fizzy Soda | Restores 20 HP | BUY: 6 SELL: 3 | foe, shop |
| Fresh Egg | Restores 80 HP | BUY: 40 SELL: 20 | foe, NPC, shop |
| Fresh Milk | Restores 80 HP | BUY: 60 SELL: 30 | foe, NPC, shop, trade |
| Giant Abalone Steak | Restores 180 HP | BUY: 400 SELL: 200 | foe, shop |
| Grilled Chicken | Restores 170 HP | BUY: 300 SELL: 150 | box, shop |
| Grilled Fish | Restores 120 HP | BUY: 150 SELL: 75 | shop |
| Hot Dog Sushi | Restores 120 HP | BUY: 200 SELL: 100 | foe, shop |
| Hot Spring Egg | Restores 100 HP | BUY: --- SELL: 30 | foe, event |
| Innit Tea | Restores 15 HP | BUY: --- SELL: --- | trade |
| Jumbo Shrimp Soup | Restores 150 HP | BUY: 350 SELL: 175 | shop |
| King Burger | Restores 280 HP | BUY: 1,700 SELL: 850 | foe, box, in the open, shop |
| Lotto Meal | When eaten in battle, anything can happen. | BUY: 104 SELL: 52 | shop |
| Lucky Rice | HP restored depends on luck. | BUY: 126 SELL: 63 | shop |
| Luxury Banana | Restores 120 HP | BUY: 500 SELL: 250 | foe, box, shop |
| Nut | Restores 5 HP | BUY: --- SELL: 1 | foe, box, trade, NPC, in the open |
| Nut Bread | Restores 30 HP. | BUY: 12 SELL: 6 | foe, box, in the open, shop, NPC |
| Nut Cookie | Restores 15 HP | BUY: 8 SELL: 4 | foe, NPC, shop |
| Pasta with a Past | Restores 190 HP | BUY: 1,400 SELL: 700 | shop |
| Peculiar Cheese | HP restored varies from person to person. | BUY: 20 SELL: 10 | foe, box, trade, NPC, in the open |
| Pickled Veggie Plate | Restores 10 HP | BUY: 10 SELL: 5 | foe, shop |
| Pork Stew | Restores 100 HP | BUY: 120 SELL: 60 | foe, shop |
| Rich Kid Stew | Restores 150 HP | BUY: 1,000 SELL: 500 | shop |
| Rich Parfait | Restores 170 HP | BUY: 1,300 SELL: 650 | foe, shop |
| Rotten Milk | Restores 10 HP | BUY: --- SELL: 3 | foe, box, event |
| Sincerity Dumplings | Restores 100 HP | BUY: 100 SELL: 50 | shop |
| Strawberry Tofu | Restores 120 HP | BUY: 180 SELL: 90 | shop |
| White Croissant | Restores 70 HP | BUY: 40 SELL: 20 | shop |
| Yogurt | Restores 80 HP | BUY: --- SELL: 35 | foe, event |

## RECOVERY ITEMS (STATUS)

| Item | Effect | Buy/Sell | Source |
|---|---|---|---|
| Aeolia's Memento | Instantly revives any KO'd person holding it. | BUY: --- SELL: --- | in the open |
| Alarm Cicada | Cures sleep status of a single ally. | BUY: 18 SELL: 9 | foe, shop |
| Antidote | Cures poison status of a single ally. | BUY: 8 SELL: 4 | foe, box, trade, NPC, shop |
| Anti-Paralysis | Cures numbness status of a single ally. | BUY: 14 SELL: 7 | foe, shop, trade |
| Cup of Lifenoodles | Cures all effects & revives KO'd ally (restores all HP) | BUY: 1,780 SELL: 890 | foe, box, shop |
| Doria's Memento | Instantly revives any KO'd person holding it. | BUY: --- SELL: --- | NPC |
| Eye Drops | Cures teary-eyes status of a single ally. | BUY: 10 SELL: 5 | box, shop |
| Flea Powder | Cures fleas status of a single ally. | BUY: 30 SELL: 15 | foe, box, shop |
| Fresh Mint | Cures sickness/nausea status of a single ally. | BUY: 16 SELL: 8 | foe, box, in the open, shop, trade |
| Ionia's Memento | Instantly revives any KO'd person holding it. | BUY: --- SELL: --- | NPC |
| Lydia's Memento | Instantly revives any KO'd person holding it. | BUY: --- SELL: --- | NPC |
| Missy's Memento | Instantly revives any KO'd person holding it. | BUY: --- SELL: --- | NPC |
| Paper Fan | Cures confusion status of a single ally. | BUY: 12 SELL: 6 | foe, shop |
| Phrygia's Memento | Instantly revives any KO'd person holding it. | BUY: --- SELL: --- | NPC |
| Razor and Lipstick | Instantly revives any KO'd person holding it. | BUY: --- SELL: --- | in the open |
| Recollection Bell | Cures forgetfulness status of a single ally. | BUY: 20 SELL: 10 | shop, in the open |
| Secret Herb | Cures all effects & revives KO'd ally (restores 25% HP) | BUY: 600 SELL: 300 | foe, box, in the open, shop |

## REVENUE ITEMS

| Item | Effect | Buy/Sell | Source |
|---|---|---|---|
| Chick | Tiny, yellow, fluffy, and chirpy. | BUY: --- SELL: 50 | event |
| Chicken | A handsome bird with stylish tailfeathers. | BUY: --- SELL: 200 | event |
| Dolphin Ossicle | A fossilized ossicle of a dolphin. (ear bone) | BUY: --- SELL: 5 | in the open |
| Dung | Trade with Wan Sum Dung for EXP. | BUY: --- SELL: --- | foe, in the open |
| Hermit Shell Crab | Home to a Hermit Crab. Return for big money. | BUY: --- SELL: 300 | in the open |
| Meteotite | From outer space. Worth a whole lot of money. | BUY: --- SELL: 2,500 | foe |
| Rotten Eclair | Not for the living. Trade item with ghost bazaar. | BUY: --- SELL: 1 | foe, NPC, in the open |

## RECOVERY ITEMS (PP)

| | | | | |
|---|---|---|---|---|
| Magic Cake | Restores 50 PP | BUY: --- SELL: 600 | box |
| Magic Gelatin | Restores 20 PP | BUY: --- SELL: 75 | foe, box |
| Magic Pudding | Restores 40 PP | BUY: --- SELL: 300 | foe, box |
| Magic Tart | Restores 30 PP | BUY: --- SELL: 150 | foe, box |

## BATTLE ITEMS

| | | | | |
|---|---|---|---|---|
| Ancient Banana | Enemy slips, inflicting damage. | BUY: --- SELL: 5 | foe, box, trade |
| Attack Attractor | Makes enemy stink and target of all attacks. | BUY: 400 SELL: 200 | foe, shop |
| Bomb | Explosive damage to all enemies. | BUY: 1,000 SELL: 500 | foe, shop |
| Bug Spray | Damages insect enemies. | BUY: 100 SELL: 50 | foe, box, in the open, shop |
| Defense Spray | Raises an ally's defense until the end of battle. | BUY: 1000 SELL: 500 | shop, in the open |
| Drago Fang | Can pierce a Drago's hide. | BUY: --- SELL: --- | NPC |
| Dragonfly | This dragonfly is the most popular among kids. | BUY: --- SELL: 70 | NPC |
| Enemy Bufferizer | Strengthens an enemy, boosts exp. pts. gained. | BUY: 800 SELL: 400 | shop, in the open |
| Enemy Wimperizer | Weakens an enemy and lowers exp points gained. | BUY: 1,200 SELL: 600 | shop, in the open |
| Honey Shower | Covers enemy in honey, causes bees to attack. | BUY: 300 SELL: 150 | box, shop |
| Made-You-Look | Tricks an enemy into turning around. | BUY: 50 SELL: 25 | foe, box, in the open, shop |
| New Year's Eve Bomb | Lowers enemies's HP to 1. It could be a dud, though. | BUY: 3,000 SELL: 1,500 | foe, shop |
| Offense Spray | Raises an ally's offense until the end of battle. | BUY: 1,000 SELL: 500 | shop, in the open |
| Pencil Rocket | Deals explosive damage to all enemies. | BUY: 500 SELL: 250 | foe, box, shop |
| Running Bomb | Deals damage to all enemies. | BUY: --- SELL: 50 | foe, box, trade |
| Saltwater Gun | Damages mechanical enemies. | BUY: 400 SELL: 200 | foe, box, shop |
| Shield Snatcher | Peels an enemy's shield away. | BUY: --- SELL: --- | NPC |
| Silver Dragonfly | Children love to chase this dragonfly. | BUY: --- SELL: 30 | NPC |
| Sprinting Bomb | Deals explosive damage to all enemies. | BUY: 200 SELL: 100 | foe, box, shop |
| Super Bomb | Deals explosive damage to all enemies. | BUY: 2,000 SELL: 1,000 | foe, box, in the open, shop |
| Thunder Bomb | Deals lightning damage to all enemies. | BUY: --- SELL: 25 | box, NPC |
| Trivia Card I, 2, 3, 4 | A riddle card. Try it on Pigmask soldiers. | BUY: --- SELL: --- | box (1-3) NPC (4) |

## PSI (HEAL & RESTORE)

| | | | | |
|---|---|---|---|---|
| Lifeup α | 5 PP | lvl 3 lvl 11 | Lucas Kuma | Restores 60-70 HP - single ally |
| Lifeup β | 9 PP | lvl 18 lvl 31 | Lucas Kuma | Restores 120-140 HP - single ally |
| Lifeup γ | 16 PP | lvl 43 | Lucas | Restores all HP - single ally |
| Lifeup Ω | 28 PP | lvl 50 | Lucas | Restores 240-260 HP - all allies |
| Refresh | 20 PP | lvl 58 | Lucas | Restores 10% of HP for 5 turns |
| Healing α | 4 PP | lvl 5 lvl 14 | Lucas Kuma | Cures one status ailment |
| Healing β | 8 PP | lvl 25 | Lucas | Cures two or more status ailments |
| Healing γ | 18 PP | lvl 39 | Lucas | Cures two+ ailments, including KO |
| Healing Ω | 30 PP | lvl 56 | Lucas | Healing γ for all allies |
| PSI Magnet α | 0 PP | lvl 27 | Kuma | Absorbs 2-8 PP from a single enemy |
| PSI Magnet Ω | 0 PP | lvl 45 | Kuma | Absorbs 2-8 PP from all enemies |

## PSI (OFFENSE)

| | | | | |
|---|---|---|---|---|
| PK Special α | 10 PP | event | Lucas | 130-150 damage to all enemies |
| PK Special β | 20 PP | event | Lucas | 230-250 damage to all enemies |
| PK Special γ | 35 PP | event | Lucas | 450-480 damage to all enemies |
| PK Special Ω | 50 PP | event | Lucas | 800-820 damage to all enemies |
| PK Flash | 12 PP | event | Lucas | Status effects to all enemies |
| PK Starstorm | 48 PP | event | Kuma | 650-680 damage to all enemies |
| PK Fire α | 6 PP | lvl 3 | Kuma | 60-80 fire damage to all enemies (10% flammability rate) |
| PK Fire β | 12 PP | lvl 23 | Kuma | 120-140 fire damage to all enemies (10% flammability rate) |
| PK Fire γ | 20 PP | lvl 43 | Kuma | 200-230 fire damage to all enemies (10% flammability rate) |
| PK Fire Ω | 40 PP | lvl 53 | Kuma | 280-320 fire damage to all enemies (10% flammability rate) |
| PK Freeze α | 5 PP | lvl 7 | Kuma | 120-140 ice damage to one enemy (10% freezing rate) |
| PK Freeze β | 10 PP | lvl 28 | Kuma | 200-230 ice damage to one enemy (10% freezing rate) |
| PK Freeze γ | 18 PP | lvl 38 | Kuma | 320-350 ice damage to one enemy (10% freezing rate) |
| PK Freeze Ω | 28 PP | lvl 51 | Kuma | 450-480 ice damage to one enemy (10% freezing rate) |
| PK Thunder α | 7 PP | lvl 12 | Kuma | 120-130 damage to one enemy (15% paralysis rate) |
| PK Thunder β | 15 PP | lvl 32 | Kuma | Two shots of PK Thunder |
| PK Thunder γ | 21 PP | lvl 49 | Kuma | Three shots of PK Thunder PSI Shields and Counters can't block |
| PK Thunder Ω | 32 PP | lvl 57 | Kuma | Four shots of PK Thunder PSI Shields and Counters can't block |
| PK Ground | 43 PP | lvl 60 | Kuma | 2-13% Max HP damage to 5 foes. PSI Shields and Counters can't block (8% trip rate) |

## PSI (ASSIST)

| | | | | |
|---|---|---|---|---|
| Shield α | 6 PP | lvl 22 | Lucas | 50% physical damage to one ally (3 layers) |
| Shield Ω | 18 PP | lvl 35 | Lucas | 50% physical damage to all allies (3 layers) |
| Counter α | 12 PP | lvl 27 | Lucas | Reflects 50% physical damage (3 layers, single ally) |
| Counter Ω | 28 PP | lvl 51 | Lucas | Reflects 50% physical damage (3 layers, all allies) |
| PSI Shield α | 8 PP | lvl 28 | Lucas | 50% PSI damage to single ally (3 layers) |
| PSI Shield Ω | 20 PP | lvl 45 | Lucas | 50% PSI damage to all allies (3 layers) |
| PSI Counter α | 18 PP | lvl 33 | Lucas | Reflects 50% PSI damage (3 layers, single ally) |
| PSI Counter Ω | 34 PP | lvl 53 | Lucas | Reflects 50% PSI damage (3 layers, all allies) |
| Offense Up α | 6 PP | lvl 14 | Lucas | Raises one ally's offense |
| Offense Up Ω | 18 PP | lvl 36 | Lucas | Raises all allies' offense |
| Defense Up α | 6 PP | lvl 17 | Lucas | Raises one ally's defense |
| Defense Up Ω | 18 PP | lvl 30 | Lucas | Raises all allies' defense |
| Hypnosis α | 6 PP | lvl 21 | Kuma | Puts one enemy to sleep |
| Hypnosis Ω | 18 PP | lvl 35 | Kuma | Puts all enemies to sleep |
| Paralysis α | 8 PP | lvl 17 | Kuma | Paralyzes one enemy |
| Paralysis Ω | 24 PP | lvl 29 | Kuma | Paralyzes all enemies |
| Brainshock α | 7 PP | lvl 25 | Kuma | Makes one enemy feel strange |
| Brainshock Ω | 22 PP | lvl 47 | Kuma | Makes all enemies feel strange |
| Offense Down α | 7 PP | lvl 15 | Kuma | Lowers one enemy's offense |
| Offense Down Ω | 22 PP | lvl 37 | Kuma | Lowers all enemies' offense |
| Defense Down α | 7 PP | lvl 19 | Kuma | Lowers one enemy's defense |
| Defense Down Ω | 22 PP | lvl 40 | Kuma | Lowers all enemies' defense |